NOVARTIS CAMPUS

A CONTEMPORARY WORK ENVIRONMENT
PREMISES, ELEMENTS, PERSPECTIVES

NOVARTIS CAMPUS

HATJE
CANTZ

Contents

Foreword
Daniel Vasella – 8

Premises

A Birthplace for New Ideas
Gottfried Schatz – 12

Inspiration or Transpiration?
The Paradoxes of Creativity
Peter von Matt – 20

The Construction of Space for
Research and Development
Mark C. Fishman
and Jörg Reinhardt – 34

Changes in the World of Work
Wolfdietrich Schutz – 38

A Short History of the St. Johann
Works
Walter Dettwiler – 44

Elements

The Master Plan: Architectural
Structure, Function, and Identity
Vittorio Magnago Lampugnani – 58

The Architects of the Campus
Marco Serra – 80

Urban Spaces: Requirements and
Design Strategies
Vittorio Magnago Lampugnani – 106

Landscape Architecture:
Streets and Squares
Peter Walker – 120

Nature under Laboratory
Conditions: The Open Spaces of
Vogt Landschaftsarchitekten
Alice Foxley, Silke Schmeing, and
Günther Vogt – 128

The Art Program: A Sketch
Harald Szeemann – 138

The Detour Art Offers Is Worth
Taking
Jacqueline Burckhardt – 144

Notes on the Appearance of and
Communication on the Campus
Alan Fletcher – 160

Cultivating Visual Identity
Lize Mifflin and Kaspar Schmid – 164

Lighting Orchestration: Between
Technology and Atmosphere
Andreas Schulz – 182

A Culture of Dining and
Communication
Andreas U. Fürst – 186

Implementation and
Management Strategies
Albert Buchmüller, Robert A. Ettlin,
Gaby Keuerleber-Burk,
Martin Kieser, Roger Müller,
Reto Naef, Markus Oser, and
René Rebmann – 192

From Rehearsal to Real Time:
The Pilot Project for
a New Workplace Landscape
Sevil Peach – 210

The Meaning-Engendering
Surroundings of the Workplace
Fritz Steele – 220

Office Space and Creativity
Roman Boutellier – 226

Perspectives

The Relocation of the Harbor and
the Consolidation of the Campus
Markus Christen – 234

The Design of the Promenade
along the Rhine
Guido Hager – 242

The Extension of the Campus:
A Possible Strategy
Vittorio Magnago Lampugnani – 248

The City and the Campus
Fritz Schumacher – 252

From the Confinement of
Heterotopia to the Urbanity of
Novartis Ville
Richard Ingersoll – 256

Author Biographies – 266

The Novartis Campus, Fabrikstrasse, 2008

Foreword
Daniel Vasella

When Novartis decided in 2001 to transform the St. Johann site in Basel, which is also where our company headquarters are located, into a "Campus of Knowledge," the project met with not only curiosity and interest, but also a reserved wait-and-see attitude.

We consciously refrained from communicating about the development of the Campus for quite some time, but our vision was nonetheless clear. Where machines and smokestacks had once occupied center stage, a location tailored to human beings and their productive well-being was to emerge. Interaction, an openness of communication, and a functional "co-location" would be assigned a special value.

Three historical facts helped in achieving this clarity: moving production out of the city district as a consequence of the fire in Schweizerhalle, the previous lack of long-term planning in the construction activity on the factory grounds, and the recognition that the physical proximity of groups who work together on a project enormously facilitates communication and, thereby, the group's concentration. In addition, it was becoming increasingly clear to us that the physical environment had a very substantial significance for the people there. An attractive work environment would also have a positive impact on our ability to recruit the best new talent.

The secondary objective is more prosaic: with its many old buildings, the site no longer met today's standards with regard to safety and the environment.

On the basis of the Master Plan developed by architect and forward-thinking urban designer Vittorio Magnago Lampugnani, Novartis's headquarters are being successively reconstructed to create a new, avant-garde work environment for our associates. The Master Plan takes a long-term view and addresses not only aspects of urban planning, architecture, aesthetics, and landscaping, but also functionality, traffic management, and sociological factors. Needless to say, the project takes into account the urbanistic and cultural context of the city of Basel.

The Campus is a work in progress. While the project is proceeding briskly, it was never our intention to force the pace when implementing the Master Plan. Thus, only those buildings that have become obsolete are to be demolished. It was always important to the company that the project remain flexible in its planning, so that future needs can be taken into account. It is therefore not yet possible to determine which of the current development scenarios will actually be realized after 2012.

All the office and laboratory buildings designed by renowned architects conform not only to the specifications of the Master Plan, but also to the specific requirements of the buildings' users in particular. Both the work environment and the largely flexible arrangement of the buildings also support the kind of interactive, project-related cooperation that aims to optimize the innovation process. Openness and transparency facilitate networking, while "multi-space" offices and "collaborative" laboratories foster interdisciplinary interaction. At the same time, parks, avenues, and streets with cafés and restaurants invite people to meet and exchange their ideas and knowledge. The well-being of associates is provided for through the creation of ergonomic workplaces and relaxation zones, and the provision of services, such as shopping opportunities and a fitness center. Last but not least, art also plays a part in helping to shape the Campus's ensemble of architecture and landscape design. As an integral part of the site, a localized collection of modern art and contemporary design is growing in close conceptual accord with the spatial design of the site and is aimed at inspiring unorthodox ideas through the power of analogy and association.

With its new Campus, Novartis is sending a signal to all its current and potential future associates that the core of our corporate culture is that ultimately unfathomable—and hence also never precisely measurable or controllable—thing called human creativity. The Campus places human beings and their well-being at the center, and signals expectations of creativity, diligence, and flawlessness in the work of all concerned through the high standards it demands of its architects, designers, and artists.

Whoever regularly passes through the Campus already senses today that a new kind of work atmosphere is emerging. This is reason enough for me to thank all those who have left their mark, and are leaving their mark, on the Campus project through their expertise and commitment: Vittorio Magnago Lampugnani, Wolfdietrich Schutz and his team, Peter Walker, Günther Vogt, Andreas Schulz, Harald Szeemann, Jacqueline Burckhardt, Alan Fletcher, Kaspar Schmid, and Michael Rock. And, of course, I am grateful to all the architects, designers, and artists involved, to the officials of the city and canton of Basel, who have always supported us, to the Campus team, and to all of Novartis's employees, because it is their work that has made it possible to realize this great project.

PREMISES

A Birthplace for New Ideas
Gottfried Schatz

So, you are one of the architects who are planning the Novartis Campus? It is nice of you to seek my opinion! We scientists are only rarely consulted about such matters. I cannot help you with architectural suggestions, but I will tell you a little about how researchers work and what they consider important. Sociologists would be able to explain to you the nanostructure of a researcher's soul and the ideal form of their work spaces, but that would only be a secondhand report. The brilliant physicist Richard Feynman once said that the philosophy of science is as important for science as ornithology is for the birds. This may also apply to the sociology of science.

We scientists all want to discover something new, but go our own ways. Research comes in many shades and colors. Applied research has a clear goal and a fixed schedule, while basic research seeks out its goals by itself and, therefore, is often not bound by timeframes. Many like to play these two kinds of research off against one another, whereby applied research is tagged as the despicable drudge of Mammon and basic research comes away as the sublime servant of science. These clichés are nonsense, however, because both kinds of research are important for our society and both require talent, motivation, and persistence. And since almost all the results of basic research are sooner or later applied, it would be better to speak of short- and long-term research. I assume that the Novartis Campus should be home to both kinds of research and that its conception is not to isolate the different researchers from each other but rather to let them mutually spur on and inspire each other. Especially in biomedicine today, the boundary between short- and long-term research is difficult to distinguish, and boundary transgression is, after all, the goal of all innovative research.

However, in spite of their similarities, short- and long-term research each have their own character and needs. The realization of a concrete, theoretically established idea can most often be greatly

"The architect that didn't read the brief," Alan Fletcher, drawing, Workshop on June 21, 2002

expedited by the smart organization and bundling of existing knowledge. Worldwide, electronically networked matrix structures and predetermined "milestones" can indeed find justification here, as long as the researchers are not unnecessarily encumbered by jet lag, overblown PowerPoint presentations, and endless meetings. A clearly defined goal can often be reached faster by a concentrated deployment of resources and rigorous planning. This is not true for long-term research. In this case, the goal is not always clear at first, and neither is how long it will take to get there or whether it will be successful. A phalanx is less effective in this situation than individual scouts who are willing to risk treading intuitively on unfamiliar ground. Networking can also be useful for these scouts, but it has to develop spontaneously and not succumb to hierarchical control from above. Long-term research flourishes most often when it is scribbled on napkins in cafeterias, rather than when it is set down in position papers in conference rooms.

Would you like to know how one recognizes a new idea? It surprises. The greater the surprise, the newer the idea. By the way, the same goes for a work of art, because artistic and scientific creativity draw from the same mysterious wellsprings that are a profound part of our individuality. Just as there is boring science, there is also boring art and—forgive me for saying so—boring architecture.

How are new ideas created? How is it, as Albert von Szent-György asked, that some of us see what everyone sees but think what no one has ever thought? I do not know, but the miracle of the human power of creativity has always fascinated me. Maybe some of us are fortunate enough to have maintained childhood's joy of play and naive curiosity. It is this joy of play that moves children to put a hat on backwards or to invent silly new words. It also helps creative researchers to intuitively sense that the way from A to C does not have to go through B, but perhaps Y or Z. Whatever the explanation may be, the history of science teaches us that gifted individuals who are not only intelligent and tenacious but also courageous are the ones responsible for new ideas, not institutions or groups. It takes courage to question generally accepted dogmas and to swim against the current. And in order that courage and intelligence can develop their power, one must also be tenacious. In other words, only those who swim against the current with tenacity and courage will discover new wellsprings.

Power and hierarchy are the mortal foes of new ideas because they impair the free contest of thought. Although research cannot do completely without hierarchy, it must constantly ensure that it is kept as minimal as possible. The ideal breeding ground for new ideas is "controlled chaos," something which only a few research personalities are capable of creating and maintaining over long periods of time. In this regard, age and official position must take a back seat, because in scientific research the carefree attitude of youth is often more savvy than the wisdom of age.

But why am I telling you all of this? Because as an architect you will decide whether or not this Campus will become a birthplace for new ideas. You have the power to contribute to the creation of the much-sought-after "controlled chaos." Researchers should meet as often and as casually as possible—broad, friendly corridors and comfortable coffee counters or cafeterias do much to encourage discussion. The greatest archictectural threat to a research institution lies

> **So, now you know what we researchers are looking for from you, the architect: The Campus should lower the threshold for the birth of new ideas. Or, to express it in chemical terms, the Campus should be a catalyst.**

not in a building's façade, but in the walls that subdivide its interior. The difference between a physical and an intellectual partition is a lot smaller than one might think. The Campus should be conceived as a reaction vessel in which human beings and ideas encounter each other as often as possible, precisely like molecules that are intended to react with each other. We chemists know that in order to achieve this, the molecules have to come as closely into contact with each other as possible and that they also have to overcome an energy barrier. Because of this barrier, most contacts are non-productive, sometimes they lead to a reaction from which something new develops. Chemists call the reaction hindering barriers activation energy, and we try to lower it by adding catalysts. So, now you know what we researchers are looking for from you, the architect: The Campus should lower the threshold for the birth of new ideas. Or, to express it in chemical terms, the Campus should be a catalyst.

The Viennese café of the past was just such a catalyst. Many poets and philosophers held court every day in "their" café at their usual table. This system may not have been formalized in an organizational flow chart, but it was scrupulously respected nonetheless. Although there was a hierarchy, it was one of intelligence and achievement. No one can now say how many brilliant, significant, and far-reaching ideas first saw the light of day in this "controlled chaos."

❚❚ A research building, however, should not just be a catalyst; it should also be an exclamation point. As all buildings do, it conveys a presence, and a self-confidence and belief in the future, as well as a claim to power. The Campus you are helping to create is a striking exclamation point for chemistry and biomedicine in Switzerland. ❚❚

Franz Grillparzer, Karl Kraus, Arthur Schnitzler, and representatives of Viennese Positivism could all be found there. Wladimir Uljanow, too, brooded over his far-reaching ideas with likeminded people at Café Central. (But maybe we should set him aside, because he later called himself Lenin and would not be a suitable mascot for the new Campus.)

A research building, however, should not just be a catalyst; it should also be an exclamation point. As all buildings do, it conveys a presence, a self-confidence and belief in the future, as well as a claim to power. The Campus you are helping to create is a striking exclamation point for chemistry and biomedicine in Switzerland.

This exclamation point comes at an opportune time, because both of these sciences are now under siege. When I was young, they were the two great magicians who could achieve anything. They yielded nylon, DDT, saccharine, brilliant colors, and potent new medications. One of them, the deep-red Prontosil, saved my life when I came down with a bad case of diphtheria at the age of five. But all of this was soon taken for granted and forgotten, because history knows no gratitude. Beginning about forty years ago, chemistry suddenly became the polluter of the environment, and modern biomedicine became a symbol for technological arrogance and a contempt for nature. Medications that are chemically synthesized or biotechnically engineered may be optimally effective, but for much of the population they have become suspect. Ever more people prefer medications that are either seductively labeled "organic" or are grotesquely diluted. Even in Basel, a world center of biomedical research, many of the trumpeted medications in the windows of the pharmacies are virtually—or even completely—ineffective. In such circumstances, an exclamation point such as this Campus cannot, therefore, be too exclamatory.

But the new Campus is also a question mark. Will it be possible to populate it with talented and enthusiastic researchers and make it a birthplace for new ideas? Will it become a vibrant place for scientific activity? We have all experienced the same sinking feeling when colleagues in ambitious developing countries proudly showed us imposing but almost empty research institutes in which the latest equipment was gathering dust in the corners. As difficult as it is to plan and build a good research facility, it is much more difficult to breathe life into one. I was therefore pleased to see that you and your architect colleagues did not want to relegate us to one of those black-glass-clad buildings, which recall a movie star hiding behind sunglasses in search of anonymity. The plans and drawings I saw show different kinds of buildings, green-lined sidewalks, and small businesses, all of which will surely contribute to a Campus where people not only work, but also feel at home. This kind of environment will go a long way toward ensuring that, in spite of great external pressure and occasional self-doubt, researchers will be able to maintain their creativity. Most experiments do not produce the desired results, and they often nullify years of hard work. In addition, many of us come from far away and have a partner who has not yet become accustomed to his or her strange new surroundings and is unhappy. A living situation in which everything emphasizes calm and reduces tension helps a great deal.

Do you really want to know what kinds of things are going to be discovered on this Campus? Well, there will certainly be many new medications, and hopefully completely new approaches not only to the healing of illness, but also to its prevention. I cannot say any more than this, however, because if I could, the discovery would not really be new. I hope that this Campus has many great surprises in store for us, and that at least one of them will occur within the buildings you are planning.

The Novartis Campus, Forum, 2008

Inspiration or Transpiration?
The Paradoxes of Creativity

Peter von Matt

Thinking happens to us. We always find out afterwards, what we have thought. The idea that thought is an instrument, which we can handle as a surgeon does a scalpel or the soloist does his violin, is an illusion. The surgeon knows where he will cut in the next few seconds or in a half hour. The soloist knows which series of notes he will play now or in the next movement. The thinker, by contrast, does not know what will be cleared from his desk in the course of the morning. If someone could tell him beforehand, he would be perplexed, surprised, and possibly disbelieving. Those who think can, of course, facilitate the process of their thinking. They determine the subject, stake out the territory, or re-tackle a problem with which they were already occupied. They can set conditions which can help them arrive at the unknown thoughts for which they are waiting, which they need and which they want. But there is no guarantee, even under the best conditions, that they will reach their goal. The goal is not even known, because I first recognize it as such only when I arrive there.

This insight is an old one, but we like to keep it at a distance. It makes us unsure about ourselves. Because if the act of thinking just happens, who is it that is doing the thinking? Am I thinking when I think or do I just log the thoughts that occur to me? Is the ego the regent of thought or is the ego nothing more than a complicated fabric of memories made up of the collected thoughts?

Georg Christoph Lichtenberg, a European physicist at the time of Goethe, Mozart, Kant, and the French Revolution, did not shy away from this insight. He was a man who could withstand any thought, even the apparently absurd, desolate, or dangerous ones, whereas we most often erase from consciousness any thought that stands in the way of our way of life and desires. In one of his famous *Sudelbücher* (waste books), in which he recorded what went through his head each day, Lichtenberg found: "One should say 'It's thinking' as one would say 'It's raining.' 'Cogito' is already saying too much as soon as it is translated with 'I think.' The assumption of an 'ego' is a practical neccessity."[1]

This means I cannot do more than to ascribe to myself a sovereign ego that is in command of its own thoughts, even if this sovereign ego is a construct, created out of a "practical need," namely, in order to conceal the eeriness of the fact that the new thought

[1] Translated from Georg Christoph Lichtenberg, *Sudelbücher II* (Munich, 1971), p. 412.

❙❙ *Einfall* (the closest thing to the English word 'incident,' which derives from the Latin verb incidere, to fall or crash in) is the designation for a sudden thought transmitted with remarkable sensuousness, both in terms of the temporal structure, with the result in a fraction of a second, as well as the riddle of spatiality, originating from outside or above. I have no idea from where the incident comes, and it crashes like a meteorite into my consciousness. ❙❙

emerges outside of all areas over which the ego might exercise control. Who or what is "it" when "it's thinking"? We know today what "it" is when "it rains." And brain research certainly knows many of the necessary preconditions for a thought to suddenly be there. But brain research prefers not to say how it is that precisely this thought, this idea, occurs, a thought which perhaps changes the world, or bestows salvation or devastation. It is similar in the case of breakthroughs in art. Today, with the right training and with forty-nine pictures of a great artist in front of me, I can manufacture a fiftieth using electronic and mechanical means that even the experts would consider genuine. But I will not be able to create an innovation like Paul Cézanne's brushstroke or Alberto Giacometti's disembodied bodies or Paul Celan's verbal sound with an experimental technical device. I can only imitate them in retrospect.

The German language has a wonderful word for the decisive procedure: *Einfall* (the closest thing to the English word "incident," which derives from the Latin verb incidere, to fall or crash in) is the designation for a sudden thought transmitted with remarkable sensuousness, both in terms of the temporal structure, with the result in a fraction of a second, as well as the riddle of spatiality, originating from outside or above. I have no idea from where the incident comes, and it crashes like a meteorite into my consciousness.

Jean Goujon, *Archimedes Inspecting the Golden Crown*, 1547, woodcut

"Eureka!"

In the history of sciences as in that of the arts, the phenomenon of the sudden incident, which under certain conditions raises research to a new level, has led to many anecdotes and testimonies. Whether the related events are historically accurate or not is irrelevant. It is only important that they bear witness to the efforts to at least narrate the mysterious event of the ignition of an idea. Among the most famous and still proverbial today is the discovery of the laws of hydrostatic buoyancy by Archimedes and Isaac Newton's discovery of gravitation as the guiding force behind the elliptically orbiting planets.

Archimedes was contracted by the ruler of Syracuse, Hieron II, to determine whether a crown of gold was really made of pure gold. The crown could not be altered in the course of the investigation. As is reported, Archimedes climbed reflectively into the bathtub, which he had filled to the brim, and submerged himself. The water overflowed the bathtub and as he reemerged, Archimedes realized that the amount of water that had overflowed corresponded to the volume of his body. If he put a piece of iron that weighed the same as his body in the bathtub, the overflow was less, because the iron was a material of greater density and needed less volume to equal his body weight. This relationship of material, weight, and volume could now be applied to the crown. Archimedes only needed to weigh the crown and then to procure a sphere of pure gold weighing the same as the crown. If the crown were really made of pure gold, then regardless of its complicated form and decoration it should have the same volume as the sphere and therefore displace the same amount of water as the sphere. If the crown displaced more water than the sphere, then the goldsmith had kept a piece of gold for himself and alloyed a lighter and less valuable piece of metal with the gold. That was in fact the case. As a result, the goldsmith was beheaded and Archimedes became famous.

It is reported that the recognition of this correlation struck Archimedes like a bolt of lightning. He jumped out of the marble bathtub and ran home, dripping and naked, through the streets of Syracuse, where he called out to his embarrassed fellow citizens: "I found it! I found it!" Since Sicily was a part of Greece at the time, he said this in Greek, so he yelled out "Eureka! Eureka!", and he has lived on through this "Eureka!" ever since.

So much for the anecdote. Most people have heard it. It is as famous as the Trojan Horse. But not nearly everyone who knows the Eureka story can also explain how someone can arrive at the idea of specific gravity from the water overflowing from a bathtub. This means that the point of the story in the collective consciousness is not the solution to the physical problem, but rather the event of the flash of insight. It was the same case with Newton, who is supposed to have come up with the laws of celestial mechanics because as he was musing beneath an apple tree, an apple fell on his head with a dull thump and triggered the recognition that the laws of gravitation must also result in an attraction between the planets and the sun.

The Boulder in Engadin and the Eagle Pub in Cambridge

There are actual stories that prove that scientific discoveries can be connected with a certain location and time, as the relevant researchers themselves remember. Sigmund Freud celebrated October 15 as a special day his whole life, because the psychological dynamic, which he later called the Oedipus complex, had become suddenly clear to him on that day in 1897. "A single thought of general significance occurred to me," he wrote to a friend. "I have also identified the infatuation with the mother and the jealousy directed against the father in myself and now consider them a general experience of early childhood."[2] Freud sometimes joked that this day be commemorated by a plaque on his house. The formulation that the thought is *aufgegangen* to him is revealing (*aufgehen* means to rise, realize, or come up, like the sun). Although the breakthrough was preceded by long and oppressive mental exertion without clear results on that day, he experienced the key to his life's work not as the consequence of that effort, but rather as an external event. It could just as easily have failed to occur.

Nietzsche's discovery of the "Eternal Recurrence of the Same," a key theory of his later development, ran a similar, if more dramaticized, course. He spoke again and again about the moment in August 1881 in the Engadin valley when the thought had come to him, a thought which he considered the most profound that had ever occurred to him and which became the basis for his philosophical-poetic work *Thus Spake Zarathustra*. In his late work *Ecce homo* he described it as follows:

> I now tell the story of Zarathustra. The fundamental conception of the work, the Eternal Recurrence idea, the most lofty formula of affirmation that can ever be attained, goes back to August 1881: it is scribbled on a sheet of paper bearing the inscription: "6,000 feet beyond man and time." That day I was walking through the forest at the lake of Silvaplana; I stopped over at a mighty boulder piled up like a pyramid near Surlei. That is where I had this thought.[3]

[2] Translated from Sigmund Freud, *Aus den Anfängen der Psychoanalyse* (Frankfurt am Main, 1962), p. 193.

[3] Translated from Friedrich Nietzsche, *Ecce homo*, vol. 6 (Munich, 1980), p. 335.

Nietzsche was so taken with the memory of the occurrence that he dedicated the poem "Sils-Maria," one of the "Songs of Prince Vogelfrei," to it at the end of his *Die fröhliche Wissenschaft*:

> Expectantly expecting nothing, here sit I,
> Enjoy the light, with good and evil long foreby,
> Enjoy the shadows, all a game,
> The lake, the noon, all time, no aim.
> When lo, my dear, the One, I see
> Is Two—and: Zarathustra passes me![4]

The way Nietzsche describes the state which preceded the point of intellectual ignition is not insignificant. It was not some desperate grasping, but rather an almost floating detachment, free from the mental shackles of society, which separates everything according to good and evil, a condition of the enjoyable observation, a waiting, as he says, but without the compulsion to produce a certain result in a certain amount of time—"all time, no aim." That means that the new thought can be promoted by the environment, the atmosphere, and the institutional framework. Since the idea occurs to me, I cannot force it. But I can put myself in the position that I know from experience is conducive to creative thinking.

It would be tempting to trace back the history of science to such moments, to compare the relevant preconditions and then derive a theory of the ideal conditions for creative breakthroughs. But the concrete cases are so varied that the beautiful proposition remains out of reach. Furthermore, the hurried anecdotal rendition, as in the cases of Archimedes and Newton, can lead to distortion. An example is the discovery of the DNS double helix structure on February 28, 1953, by Francis Crick and James Watson. This was also supposed to be a case of inspiration due to a cozy state of relaxation over a collegial mug of beer in the Eagle Pub in Cambridge. But the focus on the circumstances covered up the significance of the preliminary work of other researchers, especially that of Rosalind Franklin and Maurice Wilkins, which had set the stage for the final breakthrough of Crick and Watson.

[4] Translated from Friedrich Nietzsche, *Die fröhliche Wissenschaft*, vol. 3 (Munich, 1980), p. 649.

The Treacherous Muses

This poses the question of the relationship between the divine flash and work. It has been more passionately discussed for more than two thousand years by the poets and literary theoreticians than the scientists. The increasingly desperate author waiting helplessly at his desk for the incident who suddenly starts writing, as if he had wings, became a subject of contemplation and many conflicting theories.

Since the incident, be it poetical or scientific, is experienced as if it came from outside, as a gift, which one can neither claim with certainty nor obtain by means of certain procedures, the question since time immemorial has been, who is my benefactor? At the time of the myths one answered the question mythologically, and in scientific times, scientifically. But since, according to a well-known saying, the science of each century appears as a myth to the century that follows, at sufficient distance myth and science converge again. The eugenics of the nineteenth century is a scandalous mania for us today, black mythology, but in scientific debate at the time it was upheld by the best minds.

That is how a strange mixture of myth, phantasmagoria, and science emerges from the shifting hypotheses and theories about the incident, the inspiration, the so-called genius, in the historical overview. The book by the Italian psychiatrist and forensic physician Cesare Lombroso, *Genio e follia,* which was published in 1864 and expanded in 1877, was a bestseller well into the twentieth century. Drawing on many examples, it purports to show that the inspired minds of humanity also had a tendency to madness, became insane in old age, came from families with a history of insanity, or had progeny who were idiots. Lombroso did not distinguish between scientists and artists. Regarding our basic question about the riddle of the incident, Lombroso took the position of a psychiatric explanation of inspiration according to the state of knowledge of his time. The creative incident is portrayed as the symptom of a pathological constitution. There is supposed to be a compelling correlation between sickness, genius, and heredity. The work of Thomas Mann is still profoundly influenced by this concept, which no one can take seriously today.

Already in the earliest accounts, Greek culture posed and answered the questions of where the poets got inspiration from and who supplied them with their art. They declared the irritating notion that the incident, the inspiration, does not come from oneself, but, according to the system of the mythological explanation of the world, is attributable to the influence of certain deities. If I as a human being do not have myself or another human being to thank for the incident, then it must be a deity which inspires me. This deity must have a name, and one was also found. In the *Theogony,* the pedagogical poem about the creation of the world and the gods written and sung by Hesiod around 700 BC, there were nine female deities who blew song into the singers, including Hesiod himself.

Today the muses deserve only a trivial academic mention. By contrast, in the original myth they were formidable creatures. The first expression that is passed down to our culture from them appears to be unsurpassable in its drastic ambivalence. Hesiod was a shepherd on Mt. Helicon, on whose peak the muses lived. One day the muses spoke to him and his colleagues. They wanted to make a poet out of him. The address astonishingly begins with abuse and ends with self-determination: "You bunch of shepherds sleeping outdoors, you disgraceful bums who are nothing more than bellies, we can tell lies as if they were the truth, but when we want to, we can also proclaim the truth."[5] This sentence makes clear two things about the transcendent power that is responsible for and calls forth inspiration in human beings. First, that human beings are worthless without divine inspiration. They are lazy bums sleeping outdoors and they only think about filling their bellies until the spirit moves them. This crude address reflects the anthropological experience that the human being is helpless in the face of the incident. Enlightenment comes or it does not. Only when it does do we become anything of value. And second, that the incident, the vital breath—"enépneusan," as Hesiod says, "they breathe in," using a verb derived from *pneuma:* the breath, the breeze, respiration, the soul, the spirit—can be the truth, the unknown, a marvelous truth about the world and its secrets, or also perhaps pure nonsense, an illusion and a lie. The splendid goddesses reserve the right to promulgate both completely and without moral compunction. This is where, on the one hand, the basic suspicion about poets is engendered, the

[5] Translated from Hesiod, *Theogonie* (Stuttgart, 1999), p. 5.

suspicion about their chronic logorrhea, and on the other, the much less considered fact that the sudden incident, the divine flash, the triggering recognition when I can cry out "Eureka!", can also be a false alarm. As little as we are masters of our incidents, so do we have little guarantee that they will have the scientific or artistic character of truth, which in the final analysis is the crux of the matter. It is almost an occult event, whether it provides a boost for human knowledge or only contributes to general self-conceit.

The Intoxicated and the Sober

The chronic dispute about the relationship of inspiration and work goes back to this dubious state of affairs that always holds sway over the unexpected incident and is so spectacularly formulated in the sentence of the muses. Some say inspiration is a state of intoxication. When it makes its entrance, everything is play, and the artist looks with astonishment at what his hands create. Inspiration is all fine and good, say the others, but what counts in the end is the hard work, the hardship accompanied by sweat and groaning, which slowly, very slowly brings forth the work of art or the valid scientific result. Horace, who wrote one of the most serious theories of poetry in our history, *De arte poetica,* a treatment of the subject in verse, presents the point of view that only long, laborious polishing can ultimately bring forth a complete work. He directs this thesis specifically against the ideas about wild genius already circulating at the time—a genius that involves pursuing a state of uncombed and unwashed existence, that perceives itself as the haunt of the muses, and that takes to the pen in a creative frenzy. There was a bohemian society in ancient Rome, too, like the fin de siècle, or the beatniks and hippies in America. The connection between drugs and art—which was continuously discussed and explored in the nineteenth and twentieth centuries by Charles Baudelaire and the Surrealists, in the Berlin of the golden twenties, in the psychedelic scene in the 1960s and '70s—is a continuation of the theories of antiquity about the intoxicated nature of all real art, the Dionysian ecstasies without which artists only disseminate boredom. This was the current against which the Roman Horace wrote, and in support of which, on the other hand, William Shakespeare spoke out when he compared the poet with the lovers and the madmen. All of them are possessed. They have "seething brains," as Shakespeare says in *A Midsummer Night's Dream,* they are, in their abandonment to raging fantasy, indistinguishable from one another: "The lunatic, the lover and the poet / Are of imagination all compact."[6]

Shakespeare speaks of a specific madness of the poet in a state of creativity, a discerning, beautiful madness, "a fine frenzy":

> The poet's eye, in fine frenzy rolling,
> Doth glance from heaven to earth, from earth to heaven;
> And as imagination bodies forth
> The forms of things unknown, the poet's pen
> Turns them to shapes and gives to airy nothing
> A local habitation and a name.[7]

There is no higher, divine power standing behind Shakespeare's creative state. His madness is a purely human phenomenon, an anthropological manifestation that is difficult to describe. Plato had another opinion, when he had Socrates say: "The poet is nothing more than an interpreter of the gods, each one a passive tool of the gods, who have taken up residence in him."[8] That extends the muse theory of Hesiod, but without the ambiguity, and Shakespeare elaborates the platonic theory, but without its transcendent references.

In fact, there is evidence from poets, including great poets, for both explanations, for the ecstatic state as well as long-term hard work, as the unconditional basis for the creation of art. In February 1922, in just a few days after a year-long writer's block, Rainer Maria Rilke not only completed the *Duineser Elegien,* but also knocked off *Sonette an Orpheus*—the twenty-six pieces of Part I from the second to the fifth of February, and the twenty-nine pieces of Part II from the fifteenth to the twenty-third of February. He experienced this process as a "perplexing dictation."[9] Without being able to name it,

[6] William Shakespeare, *A Midsummer Night's Dream,* Act 5, scene 1, lines 7–8.
[7] Ibid., lines 12–17.
[8] Translated from Plato, "Ion," in *Platons Werke,* group 5, vol. 3 (Stuttgart, 1864), p. 318.
[9] Rainer Maria Rilke, letter to Xaver von Moos on April 20, 1923.

he introduced an unknown entity as his inspirer. His modern experience was the same as the experience of Hesiod more than 2,500 years before, but the interpretation must be another one, corresponding to the changed scientific world view. In contrast, Edgar Allan Poe, no less gifted an author than Rilke, contested every notion of the intoxicated and trancelike character of inspiration in his 1840 essay, "The Philosophy of Composition," and equated the creative process with the precision and the rigorous consistency of a mathematical problem. It all came down to concentration, determination, and endurance.

The often quoted saying that "Genius is ten percent inspiration and up to ninety percent perspiration"—a sentence that is always attributed to different people, on one occasion to a scientist such as Thomas Edison, and on another to an author such as Ernest Hemingway or William Faulkner—is a clear expression of the position of Poe and a criticism of the ecstasy theories as romantic ravings.

The New as Danger

The whole posing of the question is scientifically intriguing, because with every formulation of a new theory for this matter one is compelled to take a position for or against the experience of people whose qualification as principal witnesses cannot be doubted. And the old trick of the golden path in the middle, the conciliatory "x will do as well as y," is not in effect here. The work of centuries can be banished to history by a single inspired incident. In this respect the arts and the sciences seem to be dependent on inspiration as the river is on the headwaters. On the other hand, the systems of science and art can also ignore the inspired incident and nothing will happen. The ignition hisses in a vacuum; the work on existing systems goes on as before.

But one thing has become clear: there are conditions that are conducive to inspiration as well as to its rapid adoption, checking, and realization. The cozy relaxation that is posited as a precondition for new ideas in the reports about Archimedes, Newton, Nietzsche, or Crick and Watson has a significance beyond the question of whether the anecdotes are historically accurate. They indicate, namely, that the innovation processes in science and art are co-determined by material and physical circumstances. These do not require the infrastructure of a wellness spa, but they presume a feeling of security and freedom that protects the thinking individual. He must be able to

> **The incident can be dangerous for the person who has it. He who is threatened with obsolescence because of someone else's new idea will defend himself, and will be able to do so as long as the new has not yet established itself. Such processes must be avoided.**

enter into the risk entailed by the new without fear of reprisal, because the truly new also has a destructive dimension. It destroys prevailing truths, and the truths of science, as we know by no later than Galileo, are always networked in the background with the regulations and values of society. In 1847 Ignaz Semmelweis, the assisting physician in a Viennese clinic, recognized that the many cases of death among women in the pediatric ward were the result of an infection transmitted manually by the examining physician. He thereby rescued the lives of thousands of women, but had to leave the clinic. The resistance of influential doctors to his hypothesis, although it was proven immediately, delayed its general adoption by years. Semmelweis's career was damaged and he met a tragic end.

The incident can be dangerous for the person who has it. He who is threatened with obsolescence because of someone else's new idea will defend himself, and will be able to do so as long as the new has not yet established itself. Such processes must be avoided. That is not the least significant consequence to be drawn from the remarks made here.

The Novartis Campus, Forum, 2008

The Construction of Space for Research and Development
Mark C. Fishman and Jörg Reinhardt

An Interview of Mark C. Fishman and Jörg Reinhardt conducted by Simon Heusser

Simon Heusser: In his essay for this volume, biochemist Gottfried Schatz describes the ideal working environment for scientists as one of "organized chaos." Is the Campus an attempt to organize the chaos or to make the company more chaotic?

Jörg Reinhardt: No, it's not about the organization of chaos, but about creating an environment for a modern means of collaboration that is the most efficient possible. We want to achieve this by designing the working environment so as to provide an optimum stimulus for communication and creativity. Furthermore, this objective is not limited by any means to scientists, but applies equally to all other associates in our company, on whose energy and wealth of ideas Novartis is no less dependent. I firmly believe that a stimulating and attractive setting helps to shape the whole company in a positive way.

Mark Fishman: Perhaps a distinction should be drawn on the Campus between an artistic, creative aspect and a sociological one. The artistic aspect is important for a reason that sounds trivial and is often omitted from the debate, but is of key importance: the associates spend a large part of their lives on the Campus. Therefore, an inspiring work environment is of the utmost importance. I also firmly believe that an unusual project such as the Novartis Campus makes associates feel they are part of something bigger. The sociological aspect is perhaps less spectacular, but it is just as important: it is about enabling "chance" encounters that are an indispensable precondition for processes of scientific discovery. Those people one did not necessarily meet regularly before now enter into discussion more often, and those one always had something to do with are now offered a more pleasant setting for these encounters.

SH: The environment helps people to generate ideas—this is the implicit premise of the Campus project. Can you confirm, on the basis of your personal experience, that it does actually work this way?

JR: Yes, I can. I have been working for about four years in an open-space environment, and I appreciate it enormously. Before, when everyone was locked away in their offices—I'm exaggerating slightly—ideas did not flow even close to as freely as they do today. The hierarchies were unmistakably reflected in the communication structure. Today everyone often sits at a table without any regard for hierarchical position, and I get to know what people are working on at that moment, what occupies them, and what worries they have. That is a major step forward, in terms of both the approach to work and the working atmosphere.

MF: I recently moved into my office in the Krischanitz building and am very impressed both by the lighting and by the numerous meeting places. For example, I hold a lot of my meetings in the atrium. I am also convinced that the open structures have a productive influence on the way people collaborate. Especially in science, hierarchies count for little; what matters is the quality of the ideas.

SH: But a glance back in time shows that numerous discoveries were made in working environments to which one would hardly dedicate a volume of essays.

MF: It is true that a lot of exciting discoveries were made in the past in laboratories that were crowded and, not infrequently, downright ugly—laboratories that one actually ought to have banned! But this must not be misunderstood as making a case against an aesthetically pleasing workplace. On the contrary, beauty motivates people; in today's highly competitive market, it also helps us with the recruitment of specialists. But from a scientific point of view, the great physical closeness between researchers is crucial, and this is the core idea behind the Novartis Campus. It is not absolutely essential to have both beauty and proximity in order to optimize the innovation process, but it is ideal, of course, if both coincide.

SH: What about the taciturn thinker type in this beautiful new world of communication? Do introverts also thrive in the "collaborative workspace" or do those who like to talk most simply dominate?

MF: Actually, I do worry about this. We also need to concern ourselves about those scientists who need more quiet for their work.

JR: I also believe that the open-space environment is not equally suited to everyone. It is naturally of particular advantage to people who interact a lot with others or for teams that are in very close contact. But there are also those who primarily produce individual contributions, and often do so in an excellent manner. These people get little out of the open-plan environment, and we shall have to address their needs to a greater extent in the future, probably by means of separated areas. But this is quite feasible.

SH: Even in a working environment that is aesthetically very attractive and functionally stimulating, leadership and corporate culture remain crucial elements of innovation management. Or do you see it differently?

MF: Yes, I do see it a little differently. Leadership is crucial in the innovation process above all because it can be hugely disruptive if the leadership is bad. The same is true of corporate culture. But when we talk of genuine innovation, I'm skeptical about the level of active influence, because this is the result of a strange mix of individual discoveries and insights, the chemistry in a group, and the right mix of enthusiasm and criticism—no architecture, no leadership, and no corporate culture in the world can consciously produce such an amalgam.

SH: Does this apply to Development in the same way as to Research?

JR: No, in Development things are a little different. It even requires very strong leadership to take a discovery and make it into a product ready for the market. But as far as the actual process of discovery is concerned, I agree entirely with Mark.

SH: To innovate successfully, one has to take ideas from both outside and inside an organization and fit them together. What would you say to critics who feel that this "network innovation" approach is being undermined by the character of the Campus, which is cut off from the city—that is to say, from "real life"—with its numerous stimuli and its inspiring unpredictability?

JR: I feel this is a huge misunderstanding. The Campus is by no means cut off. On the contrary, it is far more open than before.

MF: It is positively inviting now.

SH: This view of the Campus project is not necessarily capable of securing a majority, at least not within the region.

JR: Why not? People forget that the Novartis buildings were surrounded by high fences before.

MF: Now people feel drawn in. There is a Visitor Center, where you can find a lot of information about our activities.

SH: So how do you explain that a lot of people appear to see the Campus as an enclave?

MF: The global issue of "security" must not be confused with the Campus. The security level in recent years has increased all over the world, in hospitals and universities, in research institutions and in company headquarters. That has nothing to do with the Campus. I can assure you, the Campus is more visitor-friendly than many other headquarters of global companies.

JR: There are various aspects. The site gives a much more accessible impression than it did when Novartis was founded. The signal to the outside world is clear: we are open, we invite you in. But one must not be naive: our company operates in business with intellectual property. We do not sell washing powder that can be imitated and sold by others without any problem. We sell knowledge that has been accumulated over generations and in which billions of dollars have been invested. This knowledge has to be protected. If we are careless in our handling of the security issue, we risk nothing less than the loss of everything upon which our business is founded.

SH: Research today is very much a team performance, and most scientists with their teams will never in their lives find a substance which makes it to the marketplace as a full-fledged product. How do you actually motivate researchers in a highly individualized company that has made the measurability of success into a fetish?

MF: Indeed, we often talk about this, so it is acknowledged as being a problem. Nevertheless, I remain of the opinion that the best scientists derive a large measure of motivation from within: they want to help discover something pioneering, they want to contribute to a medicine, even if they are very much aware of how limited their influence is on the end product. Needless to say, they would love to be able to say "I was part of a team that discovered this medicine," but the circumstances of the innovation process are often not entirely clear, added to which the process takes around twelve years in the case of medicines. So they have to enjoy the discovery process in itself and in its incremental progress—and they do so.

SH: But does this not mean that the working environment is more important for researchers than it is, for example, for people in marketing or finance who have short-term and at least partly measurable objectives?

MF: I believe an attractive workplace is important for all associates, because they spend a large part of their active lives there. But perhaps the environment is indeed a little more important for people who very rarely, if ever, go out into the world.

JR: I also firmly believe that a stimulating environment helps everyone to achieve a better result—regardless of the field in which they work. This has to be seen against the background of the discussion about the so-called work-life balance. I say "so-called," because I don't like this inflationary use of the term "work-life balance." I believe it misses the point.

SH: So work and life can no longer be separated?

JR: Yes, work is life—at least, this is true for very many people, and I cannot see anything bad about this. With the Campus, we are creating an environment where associates feel at ease and where they like to be—an environment, therefore, which they don't want to leave again as quickly as possible. I believe that work and life will grow ever more entwined in the future. Even today, people spend their time at the workplace much more consciously than they did twenty years ago, when—as in our own case—they had a rather ugly environment in which to work. Today they feel comfortable here, they like to spend their time with the company and, I am convinced, they also produce a correspondingly better performance. That is part of the "business case" for the Campus.

SH: The "business case" also includes easier recruitment of sought-after top people. What role does the Campus play in the motivation mix that prompts a graduate from MIT or Harvard to join Novartis instead of another attractive employer?

MF: My experience with scientists shows unequivocally that they much prefer to go where outstanding scientists work. To this extent, the Campus is important, because it is an impressive signal to researchers that this is a fantastic place to do research. This signal is all the more important since not every company is so strongly committed to innovation today as Novartis. What also seems to me to be important is that the Campus, with its open structures, enables associates to interact with people from a wide variety of fields, whether these are basic research or marketing, or law or development. To know that all these competencies are gathered together in such a small area is fantastic! It also shows all associates every day just how diverse and exciting a process innovation is.

SH: For a few years now, the horizon for the pharmaceutical industry has appeared to have grown bleak. The FDA is becoming ever more conservative in its criteria, the pressure on prices is increasing as a result of demographic change, and intellectual property is threatening to lose its legitimacy. Can a company like Novartis be innovative in a society that is increasingly skeptical about the idea of progress and is threatening to weaken the incentives accordingly?

JR: The only correct conclusion to be drawn from the difficulties you mention is that we have to be better. We have to be even more innovative. What would have been regarded twenty years ago as an acceptable level of innovation is not nearly enough today. The proverbial "low-hanging fruit" has long since been picked. This also means that we need the best people, and that we encourage them and provide them with the incentive to do their best. We need people who want to think and understand beyond the confines of their own specialty. We have integrated teams in all areas of the company that are developing a holistic perspective and motivating each other to come up with new ideas. All these activities are stimulated by the open environment which we are currently creating.

SH: So the Campus can thus be seen as an important response to the ever greater challenges in the healthcare sector?

MF: Definitely. Interfaces are currently emerging between disciplines which have always been kept historically separate by the universities—and are still kept separate—and which can only come together at all in the kind of environment found at Novartis. The opportunities for scientific discoveries today are greater than they have ever been before. The discovery of medicines is the *frontier* of science today. In addition, of all the institutions that maintain they make medicines, it is still the pharmaceutical companies which are really capable of doing so on a large scale. All of the negative developments in society that you have mentioned cannot the outweigh fact that there are still huge, unmet medical needs, and that we are the only ones who can really help.

Changes in the World of Work
Wolfdietrich Schutz

The three-sector hypothesis developed by the French economist Jean Fourastié in the 1930s divided the advanced sector economies into three areas of value creation: a primary sector (raw materials extraction and agriculture), a secondary sector (production and processing), and a tertiary sector (services). The primary sector dominated the economic life of Europe until the mid nineteenth century. There were no factories and the majority of people worked on farms. Beginning in England with the continued development of the steam engine, this situation changed in just a few decades. With the breakthrough of industrial development and the ensuing Industrial Revolution of the second half of the nineteenth century, large manufacturing plants and factories were erected everywhere. Until the reign of Wilhelm II and the beginning of World War I, the percentage of the second sector grew to almost seventy percent. Over the course of the twentieth century, technological progress increased rapidly and led to enormous gains in productivity. The percentage of employment in the secondary sector in the older industrialized countries is dropping dramatically due to continuing globalization and rising, in contrast, in the emerging economies, such as those of China and India. Whereas industrial productivity and value creation has continued to increase, the percentage of secondary-sector employment in advanced economies has dropped to less than thirty percent.[1]

Agriculture today contributes less than five percent to the creation of value. For instance, in the United States there are more people teaching in universities than working in the agricultural sector. Less than two percent of the working population work in agriculture, which, considering the sector's high returns, indicates the extreme efficiency of agricultural production in the United States.[2]

[1] B. R. Mitchell, *European Historical Statistics 1790–1975* (London, 1978), p. 433.
[2] Organisation for Economic Co-operation and Development (OECD), *Annual Labor Force Statistics for 2005*, http://stats.oecd.org (accessed June 6, 2008).

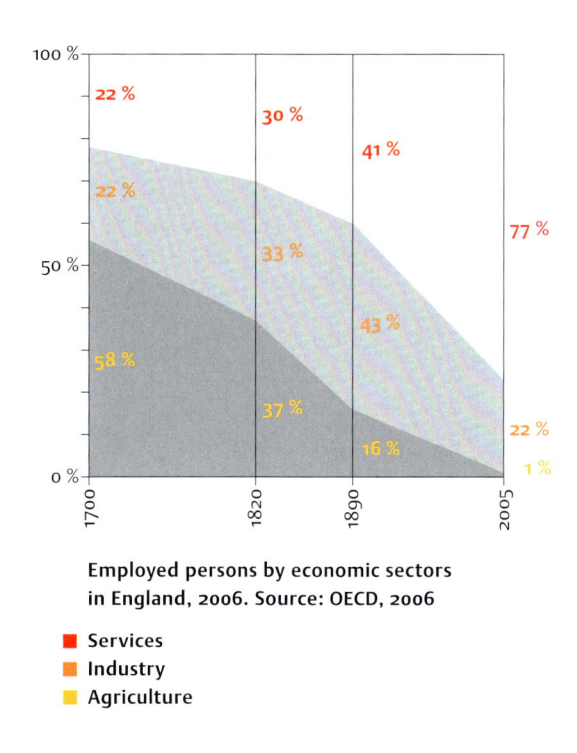

Employed persons by economic sectors in England, 2006. Source: OECD, 2006
■ Services
■ Industry
■ Agriculture

Technology and Intellectual Property: The Service Sector as an Engine of Growth

In opposition to the trend in industry and agriculture, the economic meaning of the service sector increased in significance. The service sector has become an engine of growth and employment. Alongside traditional service professions, such as that of the barber, communication and information technologies have become the sectors experiencing the greatest growth. Of every Swiss franc of value created today, about seventy percent is earned in the service sector, and almost three out of four working people are employed in services.[3] Along with—and because of—this development, intellectual property, the result of creative and innovative work protected by patent and copyright law, has become a significant economic factor. The value of intellectual property in the United States is estimated today as representing about forty-five percent of the gross domestic product and represents an important, dependable basis for the growth of this economic zone.[4]

[3] Ibid.
[4] OECD (as in n. 2), *Intellectual Property as an Economic Asset* (Paris, 2005). Available at URL: http://www.oecd.org/dataoecd/45/13/35043640.pdf (accessed June 6, 2008).

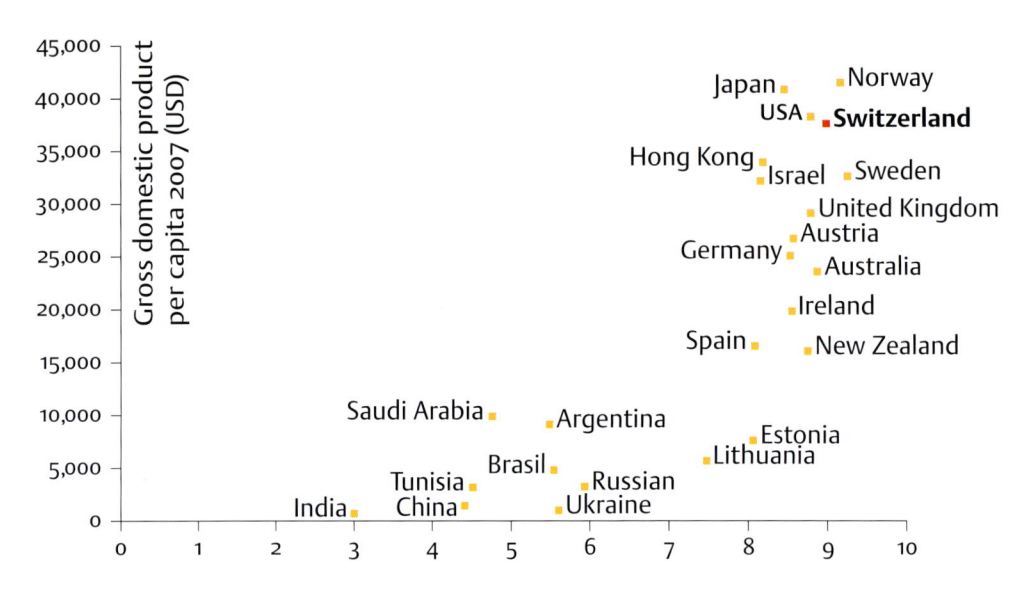

Knowledge Economy Index, 2007: The index was determined for 128 countries and measures the capability of a country to turn its intellectual resources into economic growth.

Chart: Gross domestic product per capita 2007 (USD) vs. Knowledge Economy Index, 2007. Countries plotted include: Norway, Japan, USA, Switzerland, Hong Kong, Israel, Sweden, United Kingdom, Austria, Germany, Australia, Ireland, Spain, New Zealand, Saudi Arabia, Argentina, Estonia, Lithuania, Brasil, Tunisia, Russian, Ukraine, India, China.

Success through Innovation

Only the capacity to innovate can guarantee the prosperity of a highly developed national economy. In short, growth needs innovation, especially against the backdrop of the emerging demographic challenges. The preconditions for this in Switzerland are good. In addition to the guarantee of a high level of education, both the state and the private economic sector invest a great deal in order to stimulate innovation and research. A top rating for Switzerland in the current Knowledge Economy Index (sixth place) shows that these investments are bearing fruit.[5]

Financial analysts are following the product pipeline of pharmaceutical companies with an eagle eye. This makes the meaning of innovation for businesses like Novartis clear. For a group like Novartis, whose ability to generate value is based substantially on its intellectual property, innovation is of vital significance. Only through innovation can Novartis reach its primary goals: progress in the successful treatment of patients in need and the economic growth that accompanies this.

[5] See the Knowledge Assessment Methodology (KAM) 2007, Worldbank (2008), http://www.worldbank.org/kam (accessed June 6, 2008).

The Preconditions for Innovation

Innovation is the result of the generation and transfer of knowledge. My estimate is that about eighty percent of the total worth of the pharmaceutical industry is based on it. In order to best use knowledge to the benefit of the company, it must be combined synergetically. The fertilization of knowledge occurs with increasing interdisciplinarity; there are hardly any more borders that we are not willing to cross in order to advance our interests. For this reason it is important to support encounters and the exchange of knowledge as much as possible, in order to improve the conditions for communication on an ongoing basis and thereby guarantee efficient and inspiring collaboration.

A Stimulating Work Environment

With this knowledge, a long-range view, and much courage, Daniel Vasella and the management of Novartis initiated a pioneering endeavor in 2001. The goal of the long-term Novartis Campus project was clearly defined from the beginning: the St. Johann site in Basel was to be remodeled as an ultra-modern, functional, and attractive R & D and management center, an optimal environment for creativity and innovation. This "Campus of Knowledge" is above all intended to provide an optimal working environment for employees.

Visionary thinking and the will to blaze new paths serve as the foundations of the new initiative. For Novartis—and ultimately for the economy as a whole—it is vitally important to open up new sources of income and to create the necessary preconditions for this kind of activity.

The Novartis Campus is intended to be a place where people can enjoy working together and be successful. It is supposed to become a community, not a partitioned social space or retreat. In order to encourage communication and interaction, new and modern places of work are needed.

|| **With each new workplace that is created, with every new building erected, the learning process is renewed. The demand for 'openness to new and better ideas' is also valid for development within the Campus project itself.** ||

Collaboration, Variety, and Stimulation

The new work environment created by the Master Plan on the basis of these goals and the newly created buildings and public spaces have been very positively received. The employees value the functional, friendly, bright, well-ventilated work rooms, which are the ones best suited to collaboration and which, at the same time, offer sufficient individual areas to which to withdraw and in which to concentrate. The varied settings in which one can work—a desk, a public meeting area, closed conference rooms, or just on a couch—accommodate the individual desires of the employees. It has been shown that communication occurs more efficiently and decisions are made faster in these new rooms.

Every epoch in the modern economic history of our society has required an architecture that accommodated the needs of the time. During the period of industrialization, factory buildings best served the purposes of production and the storage of goods. The post-industrial era, however, needs its own work places. In this regard, with the creation of the Campus, Novartis is setting an example and achieving a significant milestone. The company is building a place of work for the future for its employees in Basel. There are no patented solutions for this. The project will remain an ambitious, far-reaching, controlled experiment, in which new paths are forged and the development of the world in which we work is advanced. With each new workplace that is created, with every new building erected, the learning process is renewed. The demand for "openness to new and better ideas" is also valid for development within the Campus project itself.

At the heart of these efforts, from the first project sketches to the Campus's final completion, are Novartis's goals of minimizing suffering, and extending and improving the quality of life.

Visitor Center, 6 Fabrikstrasse, 2008

A Short History of the St. Johann Works
Walter Dettwiler

With the exception of sulphur manufacture, industrial chemistry started out as dye production. The synthesis of the first artificial dyes in 1856 triggered a gold rush mood in Europe. Every dye expert in the dye works and cloth printing industries tried to discover similar substances, or at least to acquire the formula. In 1859, the silk dyer Alexander Clavel-Oswald in Basel started producing synthetic dyes. In the 1860s other Basel companies started producing artificial dyes. In 1886, Chemische Fabrik Kern & Sandoz started production in the northwest part of the city. Like the other dye factories, it was built outside the former Basel residential quarter on an approximately 11,000-square-meter lot. Next door, the hide broker Gebrüder Bloch & Cie., the chemical factory Durand & Huguenin, and the municipal gasworks were located. At the time it was not known that the new dye factory and its neighbors were occupying grounds that the Celts had settled between 150 and 80 BC. This settlement had reached a maximum extent of fifteen hectares, between the Rhine and what today is Voltaplatz. The archaeologists have unearthed several thousand individual pieces on the site, including coins made of gold and silver.

A Fabulous Beginning

The factory of the chemist Alfred Kern and the salesman Edouard Sandoz consisted of an office building with an adjoining laboratory, three connected sawtooth-roof production buildings, and a boiler house with a twelve-horsepower steam engine. Unlike the Basel chemical factories in the early years, the new company enjoyed dynamic growth from the very beginning. Ten years after the factory's foundation, its grounds had expanded to over 63,000 square meters. The unpaved streets linking the grounds were, according to an eyewitness report, dusty when the sun was shining and impassable when it rained: "The many vehicles which daily delivered ice, coal, and other loads transformed the streets into a morass. It was almost impossible to make one's way without wooden shoes, and just about everyone who had anything to do with the factory went the whole year in wooden shoes."[1]

[1] Oskar Knecht, "Lasst hören aus alter Zeit," in *Unser Weg und Werk. Hauszeitung der Sandoz AG* 4 (October 1948), p. 80.

Left: In the summer of 1885, Alfred Kern submitted a request for a building permit to the local Basel government. In September the government approved the building of a factory, which was begun already that fall and completed in the spring of 1886. The photograph shows the first factory plant around 1890.

Below: Site plan of the St. Johann grounds by Ernst Eckenstein, between 1926 and 1935

Following double page: Manufacturing Plant I, built 1917, ca. 1925

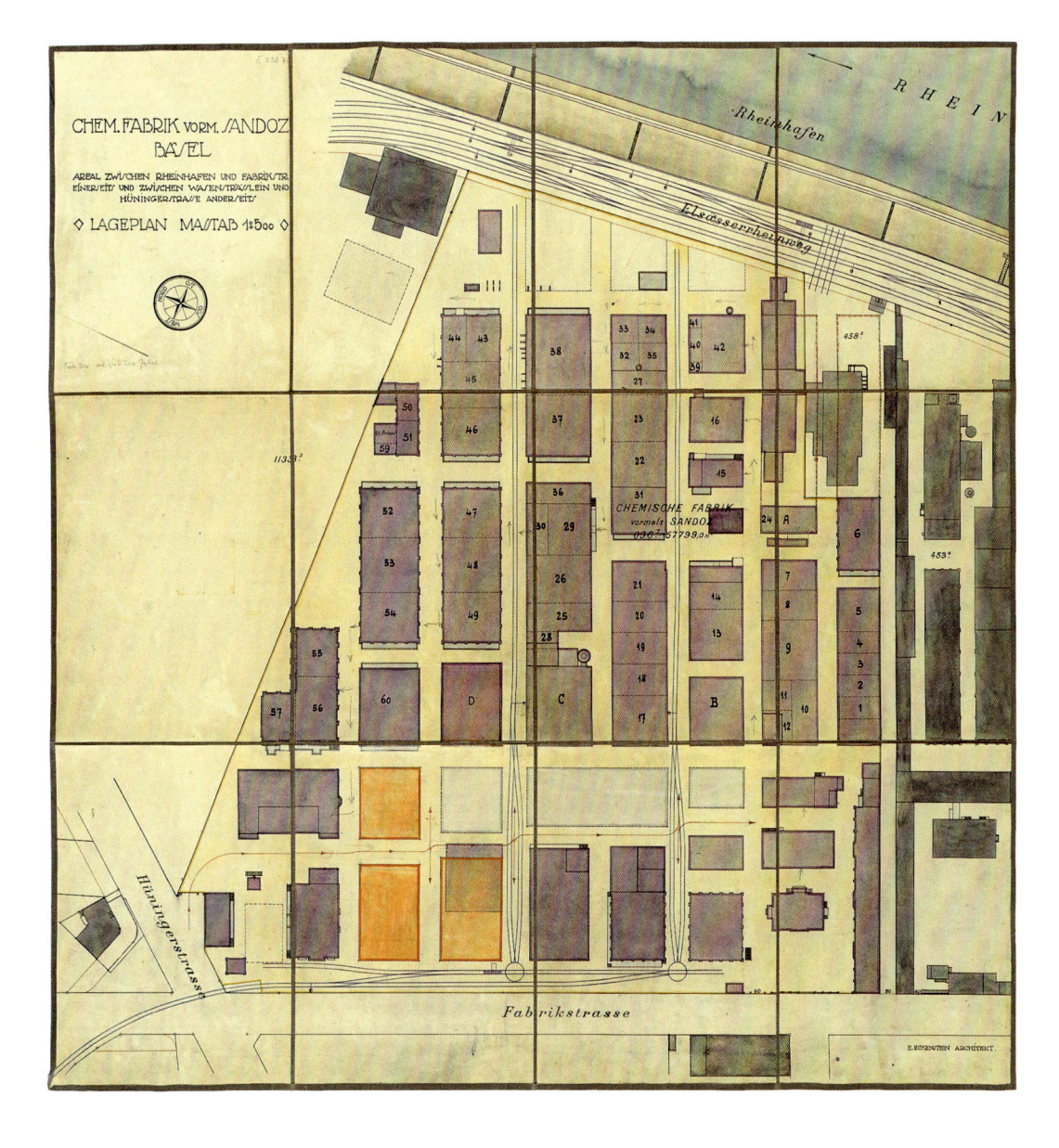

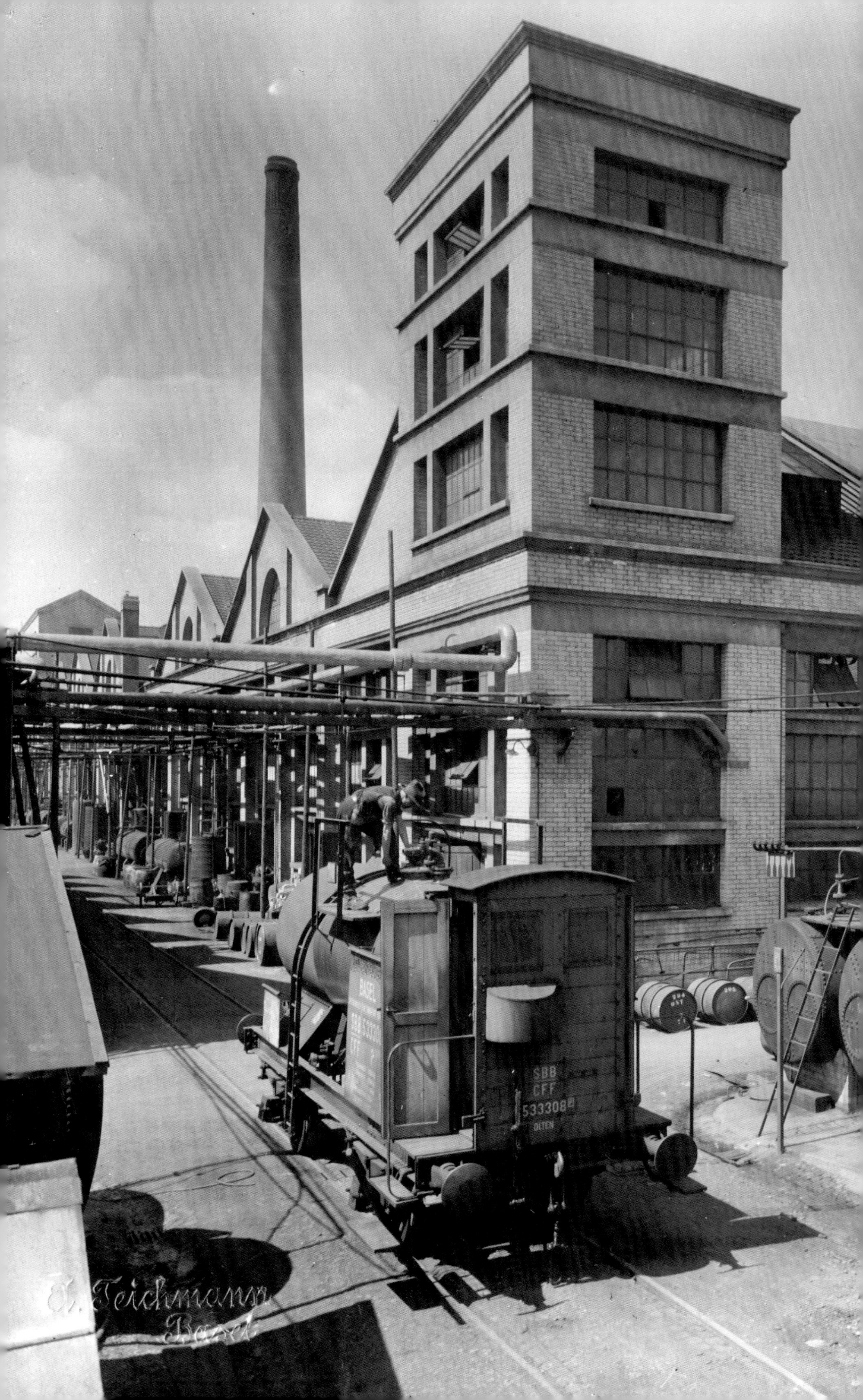
SBB
CFF
533308
A. Teichmann
Basel

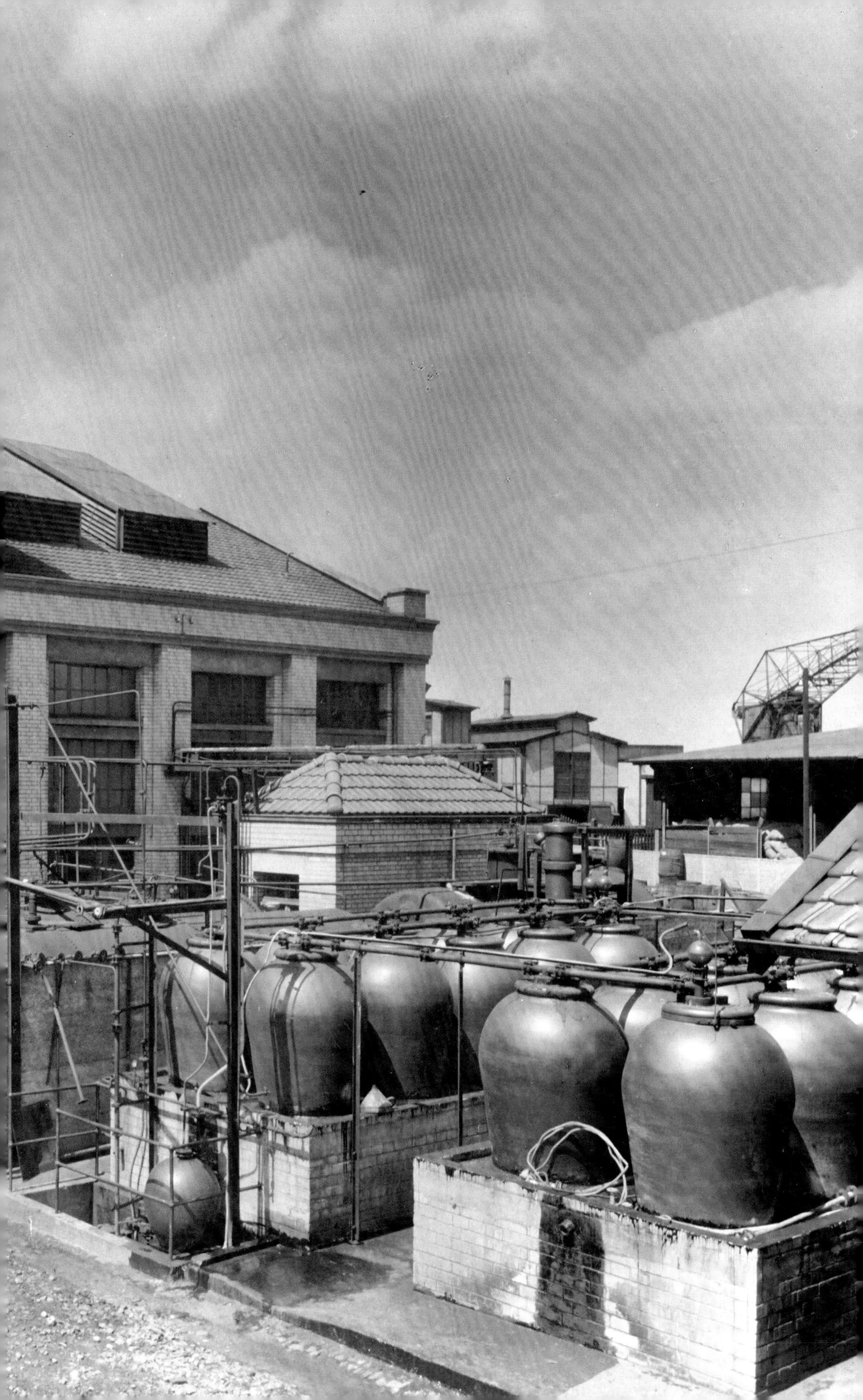

3 Arealstrasse, summer, 1920: In 1889 there were 50 employees, and ten years later there were 238. In 1920 the number of employees at the St. Johann plant was about 900.

World War I: Takeoff at the St. Johann Works

World War I was a bonanza for the chemical industry in Basel. Since the dominant German competition was no longer a factor, the Basel chemical factories became the main suppliers overnight, so to speak, for the English textile industry, the market leader at the time. While in 1914 the turnover of the Chemische Fabrik vormals Sandoz was just 6 million Swiss francs, by 1916 it had already reached 29.5 million, growing in 1918 to 37 million francs! Thanks to the sensational increase in business, a far-reaching modernization and expansion of the production apparatus was implemented during World War I at the St. Johann Works, which was extended from the 1920s to the 1930s. The old sawtooth-roof buildings gave way to multi-story manufacturing locations in which vertical operation was implemented for the first time. According to a contemporary Swiss architecture magazine, these new industrial buildings took into account "the demands of our time," because they fulfilled "in reference to their exterior the striving for beauty, and in reference to their interior, the desire for practicality."[2] These were the industrial buildings of Ernst Eckenstein, who was the house architect of the company from 1915 until World War II. His last project on the St. Johann grounds was the administration building designed by Wilhelm Brodtbeck and Fritz Bohny. This triangle-shaped building, which was completed in 1939 and later called "Gebäude 200" (Building 200), was extended to form a rectangle through the addition of two wings after World War II.

[2] "Industriebauten von Ernst Eckenstein, Architekt in Basel," in *Die Schweizerische Baukunst* 11 (1919), p. 166.

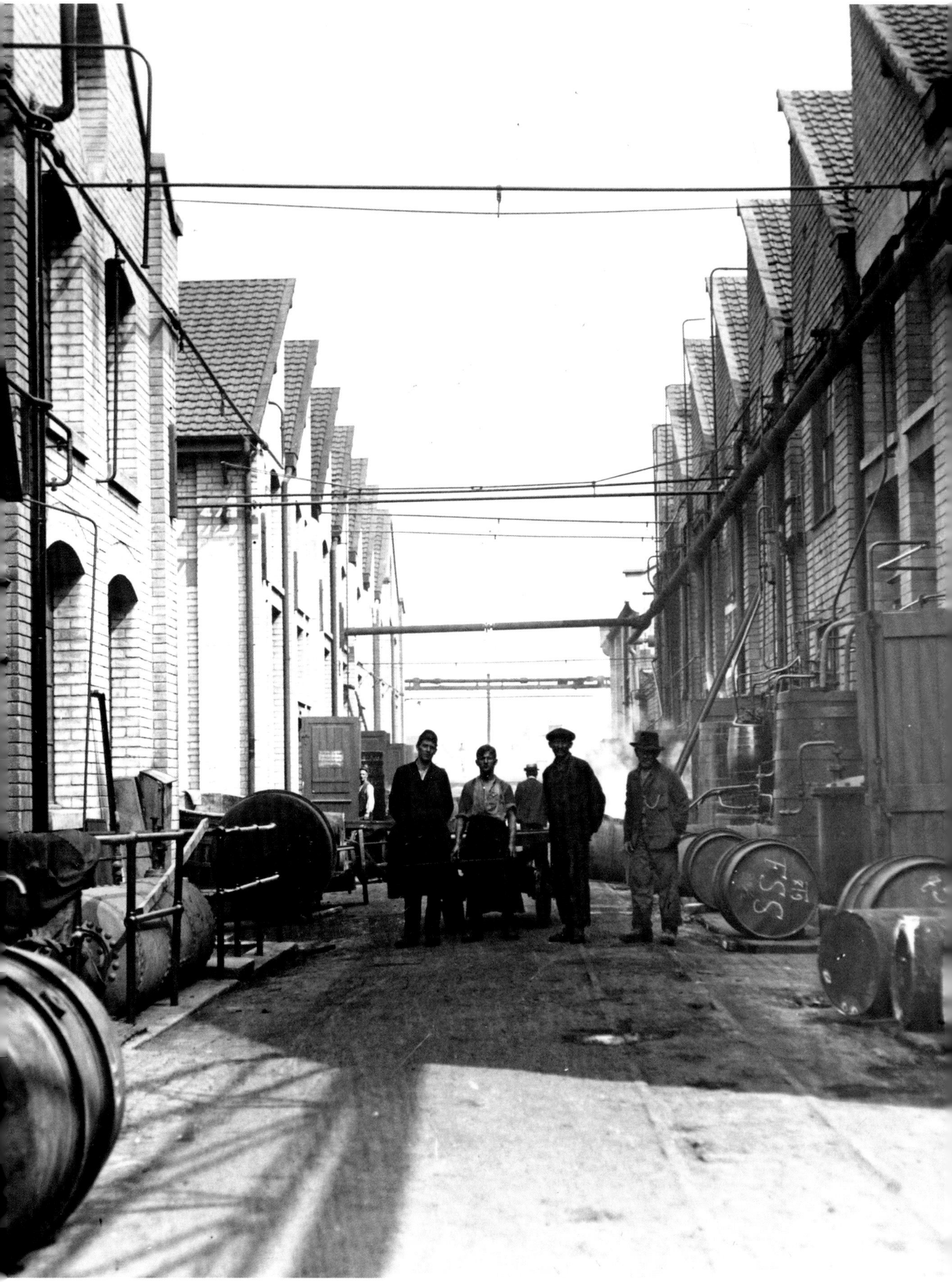
FSS

1 Gasworks and factory facilities by Durand & Huguenin and Sandoz & Cie.: The photograph was taken from an altitude of 450 meters from the balloon *Urania* on June 16, 1895.

2 Aerial photograph, between 1914 and 1920

3 Aerial photograph with the St. Johann grounds in the left background, ca. 1926

4 Aerial photograph, 1936

5 Partial view of the St. Johann grounds, aerial photograph, September 1958

6 Aerial photograph, 1995

Former warehouse building for raw materials and semi-finished goods designed by Conrad Müller, today Building 103, between 1955 and 1960: In 1952 Sandoz bought the property of the Kohlen- and Brikett-AG, which was located between the factory grounds and Hüningerstrasse. This made it possible to build a central, intermediate storage building and consequently to design a more efficient raw materials transportation system within the facility.

The 1950s and 1960s: The Boom Years of Building

These were the times of economic boom, when the Basel chemical group grew rapidly. The respective pharmaceutical branches grew into a giant corporate phenomenon. From 1950 to 1969 the group turnover of Sandoz AG grew from 278 million to 2.5 billion Swiss francs.

The appearance of the St. Johann Works changed fundamentally and at breakneck speed: the area was consolidated, unused lots were built upon, and old buildings were torn down and replaced with modern high-rises. Up until 1956 expenditures in the order of 20 million Swiss francs per year had been made for only the most urgent needs. However, by 1960 the investment in construction had doubled, rising to 80 million francs per year in 1965.

In 1960, construction was begun on Area 5. The office and laboratory Building 503 was built here in two stages between 1961 and 1968 by Burckhardt Architekten and, at a height of seventy-seven meters, was extraordinary by Swiss standards. In 1965 the Burckhardt Architekten–planned offices of Building 202 were completed: the structure today called Forum 2 was supposedly the first Basel industrial building to be built from prefabricated parts. In the same

Laboratory in Building 506, ca. 1965: Building 506 was occupied at the end of 1963. In it Sandoz conducted work on current scientific problems of applied microbiology, for instance, microbiological research on the ergot fungus.

Following double page: Partial view of Areal 3, March 28, 1957: In the 1950s Fabrikstrasse still ran off from Hüningerstrasse, between Areal 3 and 4, to the national border.

year the new restaurant for factory personnel run by Conrad Müller and his coworker, Guido Doppler, went into business. In 1969 Sandoz finally took over the neighboring dye manufacturer, Durand & Huguenin, and the surface area of about 29,000 square meters this accrued rounded off the St. Johann grounds in a useful fashion.

In the 1970s the last significant aboveground buildings in the Basel Sandoz Works were built by Burckhardt Architekten and Burckhardt + Partner: Building 360's laboratories and the office high-rise Building 210 were erected in 1973, and the research spaces of Building 386 were constructed in 1976.

From Building Slump to Campus Kickoff

With the advent of the oil crisis in 1973, the long period of economic boom came to an end and gave way to an economic situation that was determined by much shorter upward and downward swings. After the great fire in the Schweizerhalle works on November 4, 1986, additional security and fire-protection measures were instituted at the St. Johann site as well. As a consequence of the recession, Sandoz massively curtailed group-wide investments in buildings, facilities, and real estate beginning in 1975. This put a substantial brake on the formerly busy construction developments at the St. Johann Works.

In the 1980s, investment activities started up again, whereby modernization of production facilities and projects for environmental protection and security took center stage. The only "visible" new construction on the St. Johann grounds until the merger in 1996 from which Novartis emerged was Building 25. This building, which went into operation in 1993, served the production of prioritized active pharmaceutical ingredients.

The renovation and reconstruction of Building 200—today called Forum 1—was completed in 2002, and at the end of this reconstruction phase the inner courtyard of the building was also redesigned. These last projects were simultaneously the starting point for the redesign of the entire St. Johann grounds into a "Campus of Knowledge."

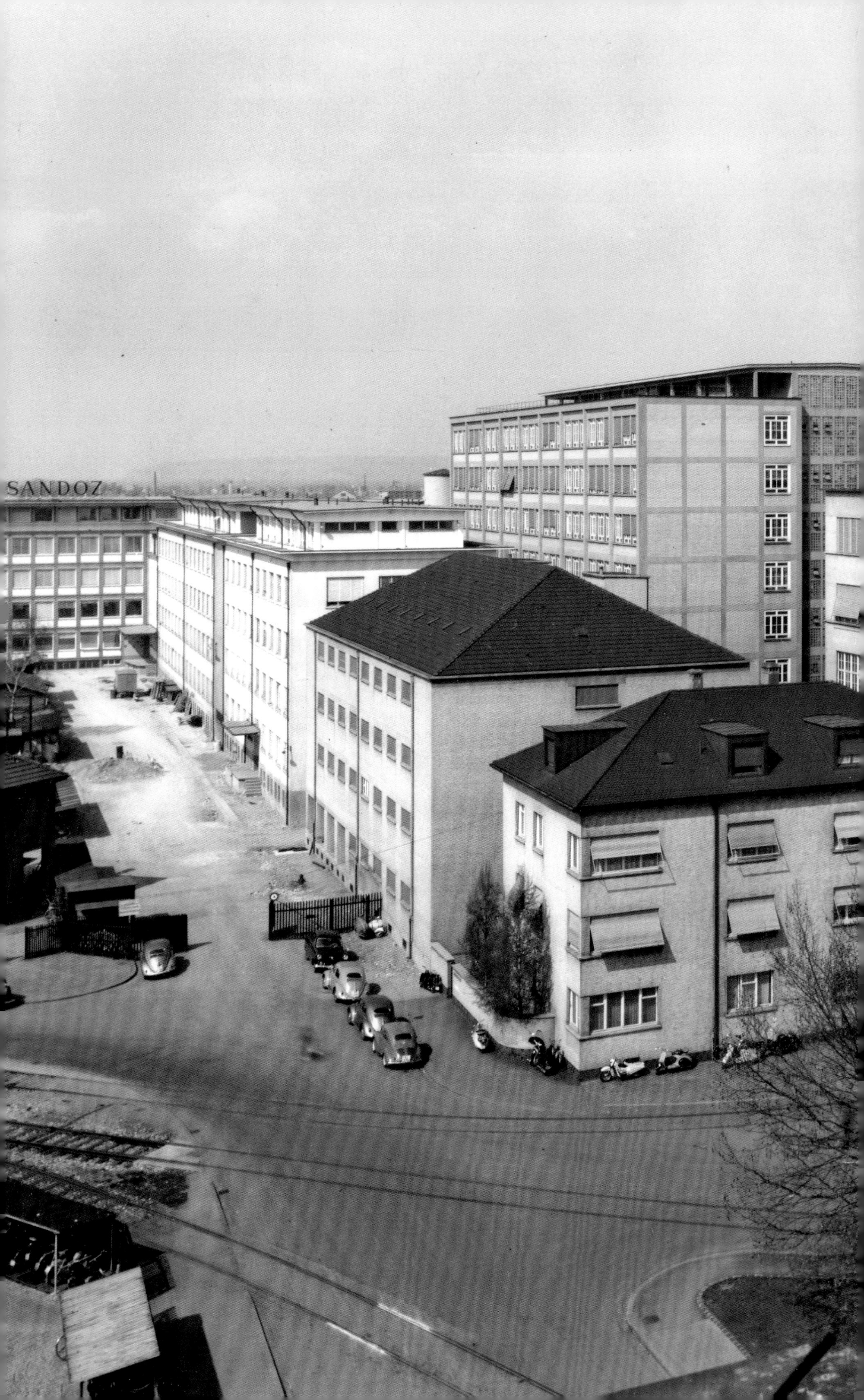
SANDOZ

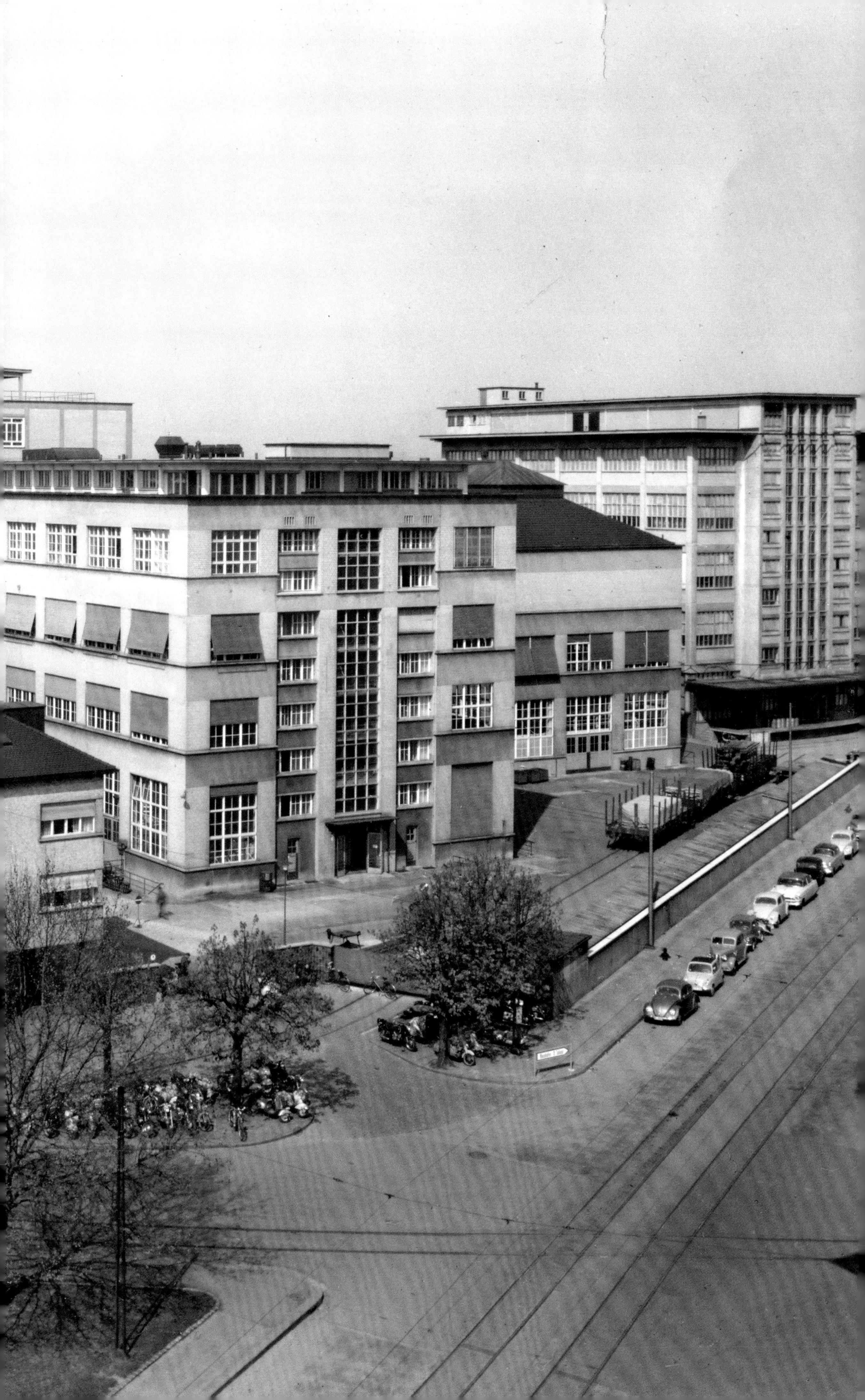

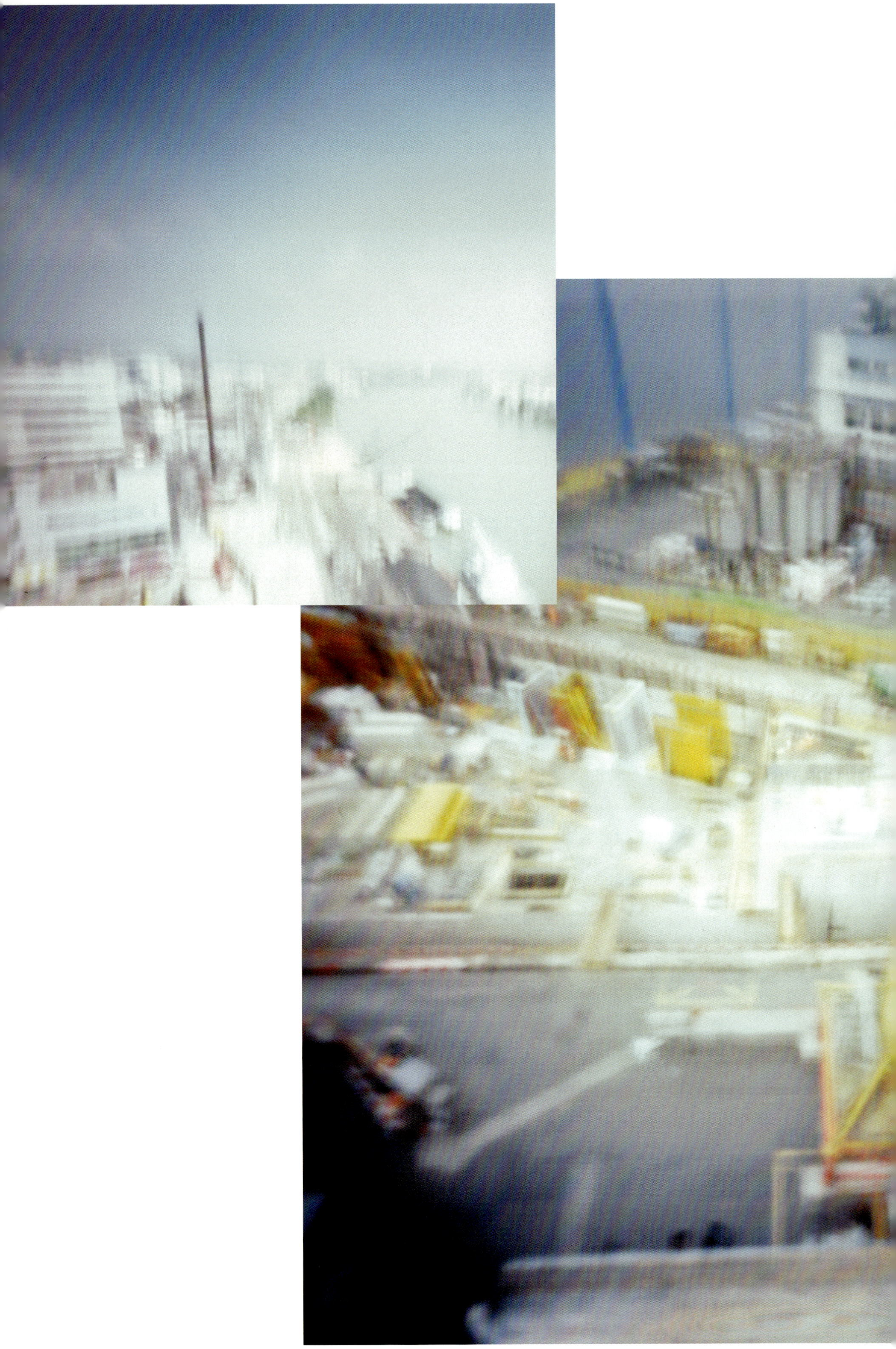

ELEMENTS

The Master Plan: Architectural Structure, Function, and Identity
Vittorio Magnago Lampugnani

At the end of the year 2000, the management of Novartis decided to carry out a fundamental architectural restructuring of one of the areas owned by the company in Basel–St. Johann. It was to be transformed from a production site into a location for innovation, knowledge, and encounters. This functional re-designation was to be reflected in the urban planning, architecture, and atmosphere of the site.

The History of the Area

The area between Elsässerstrasse, Voltastrasse, the national border, and the Rhine had been owned by the Chemische Fabrik Kern & Sandoz since 1886. The company was later renamed Chemische Fabrik formerly Sandoz, and during the nineteen-forties became Sandoz AG. In the early twentieth century, the area had quickly developed into a remarkable complex of factories, with impressive brickwork shed buildings. In the mid nineteen-twenties, these low buildings started to be demolished and replaced with taller ones. The plain, elegant main administrative building, by Eckenstein & Kelterborn of Basel and Brodbeck & Bony of Liestal, was opened in 1939. Subsequent developments in the area continued in a more or less unsystematic way, so that by the eighties and nineties, the area had the appearance of a fairly random accumulation of buildings with varying uses, heights, and signatures.

The Task

The task essentially consisted of systematizing and rationalizing the future development of the area and guiding it into comprehensible urban-planning pathways. The new architectural measures required by the restructuring and expansion of the company were to be coordinated with each other. Examples of bad planning resulting from poor coordination and insufficiently flexible usage, as well as expensive provisional facilities, were to be avoided in the future. This was also intended to make the building facilities more economically efficient. An ultramodern, functional, and at the same time attractive, friendly environment for intensive collaborative work and communication was to be created both for Novartis employees and for visitors. The roots and also the ambitions of the international company were to be given architectural expression. A new, open, and exciting style of work was not only to be made possible through the spatial design, but also specifically encouraged.

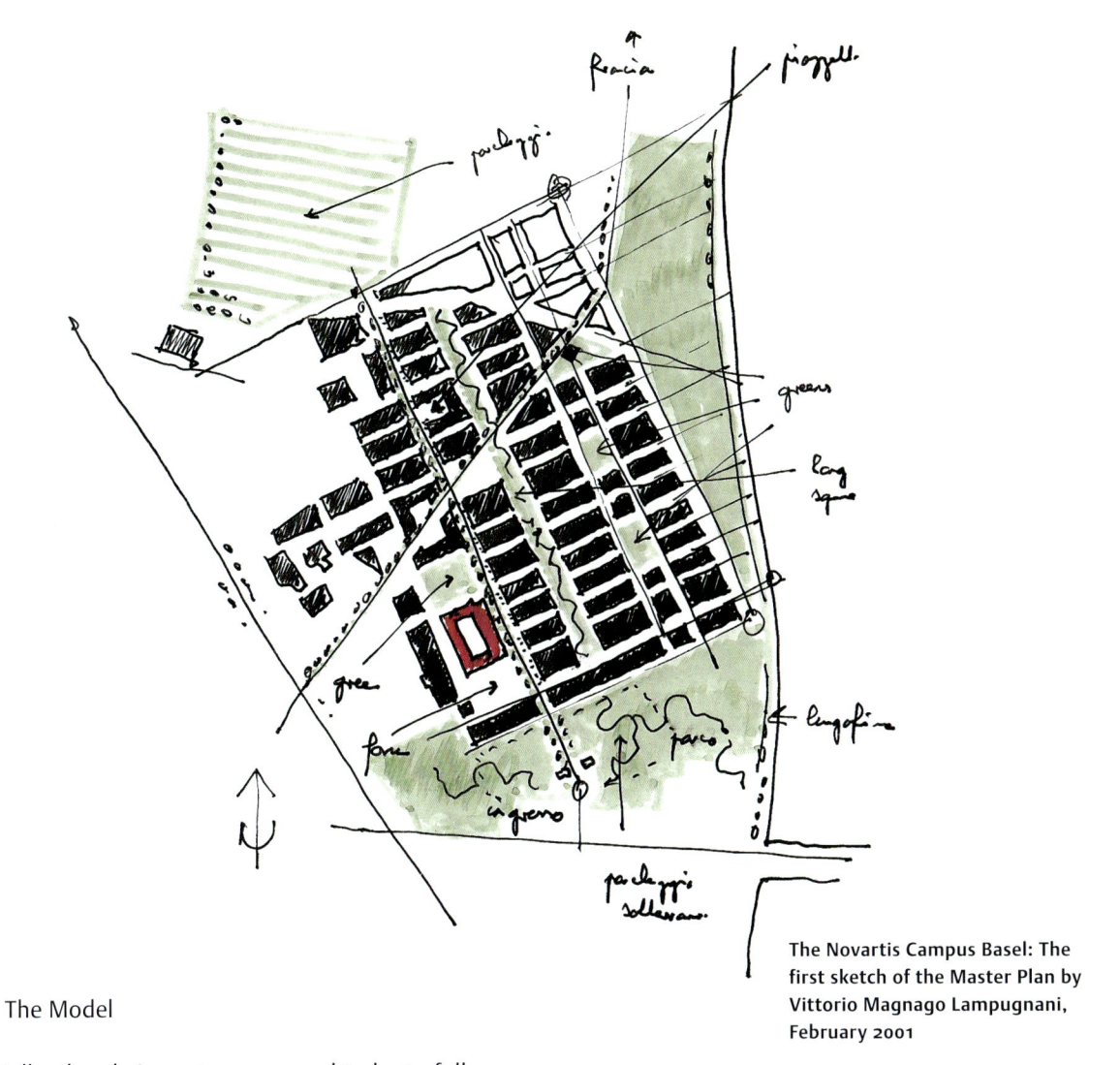

The Novartis Campus Basel: The first sketch of the Master Plan by Vittorio Magnago Lampugnani, February 2001

The Model

Initially, the obvious step appeared to be to follow on from the existing heterogeneous building structure and to systematize, or even intensify, the existing irregularity. This would have allowed the greatest possible flexibility both in dealing with the existing architectural fabric and in placing and scaling the new buildings, which could have been precisely matched, or even tailor-made, to fit operational and usage requirements.

Upon more detailed reflection, however, and after numerous alternative options had been investigated, it was decided to take the industrial sociology of the task as the starting point and to focus on communication as the central aspect of the project. This led to the model of a city, as this is the location par excellence where people enjoy meeting and talking to each other, and it is therefore the ideal architectural implementation of the imperative for social interaction. To be more precise, it led to the model of the pre-industrial city. Having arisen before the invasion of motorized traffic, the scale of the pre-industrial city is adapted entirely to human beings instead of coaches, trams, or cars. The fine network of its streets and squares not only creates short and direct connections between its various points, but also creates countless opportunities in between for planned and unplanned encounters, and thus for interpersonal exchanges.

This model of the city was geometrized, rationalized, differentiated, and adapted to the existing situation. The definitive decision favored a framework pattern, to which hierarchical levels were carefully applied and which was equipped with public spaces. Selected elements from historical cities were drawn on as a source of inspiration and as study objects, but never imitated. The intention was to produce a complex that would build on tried and tested principles of the relationship between architectural configurations and human behavior, but which would use these in an innovative and unprecedented—in short, modern—form.

The usage requirements set out by Novartis were observed, but from a more comprehensive point of view. It was neither the individual employees nor the individual departments that were to receive a tailor-made architectural mantle, but rather the dynamic and constantly changing company as a whole. Generosity and neutrality would both allow the required flexibility and also create the desired sense of well-being.

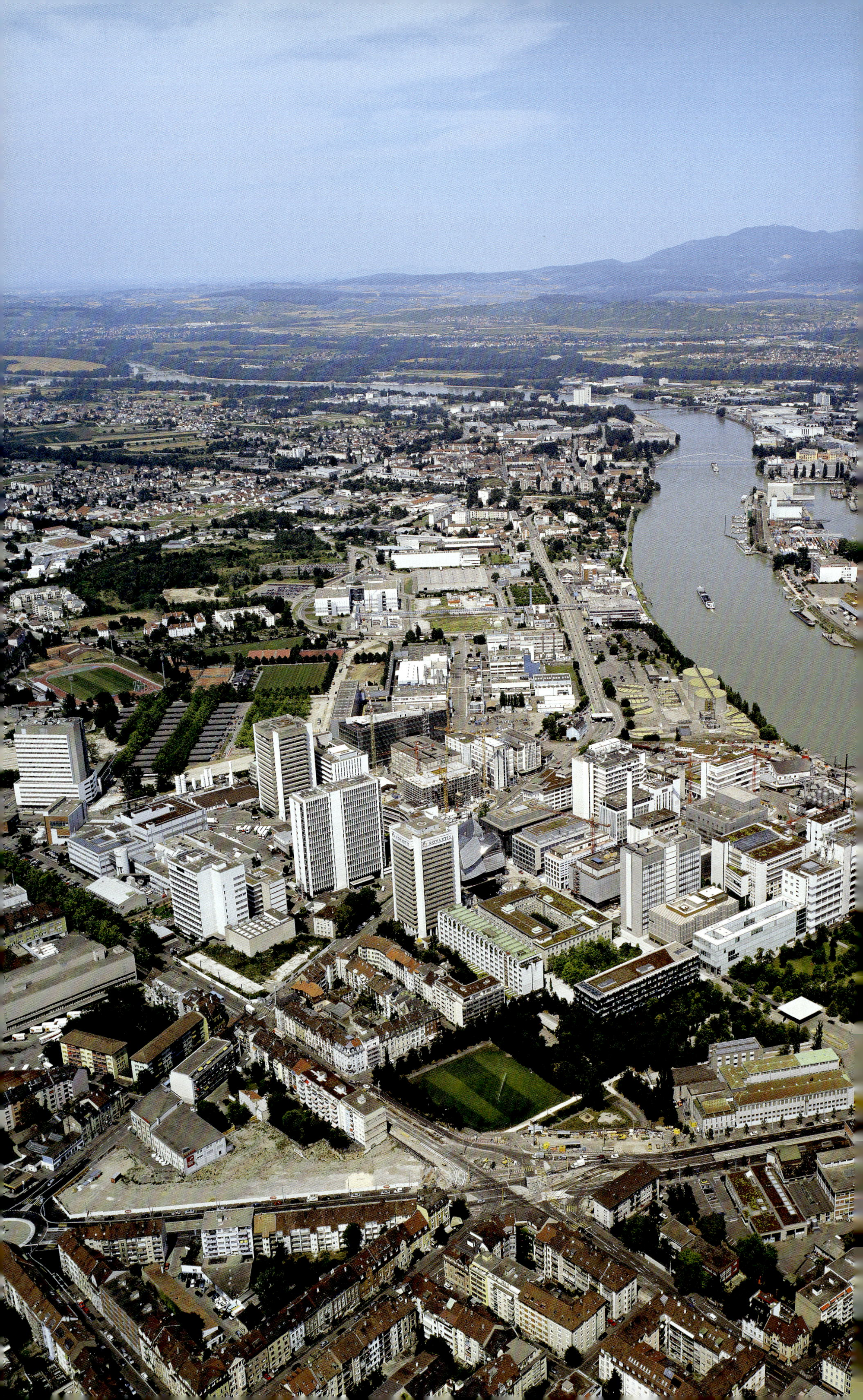

Aerial photograph of the Novartis Campus and its environs looking in the direction of France and Germany, 2008

The Master Plan

The Master Plan, which was accepted by the management at Novartis in mid 2001 and subsequently implemented, is primarily concerned with the twenty-hectare estate owned by the company. However, it also takes into account the nearby and more distant urban-planning and cultural context of the city of Basel as well. The planned "Campus of Innovation, Knowledge, and Encounters" is viewed in the context of the city's other existing and planned large educational and cultural institutions. The newly created urban space is deliberately separated from the riverside path along the Rhine in order to keep the path public, but at the same time it is oriented toward the river in such a way that the relationship between the Campus and the water is made possible and even stimulated. In addition, the special position on the border between Switzerland and France is addressed, and Basel's character as a transnational city is reflected in a proposed extension across to France in the longer term.

The basic geometrical alignment of the new, strictly orthogonal development structure is subordinated to the older alignment that defined the original factory complex. There are both functional and economic reasons for this. Existing streets are preserved, and the new ones are arranged in such a way that they correspond to existing paths, while the functioning and maintenance of the underground infrastructure is ensured. Cultural reasons were also decisive, as the grid structure also traces the pattern that characterized the Celtic settlement that existed on the site more than two thousand years ago. In addition, memories of the factory that in many ways created the foundation for today's research and development company were to be preserved in an open interpretation.

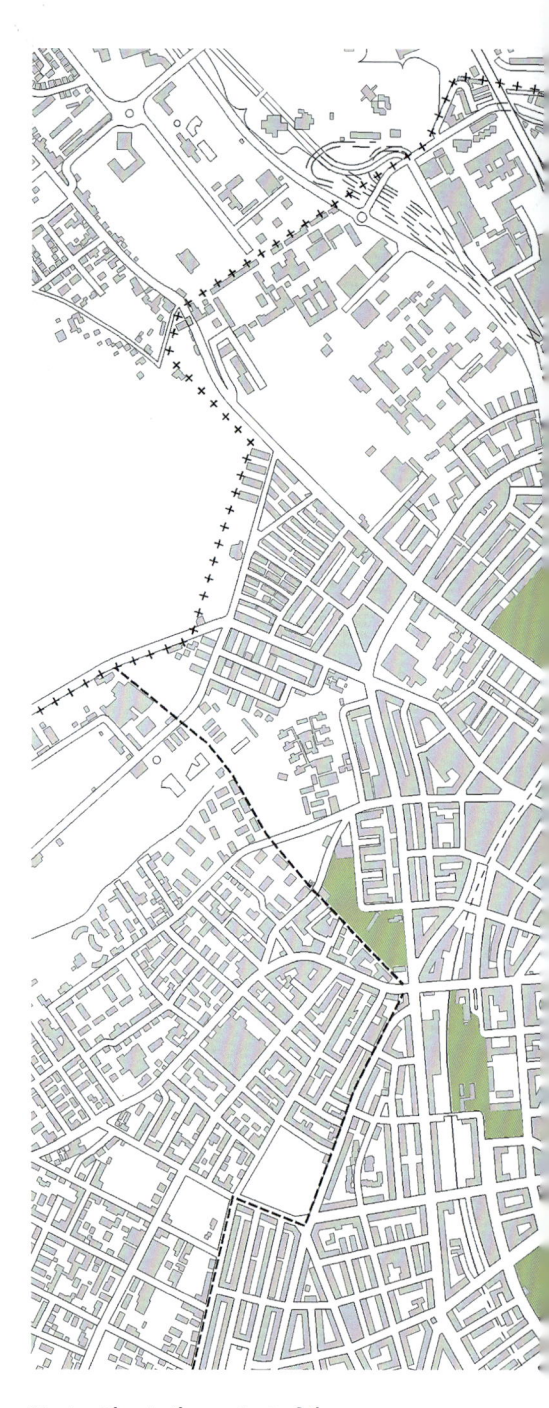

Master Plan in the context of the city of Basel, Studio di Architettura, 2002–08: The street structure and green areas fit into the preexisting plan while the building structures stand apart and create an impressive urban picture.

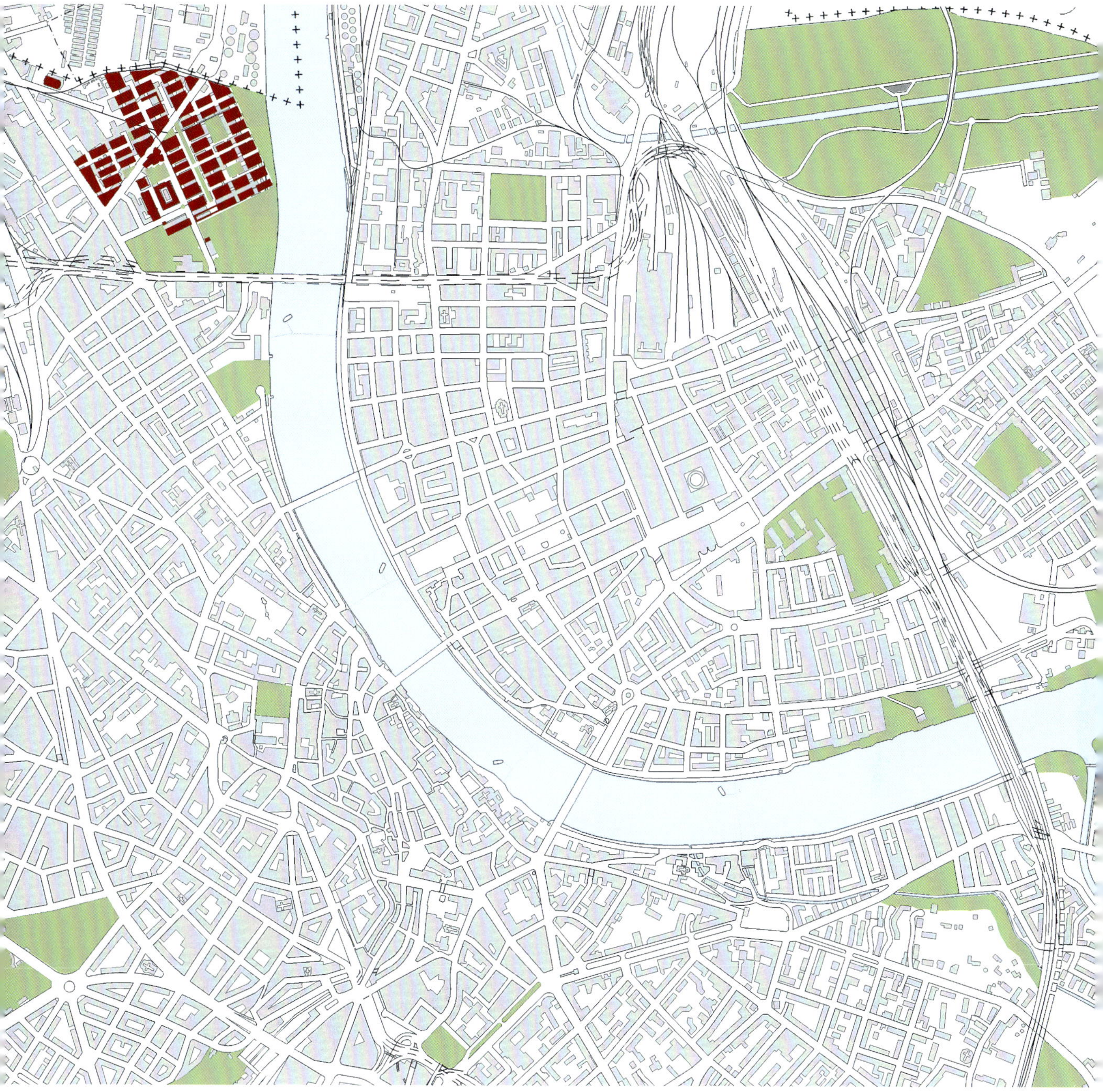

The historic Fabrikstrasse—which was called Schlachthausgasse until 1889—is being converted along its whole length of more than six hundred meters into a prestigious avenue that will form the real backbone of the new urban structure. The existing buildings to the west of it will be mostly preserved, including the high-rise buildings, which are to be supplemented with additional high-rises. The plan envisages a high-rise city *en miniature*, which will be visible from a long distance away and will correspond across the Rhine to the second Novartis area in Klybeck, with its high-rise office buildings and chimneys. By contrast, comparatively regular and small-scale five-story buildings are planned for the area east of Fabrikstrasse, and in general for most of the Campus. Buildings of this type have proved their value in most European cities, particularly as they are capable of creating well-proportioned urban spaces that offer a high quality of life. Their interiors can be efficiently divided using simple construction elements, as they are still below the limit for high-rise buildings as defined by the building regulations; they also provide naturally bright office spaces. In addition, this also allows the main building dating from 1939 to be incorporated into the new complex almost perfectly, as it is also approximately twenty meters high. However, the urban structure that is being created here will not consist of blocks, but rather of individual buildings. These are scaled in such a way that they can be used as office buildings or as laboratory buildings, although any form of zoning is being avoided in favor of a functional mixture. The largest plots are 62 by 35 meters in size, and the smallest are 25 by 18 meters.

An important consideration in establishing the urban planning structure was to allow the highest possible population density that would be tolerable in the area. This was not primarily for economic reasons, but above all for functional reasons. Above all, the Campus is intended to serve as a site for communication, and communication is promoted by density and even by confined conditions. On the other hand, overcrowding of the complex was to be avoided. For this reason, the maximum possible usage permissible under the building regulations was not fully exploited. The regulations allow buildings with a height of forty meters, but this would have led to a darkening of the comparatively narrow streets. Instead—and to compensate for the tight proximity to an extent—the plan envisaged not only a system of generous public spaces, but also two large park complexes within the system. These are intended to offer an experience of the opposite of density, namely, expansiveness and spaciousness, and here as well the urban aspect of the Campus is contrasted with a landscape aspect. The contrast has been formulated as sharply as possible, particularly since the sharpness itself has a special charm.

The most important public spaces adjoin Fabrikstrasse directly, while others lie slightly further off. They relax the dense urban structure and provide

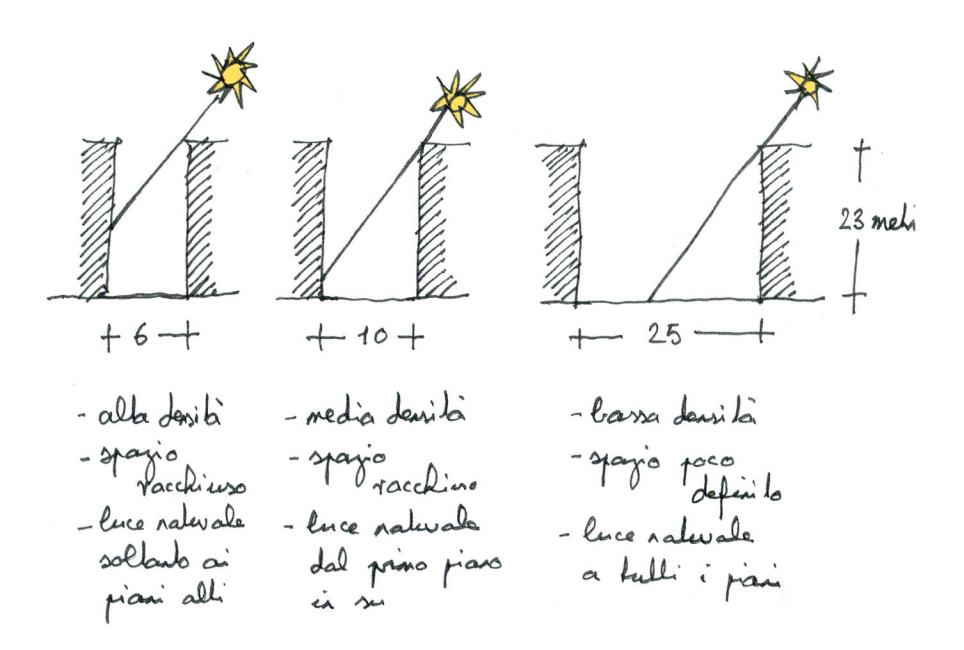

Study of street width and sun exposure, Vittorio Magnago Lampugnani, 2001: The streets were to be as narrow as possible, in order to generate spatial density, and wide enough so that the ground floor of the buildings can be naturally illuminated.

each of the buildings with a more open view on at least one side. The streets form a hierarchical network of spaces and access elements. Fabrikstrasse is fifteen meters wide, or twenty meters at some points, with four meters of arcade space in addition; the main streets are usually twelve and a half meters wide and the side streets are ten meters wide. The main streets, which run from east to west, have two rows of trees, and the east-west side streets have a single row of trees that protects the south side of the buildings from excessive sunlight. None of the streets running from north to south has any trees, with the exception of Fabrikstrasse and the esplanade-like Quinlane.

Access to the Campus from Voltastrasse is designed sequentially. You cross two squares, one belonging to the city and one relating to the Campus, walk through a wide park, and enter the Campus via a gate that narrows the street space and then opens it up again towards the Forum, the largest and most prestigious square in the whole complex. Fabrikstrasse then leads along the main buildings to the Green, which again expands the space towards the west. As it crosses Hüningerstrasse, the street narrows again before opening up towards the east this time, onto the Piazzetta. The end point of the spatial sequence is provided by a final square, in the middle of which there is a monumental sculpture that functions as a *point de vue*. Beyond the square, a passageway leads across the border to France and to the car park and sports facilities.

Following double page:
Master Plan, Studio di Architettura, 2002–08

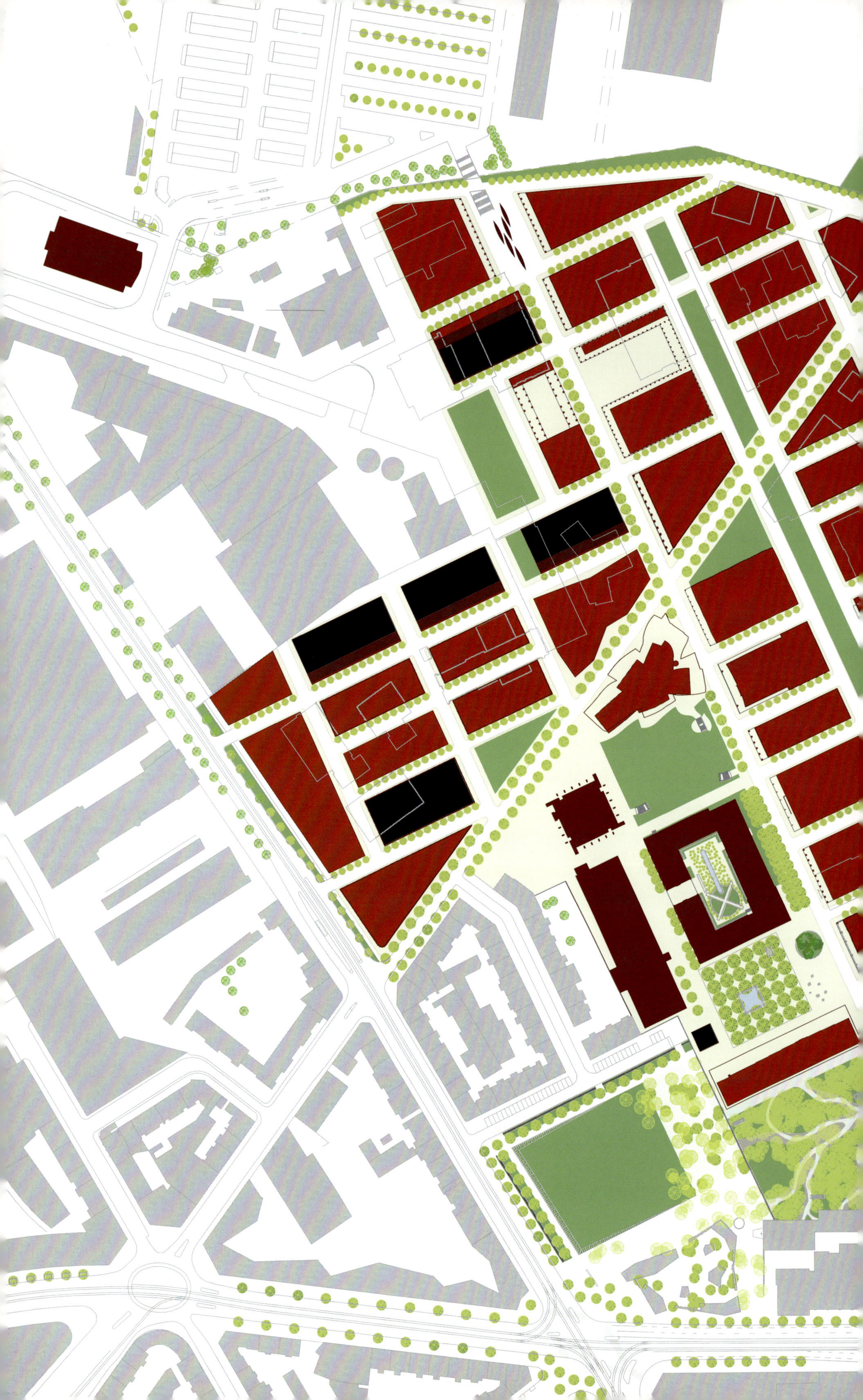

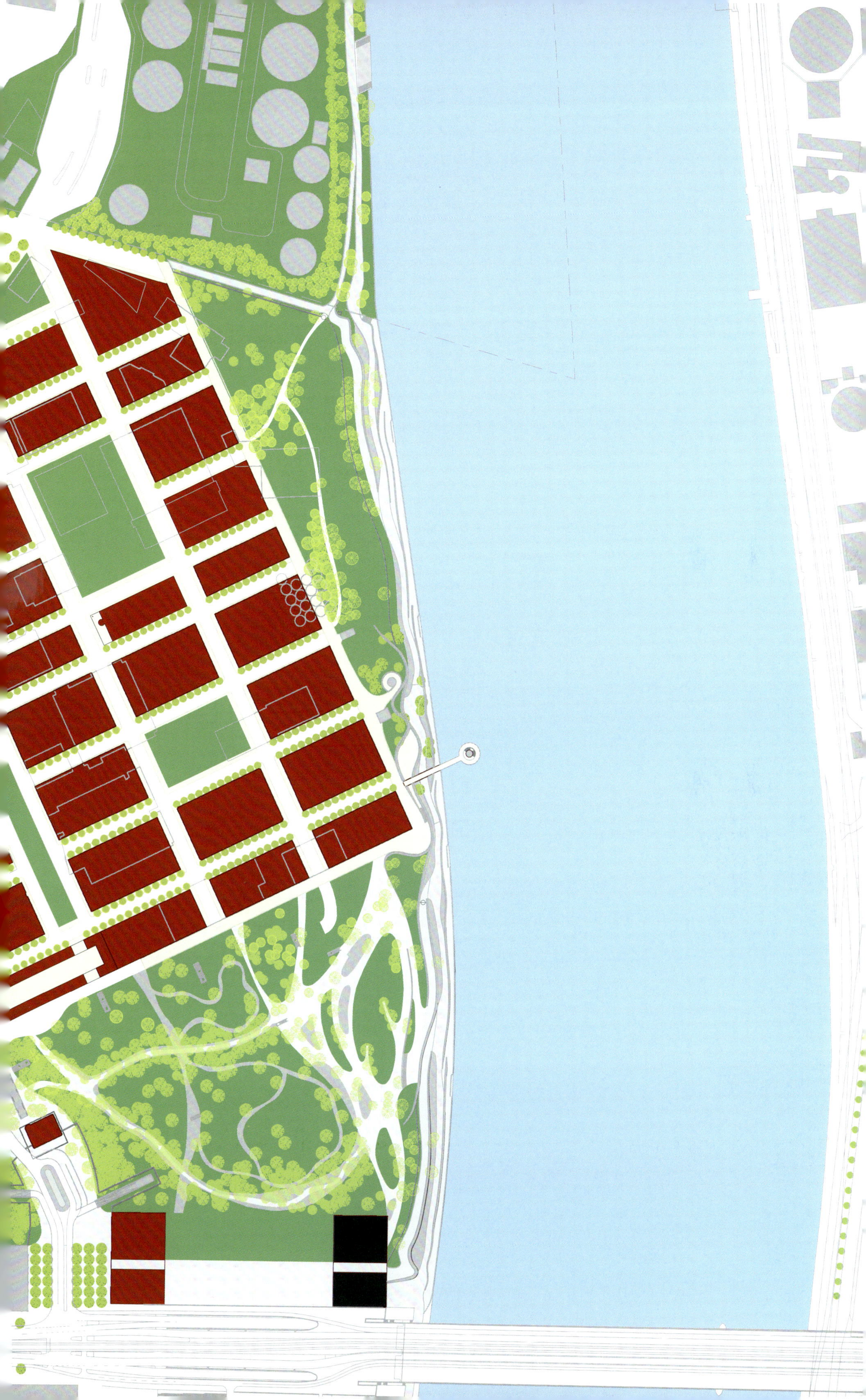

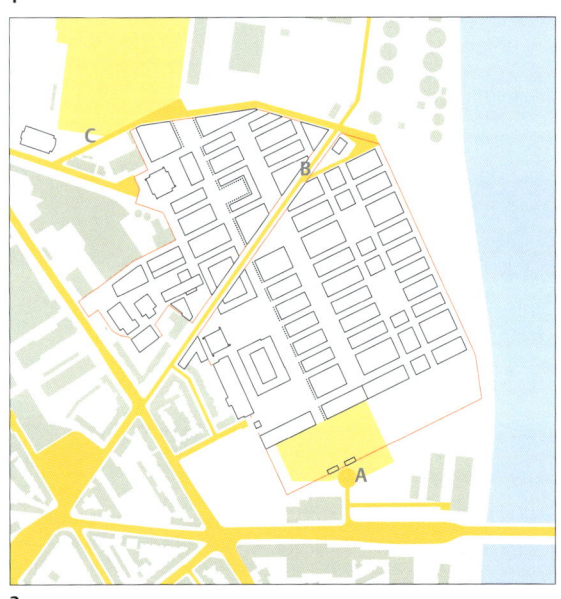

Analytical overview of the Master Plan, Studio di Architettura, 2002

1 Overlay situation (grey) and project (black outlines)

2 Green areas

3 Motorized traffic
  A Campus main entrance and underground garage approach
  B Goods delivery
  C Approach to Hüningen parking lot

4 Pedestrian area, limited vehicular traffic
  ▶ Gate
  ▸ Revolving gate
  ▪ Streetcar stop

Existing Buildings and Demolitions

The Master Plan is designed as a long-term plan. It specifies a development process that will be completed in thirty years at the earliest. In other words, it is an ideal plan. It is meant to be implemented quickly, but not forcibly. For example, only those buildings that are obsolete are to be demolished; they will then be replaced without exception by buildings that correspond to the Master Plan. The new approach thus envisages a state of coexistence between the new buildings and the remainder of the existing buildings. However, interruptions in the appearance of the complex are regarded not as threats, but rather as tolerable transitional situations, and even sometimes as beneficial.

Exceptions and interruptions of this type will be both numerous and long lasting. However, demolishing only those buildings that are completely written off and can no longer be used in any way avoids unnecessary costs and ecological waste—every destruction of a building at the same time involves the destruction of energy and produces waste. In addition, when the existing building fabric is of high quality, it represents some of the identity and memory of its location.

The decision was therefore made at an early stage to preserve a storehouse dating from the nineteen-forties alongside the still functioning, and in some cases highly equipped, research buildings. The storehouse initially had to be decontaminated and provisionally converted into an office building. The initial pilot projects for a new type of open-plan office were implemented in the process. The building, erected on a triangular plan, stands at an angle to the geometry of the Master Plan, but with its plain and memorable shape it represents a characteristic location on the Novartis Campus.

With regard to the multi-story car park that was located on Lichtstrasse directly opposite to the main building, which was built at around the same time, careful consideration was also given to the possibility of converting it for other uses. However, this proved to be difficult and would have substantially affected the character of the building. In addition, although the functional building made of exposed concrete was not unsightly, it was quite voluminous and oppressive in comparison to the main building itself. It was therefore decided to demolish it in order to make room for the generous free space of the Forum.

Parks

The parks are an integral component of the Campus—they represent the other side of a coin that has a dense urban structure on the front of it, as it were. The two larger parks mark the transition between the Campus and the city in the north, and between the Campus and the Rhine in the east. They both support and accentuate the opening of the complex towards the river space, which represents one of the most important design principles of the Master Plan. However, the artificial nature that they embody is also an antidote to the urban campus structure.

The Campus, in turn, is loosened and structured by other green areas. These squares, which are not only to have various shapes and sizes but also different designs, are placed just as precisely as the building plots. Together with the Green, the group of trees on the Forum, and the rows of trees along the streets, they join together to form a truly continuous park system that is in accord with the urban system.

Diagram of the main and auxiliary roads, main entrances, and street names, Studio di Architettura, 2004: The hierarchy of the streets, which is expressed by their width and tree cover, is underscored by the arrangement of the main façades and entrances of the buildings.

Access and Traffic

The main entrance to the Novartis Campus is no longer on Lichtstrasse, which is narrow and poorly exposed, but on Voltastrasse. A two-level underground parking garage, open to both visitors and employees, is accessed from the entrance square. Additional access points, which are, however, reserved for employees, are reached via Elsässerstrasse and the existing aboveground Hüningen parking lot. All forms of through traffic are to be kept away from the Campus on principle, although delivery traffic with small trucks, cars, and taxis is permissible. Primarily, however, the street space is to be reserved for pedestrians and cyclists, who will have to share it as amicably and considerately as possible with the few vehicles that are permitted. Those who use public transport and arrive at St. Johann Station, or at the two tram stops on Voltastrasse and Elsässerstrasse, are to be privileged with routes that are as short and attractive as possible. All heavy-goods deliveries will take place separately via Hüningerstrasse.

All of the streets on the Campus will be given the names of personalities who have made important contributions to the progress of medical science. The names have been selected and arranged in such a way that they follow the alphabet. The naming system will thus have an alphabetical order superimposed on it to allow easy orientation on the Campus. In addition, the system will become a cultural and educational facility, as the street names will be explained by information panels displaying the most important biographical data and achievements of the relevant figures. The only exception will be Fabrikstrasse, the name of which will not be changed, so as to preserve the memory of the historic origin of the factory area. Every building and each building entrance will have a number, so that people will be able to find their way around the Campus in the same way as in a city.

Art

Art on the Campus is not merely a superficial addition, but rather a component of the spatial concept as a whole. It will be used in the outer areas in such a way that it marks or interrupts thoroughfares, defines and emphasizes the space of squares, or enriches the parks conceptually. Its task is to offer perceptual aids, even it if does so by causing uncertainty or surprise. It will therefore not be "added to" the urban space, but rather planned as a component of it from the very start.

Lighting

For energy-saving reasons, as well as to create atmosphere, the illumination provided will be just bright enough to give the Campus population a feeling of safety at night without depriving the area of its sense of excitement and mystery. At the same time, the light is an architectural element that marks and characterizes urban spaces and parks, tracing and emphasizing their geometry, direction, and mood. The squares and streets will have different lighting, the main streets will be lit differently from the side streets, and the arcades differently again; the same will apply to the parks and squares. The objects used as light sources will be important, in addition to the quality of the light itself. They will therefore be developed independently and will contribute to the unmistakable quality of the Novartis Campus.

Graphic Elements

The same concepts will apply to the graphic elements in the outer areas. As for the lighting, the principle that applies will be: As much as necessary, and as little as possible. The overloading of public space with brazen, impertinent, and often superfluous written messages is to be opposed with a more subtle world on the Campus. Where signs are necessary, they will be produced independently or carefully selected so that they do not look like foreign bodies, but instead appear to be components of the urban space, the architecture, and the gardens.

1

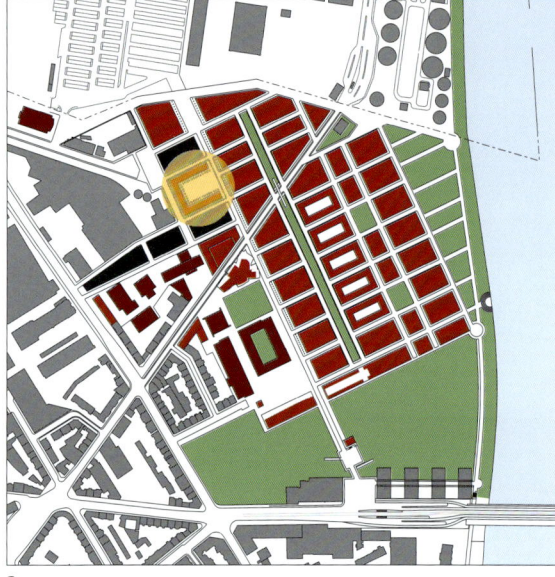

2

3

4

Studies of the design of the Piazzetta, Studio di Architettura, 2002

1 Piazzetta as a gap in the building series
2 Piazzetta captured in a building

Studies of the Piazzetta site, Studio di Architettura, 2002

3 Piazzetta west of Fabrikstrasse
4 Piazzetta east of Fabrikstrasse

5

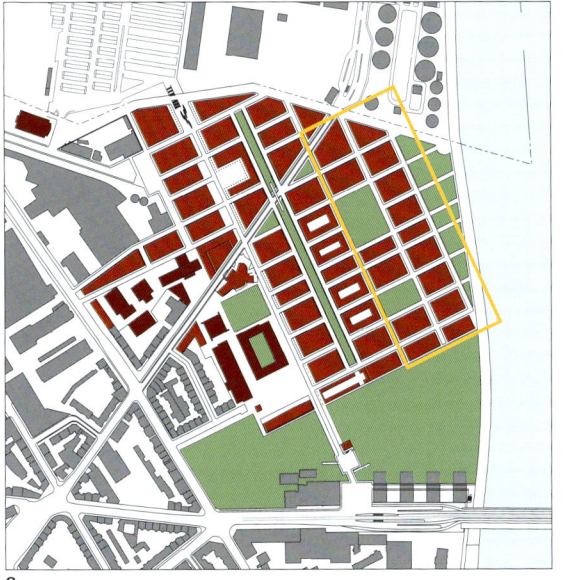

7

6

8

Studies of the building widths, Studio di Architettura, 2003

5 Narrow buildings and fourteen cross streets to the Rhine

6 Wider buildings and twelve cross streets to the Rhine

Studies of the widening of the Rhine, Studio di Architettura, 2003

7 Master Plan within the original lot boundaries

8 Expansion by about 20.8 m in the direction of the bank of the Rhine, creating a more efficient building row

A view of the arcade on Fabrikstrasse, Studio di Architettura, rendering, 2003: The public spaces on the Campus are also places for recreation, meeting, and work.

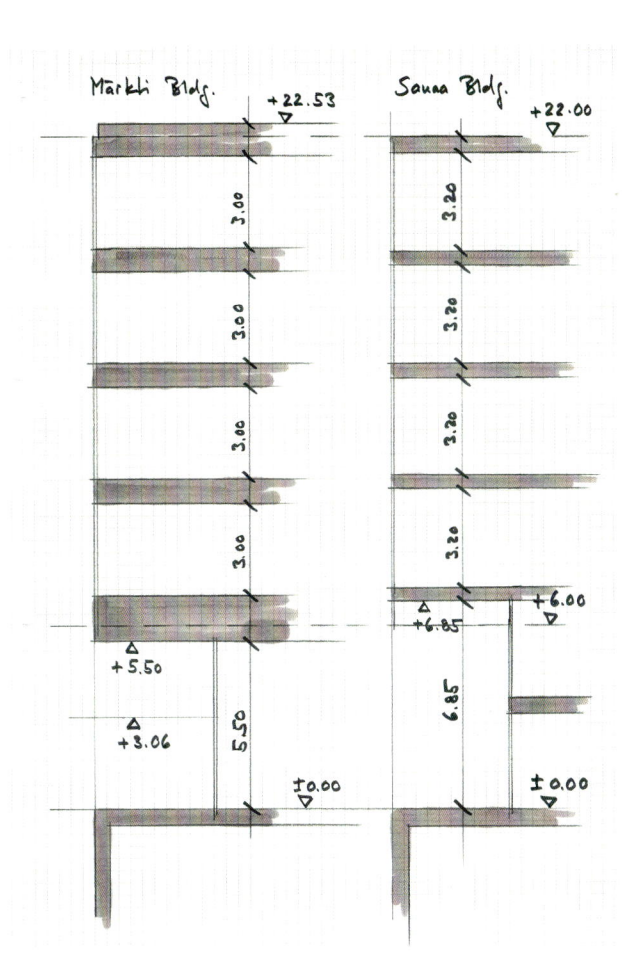

Building sections on Fabrikstrasse,
Studio di Architettura, 2005

Usage

The buildings on the Campus will be used as office or laboratory buildings. Economical but comparatively small plots were selected for this deliberately. They lead to clearly comprehensible buildings and equally comprehensible structures that can be used in a flexible way. In addition, the employees in individual departments, who will perhaps be accommodated not just in one building but in several, will be tempted by the spatial separation to use the streets more often and thus have more intensive contact with their colleagues.

Community facilities will be located on the ground floors of all of the buildings on Fabrikstrasse, ranging from the Visitor Center to restaurants, cafés, and shops, that is to say, everything that a small community needs for everyday life. This will make Fabrikstrasse not only the architectural but also the social backbone of the complex. And it will also be the place where the most movement, the most intensive exchanges—in short, the most intensive urban life—will take place on the Campus.

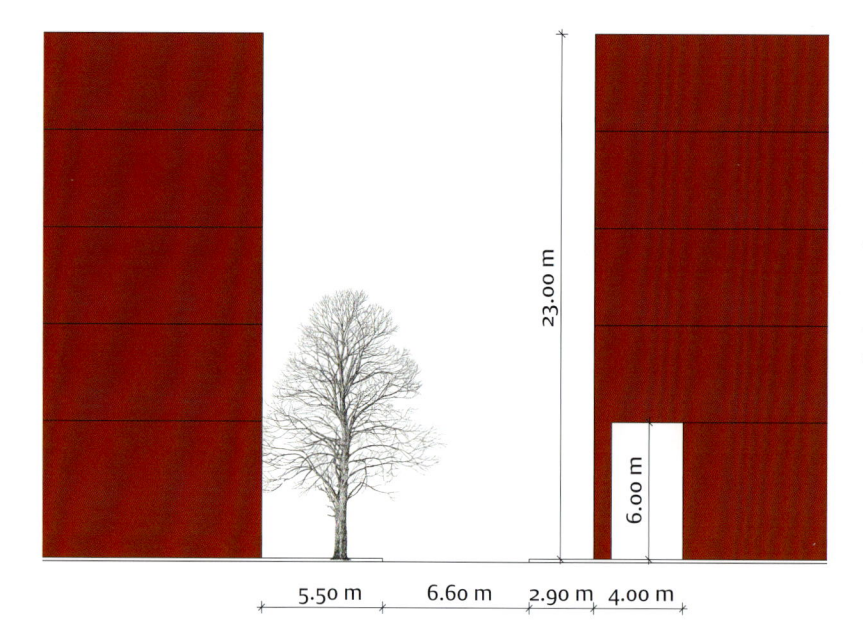

Schematic section of Fabrikstrasse, Studio di Architettura, 2002: In addition to the height of the building line and eaves for the buildings on Fabrikstrasse, the arcade space was also specified.

23.00 m

6.00 m

5.50 m   6.60 m   2.90 m   4.00 m

Regulations

The new complex will be held together by the homogeneous treatment of the streets, invigorated by the various buildings that will be erected within the plan of its plot assignments. This will require a willingness on the part of the participating architects to become involved with the plan, even quite critically, and to conduct a dialogue—which can certainly be a controversial one—with each of their neighbors. The interpretation of this fundamental attitude will be left to each individual architect. There are, in fact, neither design statutes nor set regulations for the materials or construction types to be used on the Campus. However, the building lines have to be observed, and the buildings can be below the maximum gutter height but cannot exceed it. In the design of the façades, attention should be given to their purpose, which is to limit and determine the public space on the Campus. In addition, all of the buildings bordering the east side of Fabrikstrasse must have arcades. For the arcades, the cross section that is also specified in the Master Plan is obligatory. The main access to these buildings must be from Fabrikstrasse, and in addition, as much ground-floor space as possible should be provided for public usage and face towards Fabrikstrasse. The arcade profile also establishes the height of the ground floor. For the rest of the Campus as well, the main entrances are set, corresponding to the hierarchy of squares, main streets, and side streets.

Sustainability

On the Novartis Campus, sustainability will mainly be achieved through the sustainability of the buildings themselves, which should also allow changes of use without the need for expensive conversion measures. All of the buildings are in fact conceived and scaled in such a way that they can be used both as office buildings and as laboratory buildings. This will make it possible to react to fundamental structural changes in the company without the need for equally fundamental urban and architectural policy changes. However, this will remain an exception: many more minor adjustments of the interior layouts of rubust building are to be expected.

In addition, there will be extremely low energy consumption, made possible both by relevant arrangement and by modern technology, and this will be established as a standard on the Campus. An ecologically compatible and largely naturally balanced water management system will also be an established component of the energy concept.

Implementation

A "Workshop" has been established to combine all of these various aspects, coordinate them with each other, and place them at the service of the Campus's planning. Under the guidance of a "Project Champion," the Workshop brings together the experts who are needed in order to do justice, with the greatest degree of professionalism, to the complexity of the tasks involved. In the Workshop, however, the experts do not merely represent their own discipline, but are able to participate in discussions beyond the boundaries of their own areas of expertise in an extremely open way. This will make work on the Campus interdisciplinary in the best possible sense—and it will make the Campus itself an eminently interdisciplinary project.

On the basis of ideas from the Workshop and users' requirements, the Master Plan for the Campus has been refined and modified. The re-siting of the harbor with its silos and rail connections, and the opportunity to purchase the land that consequently became available, encouraged an extension of the architectural structure towards the Rhine. This has improved not only the relationship between the Campus and the river area, but also the geometry of the plots. At the request of users, who wanted larger connected ground-plan surfaces for laboratories, the plots were modified accordingly. The changes involved went so far that one street was completely removed from the original plan, and the structure of the plots as a whole was correspondingly adjusted.

The concept of the Master Plan envisages that each building in the city should be different and should also be designed by a different architect. Prominent architects from all over the world have been and are continuing to be invited to contribute to the construction of the Campus. The buildings are meant to reflect not only different views of architecture, but also the different cultures in which these views are rooted. This is intended not least to represent the cultural variety of the buildings' users, who should also feel at home in them.

The architects received precise guidelines. These were not only based on the Master Plan, with its comparatively few rules, but also, of course, resulted from the users' functional requirements. The initial building commissions were preceded by intensive discussions regarding workplace design.

Prospects

Overall, the Novartis Campus represents a large-scale experimental arrangement for innovative urban planning, which has been conceived in a three-dimensional way from the very start and includes architectural, landscape, artistic, graphic, and lighting aspects, but which above all forms part of an equally innovative and comprehensive company strategy. To this extent, the Campus is in the tradition of the great urban-planning enterprises of the past, which have always been not merely artistic, but also economic, social, political, and ideological projects. As the experimental arrangement has been set up in an extremely—and unusually—long-term fashion, it will only be in a few years' time that it will be possible to discuss results that are in any way definitive. The results that are already visible today on the building site on the Rhine give grounds for confidence that it is still possible even today to plan and implement an urban planning project that is not compromised by short-lived fashions and alleged external constraints, is free of short-term thinking and personal vanities, corresponds to the needs of its users, pursues a community-based idea, and represents high cultural standards.

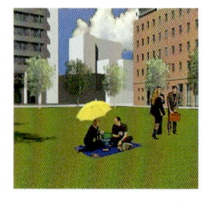

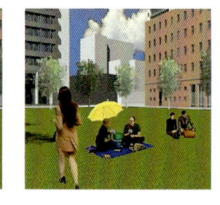

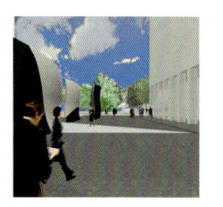

Stills from the simulation film
Novartis Campus, Studio Azzurro
with Studio di Architettura, 2003

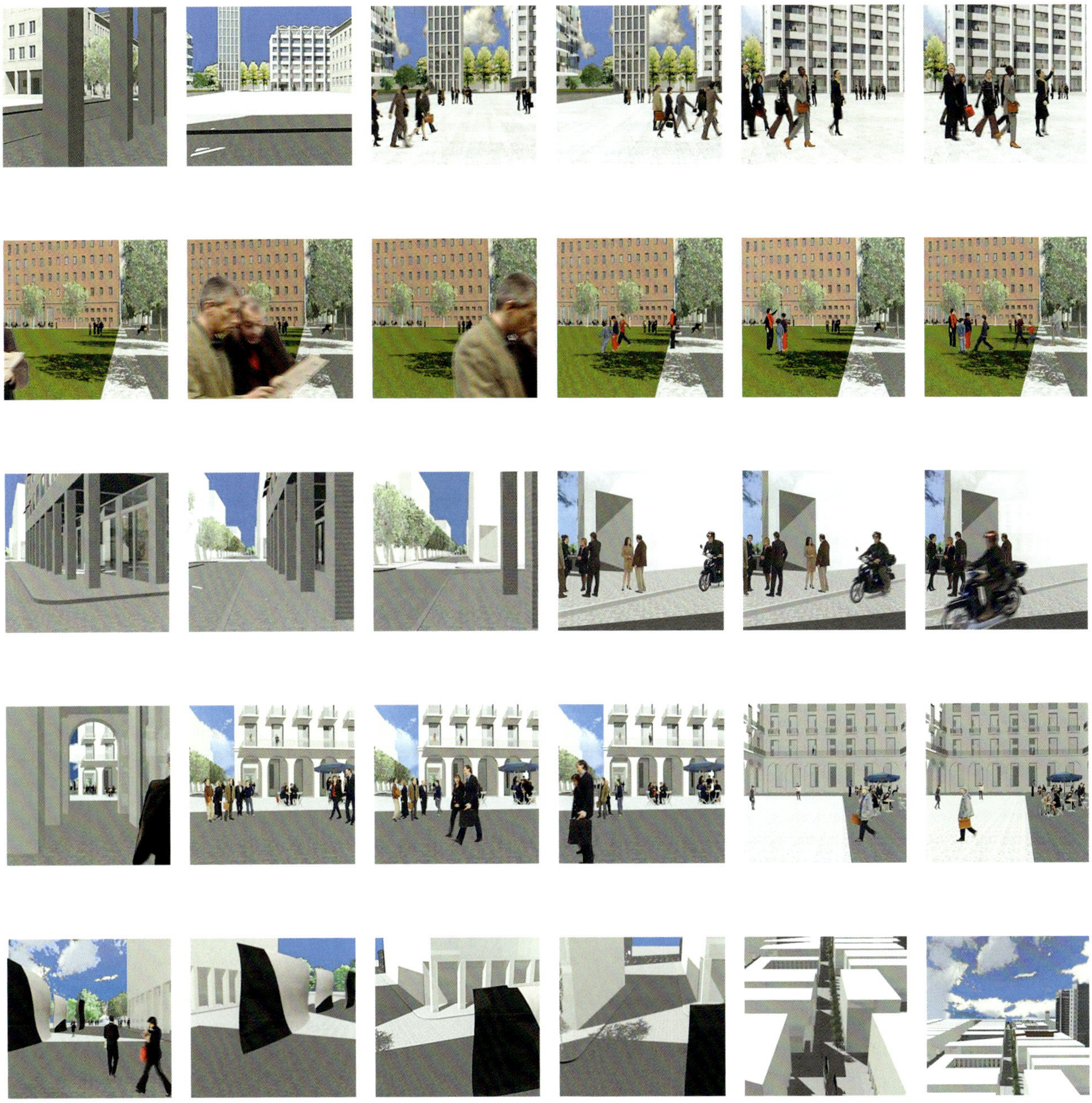

The Architects of the Campus

Marco Serra

In spite of, or perhaps especially due to its urban planning clarity and stringency, the Master Plan is capable of meeting individual needs. It is conceptualized in such a way that changes can be undertaken without having to relinquish the basic idea. The original building organization was already modified and further developed in many ways during the first realization phase, but the character of the Master Plan was kept intact and the urban planning basics have become more valid than ever before. The selection of the architects who are to realize the individual buildings plays a fundamental role with regard to the changes. Several examples serve to illustrate how specific building decisions—suggested by the architects themselves or the users—can have a direct and positive influence on the development of the overall Master Plan and thereby leave a mark on its character.

It was clear from the beginning that this project was not the result of a tabula rasa approach nor was it the work of a single guiding hand. The initially very homogenous-looking visualization concentrated on the representation of streets, proportions, and a constellation of open squares. At that point, the architecture and any appearance it might have had was secondary. The only thing that was clear was that the Master Plan would not be designed and built by a single architect. It was only after the urban planning design was consolidated that the question was posed regarding the appropriate method of selecting the various architects who would emphasize the many facets and excellence of the company. Vittorio Magnago Lampugnani was assigned the execution of one building, and renowned architects from different cultures were sought for the rest of the projects.

The architects of the first four buildings were selected by means of competitions. The number of participants for each competition was set at a maximum of six architecture firms through a screening process. Architects from Basel, Switzerland more broadly, Europe, Asia, and America were considered. In addition to an extensive demand specification profile to which the architects had to conform, reference projects played a decisive role; different properties were evaluated before a decision was made. The jury was composed of the eventual users of the buildings to be constructed, those responsible for the execution of the projects, and architectural professionals. Although the competition procedure seemed to open up a relatively large spectrum of suggestions and discussions, the influence of the builders on the final result was for the most part completed through the appointment of the architects. Although the jury was confronted with a multitude of suggestions, structural changes could hardly be taken into account. In contrast, especially in the selection phase of the architects and in the evaluation of the contributions, this strategy provided the occasion for an exciting discussion about the architecture. This process intensified as the number of participants grew, where-by not only the compatibility of the proposed architecture with the Master Plan was discussed/debated, but also the compatibility of the various architectural works in relation to each

> **The project has been developed in continuous dialogue with a large number of participants. . . . The debate with the users, the scientists who will actually work in the building, has been especially intense and productive.**
> *Álvaro Siza*

> **Building 153 developed from the signal importance that the laboratory space had for the building, and the goal we had in making that workspace both efficient and focused and simultaneously open and extroverted. . . . We understood that the desire to evolve the concept of the workspace was a key goal. 153 addresses this issue. . . . It is now the responsibility of the people of Novartis to insist on this latent potential in the building so that the labs do not just simply repeat the typical configuration found everywhere else.**
> *Rafael Moneo*

other. The interdisciplinary debate about the projects conducted by the jury, of which the art curator Harald Szeemann and the designer Alan Fletcher were members, often led to unexpected results.

The first Campus project was awarded to Diener & Diener Architekten with a 1:1 façade model. On this basis it was determined that the architects to follow should also be given the opportunity to make this kind of presentation when proposing their own projects.

Peter Märkli won the next competition, and his well-reasoned design did not undergo any radical changes during the execution phase. A very friendly building that users like to visit was the result of a project that was represented as rather challenging in the competition.

Kazuo Sejima and Ryue Nishizawa (SANAA) were successful with their project for the next building. The Master Plan's specification that an office building must demonstrate a minimal building depth of twenty-two meters was waired in this case. A building with an eleven-meter-wide courtyard and office depths of five and a half meters became the new typology for the Campus. The last commission to be awarded as the result of a competition was given to Adolf Krischanitz.

> **I think this is one of the rarest opportunities that we have been given to design a building on every level; from responding to a Master Plan, to pushing the limits of technology in terms of the use of glass and sustainability, to inventing an interior workspace down to the details of building graphics and work station design together with the client. So in this sense, it's one of the most holistic and complete design processes that we have been involved with in the history of the office.**
> Frank O. Gehry

Up to this point, all of the projects were executed by the architects selected by the competition juries. The project for the entryway pavilion and parking lot marked the definitive end of the competition procedure. It was extremely complex and involved many interfaces. The Master Plan had specified the location and form of the reception buldings. But in contrast to the rest of the Campus buildings, the area's interfacing with the surrounding public areas had to be considered and was an integral component of the proposal. The relationship of the parking lot to the Park was an important aspect of the project, particularly since there were already clear ideas about the latter. Hiring the architect Marco Serra, which made it possible to have very close contact with the users and the landscape architect, led to a satisfactory result.

With this information as background the following architects were found based on the selection principle of direct commissioning. Not only new architects, but also architectural firms already known from the earlier competitions were considered, including David Chipperfield and Eduardo Souto de Moura. Each of these architects realized one laboratory building for the Novartis Campus. Above all, this kind of direct commissioning had the goal of coordinating as closely as possible the collaboration between architects, users, and clients from the very beginning, a goal that was achieved. Various developments that would not have occurred without the direct intervention of the architectural firms underscore the positive effect of this modus operandi.

The first two direct commissions were given to Tadao Ando and Frank O. Gehry. Different construction sites with different use possibilities were suggested to Ando. There were several reasons that a decision was reached in favor of the two buildings on the north end of Fabrikstrasse: first, for their strategically important location and challenging floor plan, and second, for the sculpture by Richard Serra that was already in place there by this time. The result was that Ando designed two buildings for the north Campus entrance, which simultaneously created a sort of gateway. No great discussion was necessary when the architect—in opposition to the Master Plan—suggested that both buildings be raised from an original planned height of 23.5 meters to 38 meters. The reason that the architect's proposal was accepted so swiftly is that the Master Plan was designed to be flexible enough to allow for change when the request for it is justified.

The determination of the construction site to be assigned to Gehry ran a similar course. In this case, too, different construction sites were considered based on several use scenarios. However, this time the architect was offered a location with great room for maneuvering. A decision was made to have Gehry design a building in the geographic center of the Campus—a location where his architectural style could escape the stringency of the road building lines and building heights without running the risk of being perceived as "incongruous." During the process of collaborating with the architect, the fact

> We have interpreted the building task as a window onto the research world, as an architectural connection that links the international group to the location by which it is influenced and which it itself influences. Our assignment was to seek the kind of sensual energy that radiates architectural openness and focus.
> *Roger Diener*

> It was crucial for me that Novartis had assigned a cultural value to the workplace. The architect's task is to realize this attitude in a concrete form and to provide the interior spaces [of the Campus buildings] with a structure, an imprint, an expressivity. The result is that the [Campus's] workplaces are very human.
> *Peter Märkli*

that the site bordered on a public place led to the decision to add an underground auditorium for six hundred people that had not originally been planned for the project.

The projects of Yoshio Taniguchi and Rafael Moneo present an interesting juxtaposition. Both projects were given the same parameters but led to completely different solutions. With his spatial layout, Moneo has created an extremely suspenseful and extroverted building, because the laboratories and offices are connected via corridors oriented along the façade. In contrast, with his enclosed glass façade, Taniguchi has evoked a very sculptural and unusual look for a laboratory building.

The project designed by Álvaro Siza represented a particularly positive development through the cooperation of the users, architects, and master planners. It was created at the same time as "Campus Plus," the joint project being carried out by Novartis and the city of Basel for the revamping of the areas adjoining the Campus. The building is located exactly at the transition to the current property border. In the spirit of a trade-off, the city of Basel granted Novartis the right to extend the Campus in the direction of the Rhine. From a long-term perspective, the initiative's very great potential ran the risk of not being realized in the short term, because railroad tracks were blocking the immediate commencement of construction. However, an unusual collaboration between the architects and the master planners permitted the development of a project that could be realized on a short-term basis without compromising the Master Plan in the long term. Fumihiko Maki is building an impressive building near Siza's that corresponds to the specifications of the Master Plan.

The next project in the framework of the Master Plan involves two high-rises, whose designs have been commissioned from Renzo Piano and Jean Nouvel. Contact has also been established with Rem Koolhaas for another building. In these cases also, the goal will always be to create exceptional working conditions for innovation and exchange within the vision of Novartis's "Campus of Knowledge" and its future-oriented workplace.

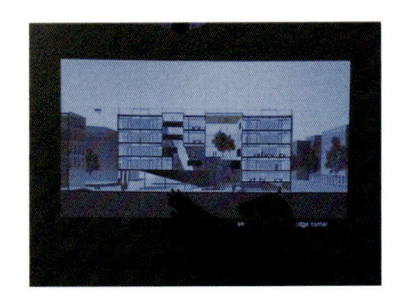

Video sequences from different
workshops and feedback meetings,
2003–04

Mock-ups, from left to right, designed by Fumihiko Maki, Yoshio Taniguchi, Rafael Moneo, Álvaro Siza, and Eduardo Souto de Moura, 2008: For each new building of the Campus, a partial model is first made in a scale of 1:1, which is used to go over all design decisions.

Aerial photograph of the
Novartis Campus, 2008

1   Diener & Diener,
    Gerold Wiederin,
    Helmut Federle
    Forum 3
    Study from October 2001
    Planning from October 2002
    Construction from October 2003
    Occupation in May 2005

2   Peter Märkli
    6 Fabrikstrasse
    Study from November 2002
    Planning from April 2003
    Construction from September 2004
    Occupation in May 2006

3   Sejima & Nishizawa (SANAA)
    4 Fabrikstrasse
    Study from November 2002
    Planning from January 2004
    Construction from March 2005
    Occupation in September 2006

4   Marco Serra
    2 Fabrikstrasse
    Study from July 2002
    Planning from October 2003
    Construction from October 2004
    Occupation in May 2007

5   Adolf Krischanitz
    16 Fabrikstrasse
    Study from March 2003
    Planning from January 2004
    Construction from July 2005
    Occupation in February 2008

6   Studio di Architettura
    12 Fabrikstrasse
    Study from January 2005
    Planning from October 2005
    Construction from October 2006
    Occupation in October 2008

7   Rafael Moneo
    14 Fabrikstrasse
    Study from January 2005
    Planning from December 2005
    Construction from October 2006
    Occupation in January 2009

8   Frank O. Gehry
    15 Fabrikstrasse
    Study from October 2003
    Planning from September 2004
    Construction from March 2006
    Occupation in July 2009

9   Tadao Ando
    28 Fabrikstrasse
    Study from May 2004
    Planning from October 2005
    Construction from August 2006
    Occupation in July 2009

10 Fumihiko Maki
    Square 4
    Study from July 2005
    Planning from August 2006
    Construction from November 2007
    Occupation in August 2009

11 David Chipperfield
    22 Fabrikstrasse
    Study from October 2005
    Planning from October 2006
    Construction from November 2007
    Occupation in October 2009

12 Yoshio Taniguchi
    10 Fabrikstrasse
    Study from January 2005
    Planning from December 2005
    Construction from March 2007
    Occupation in November 2009

13 Eduardo Souto de Moura
    Physic Garden 3
    Study from July 2005
    Planning from October 2006
    Construction from February 2008
    Occupation in July 2010

14 Álvaro Siza
    Virchow 6
    Study from July 2005
    Planning from August 2006
    Construction from February 2008
    Occupation in October 2010

15 Renzo Piano
    WSJ-526
    Study from October 2008
    Planning from March 2009
    Construction from July 2010
    Occupation in July 2013

16 Jean Nouvel
    WSJ-536
    Study from October 2008
    Planning from March 2009
    Construction from July 2010
    Occupation in July 2013

17 Tadao Ando, in planning

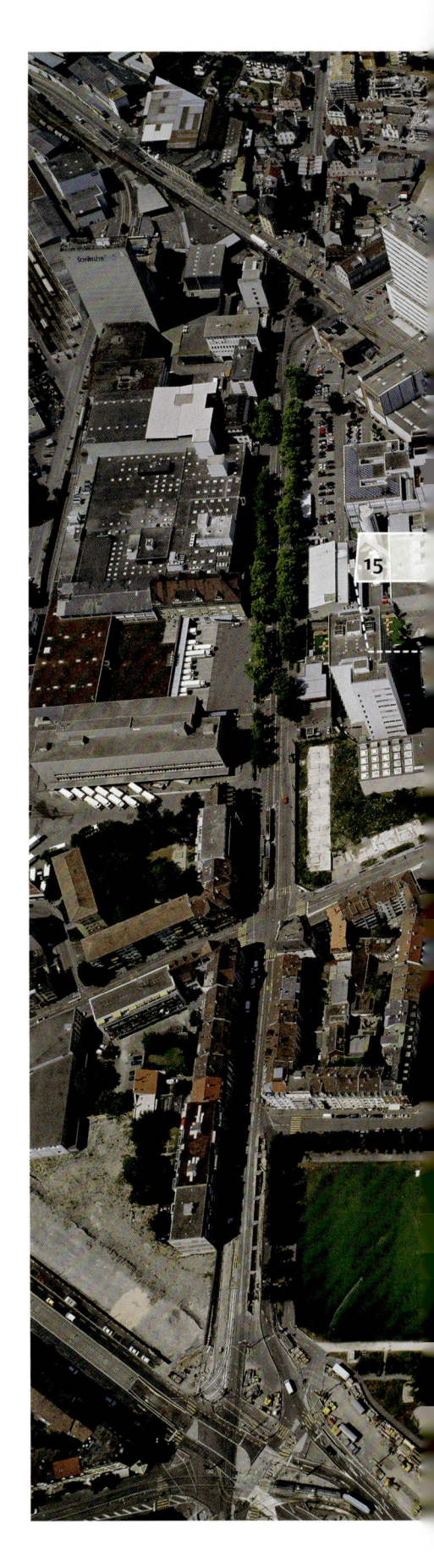

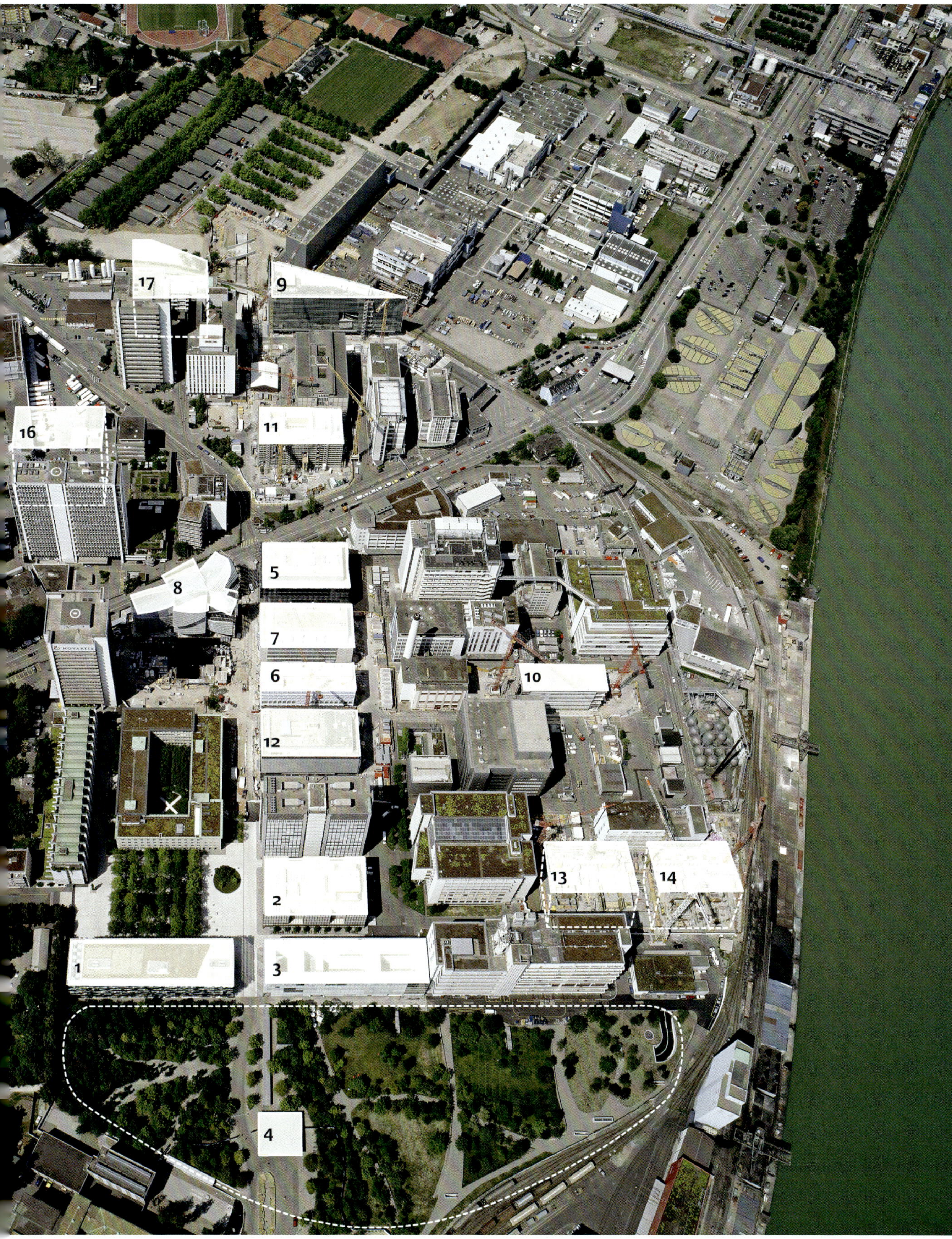
17
9
16
11
5
8
7
6
10
12
13
14
2
1
3
4

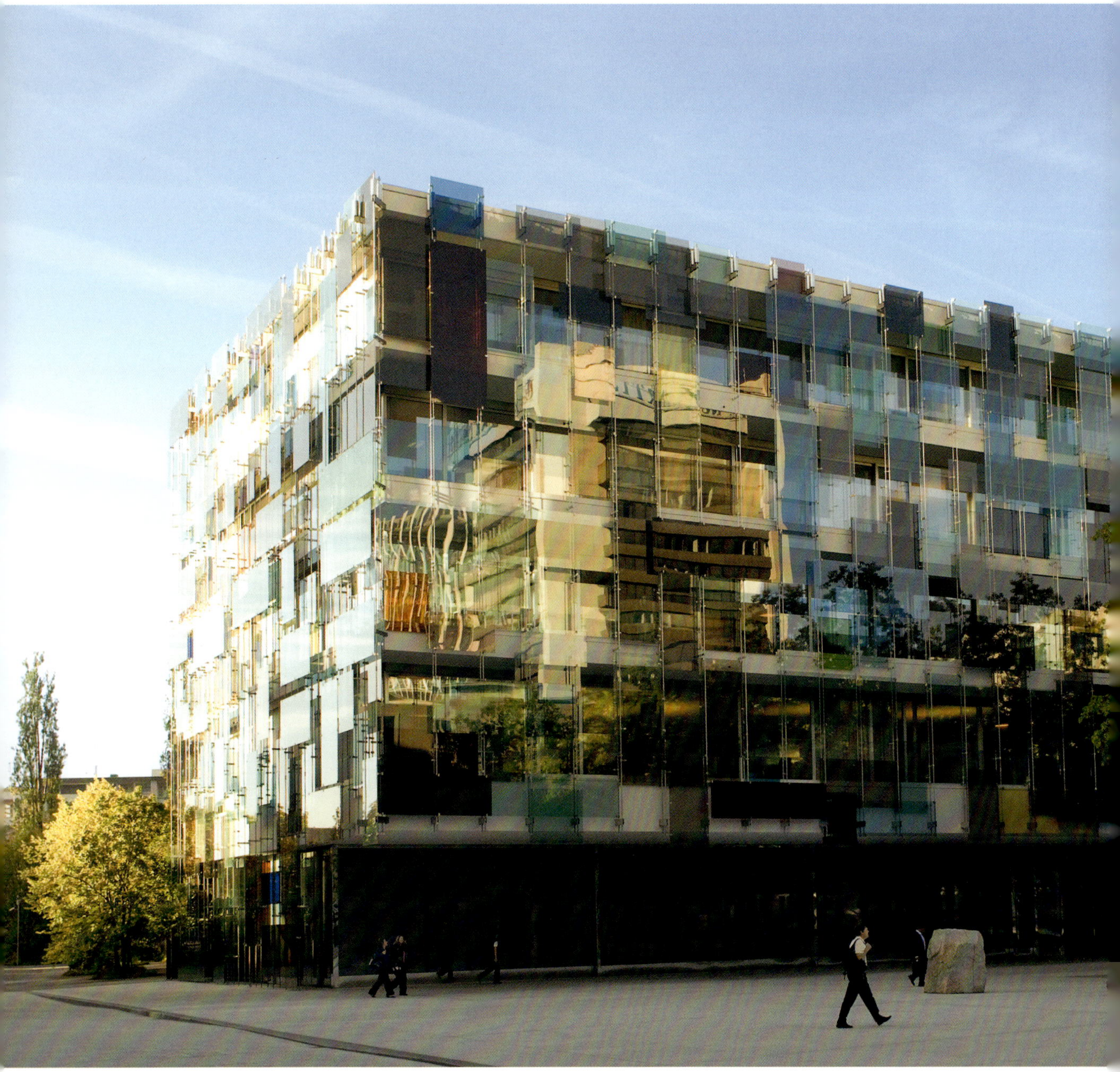

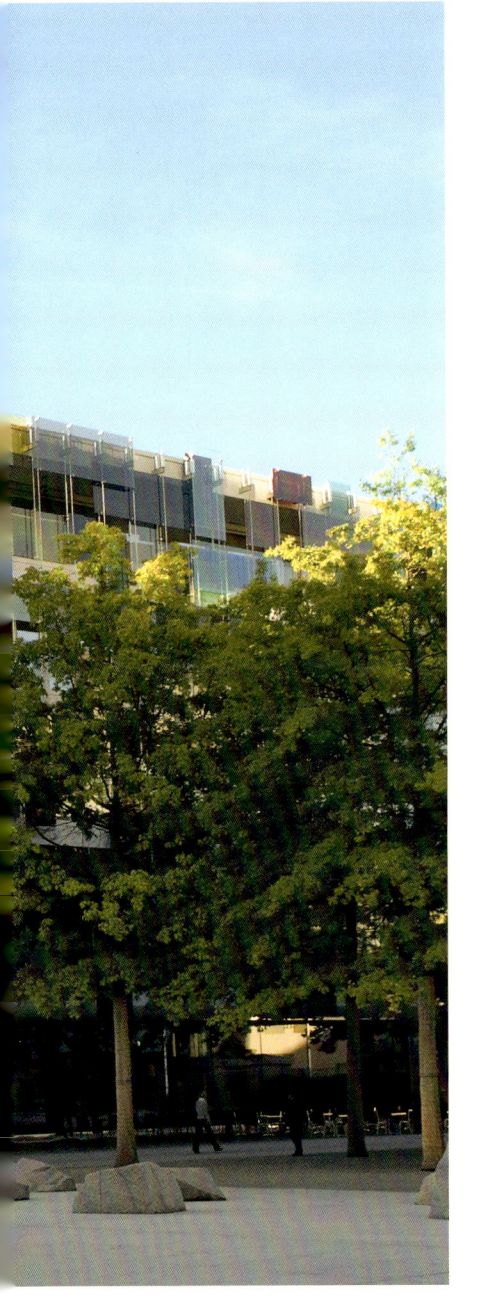

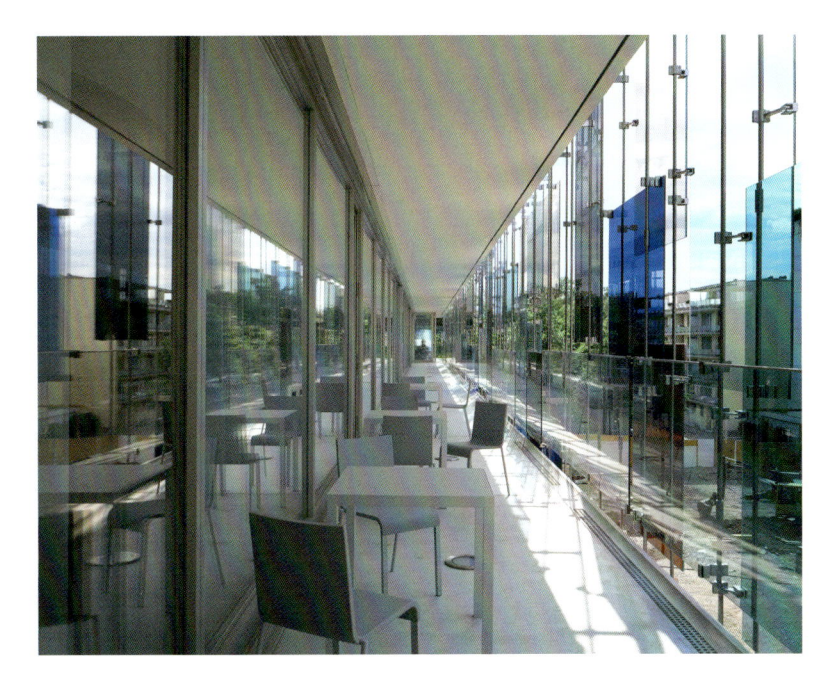

Diener & Diener, Gerold Wiederin, Helmut Federle, Forum 3, 2005

Left: Main façade of the Forum

Above: Interior view of the stairwell

Below: Loggia in the south façade: The interior and exterior interpenetrate one another.

Peter Märkli, 6 Fabrikstrasse, 2006

Above: Main façade on the Forum

Above left: Interior view of the stairwell

Left: Interior view of the auditorium

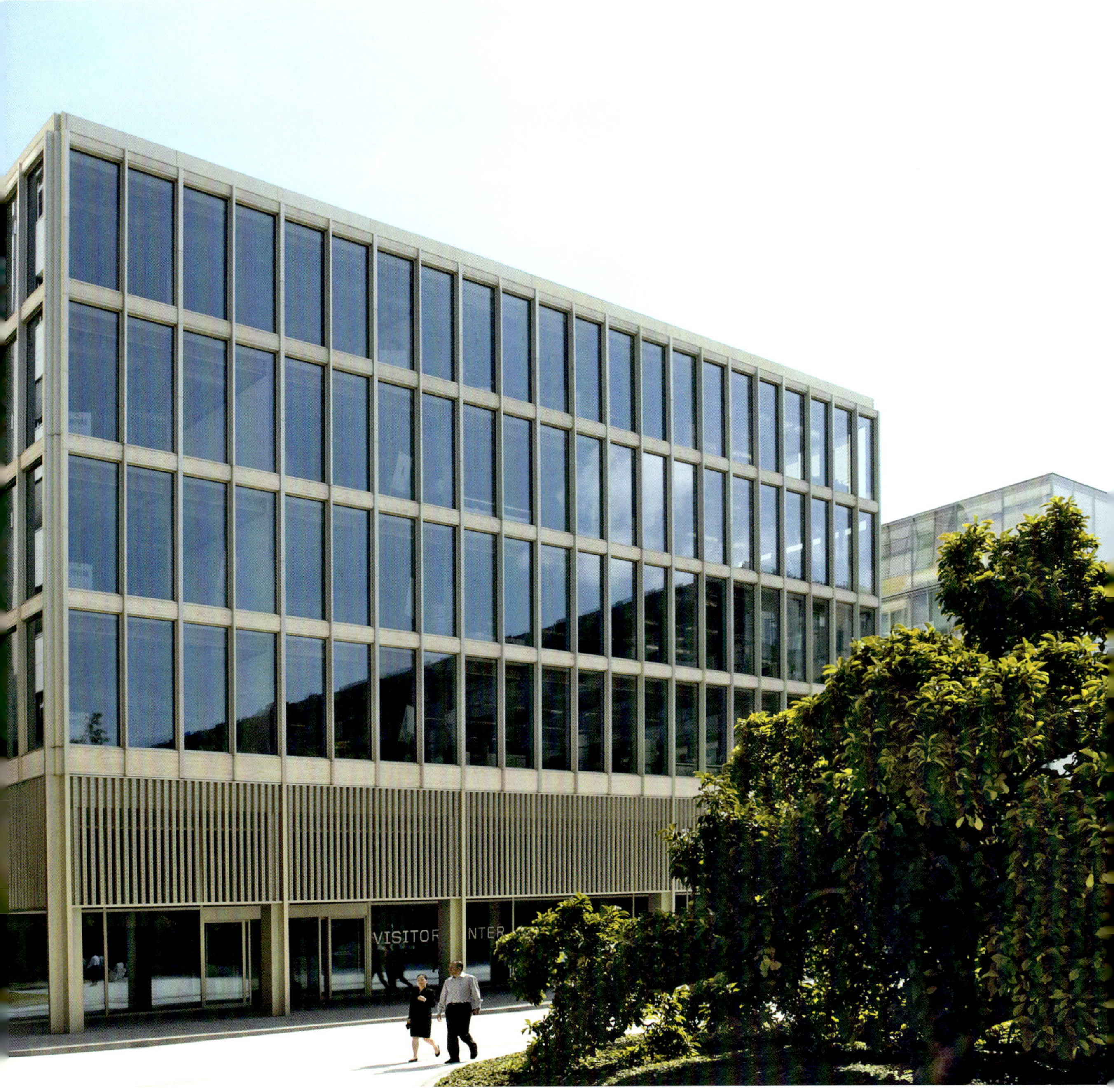
VISITOR

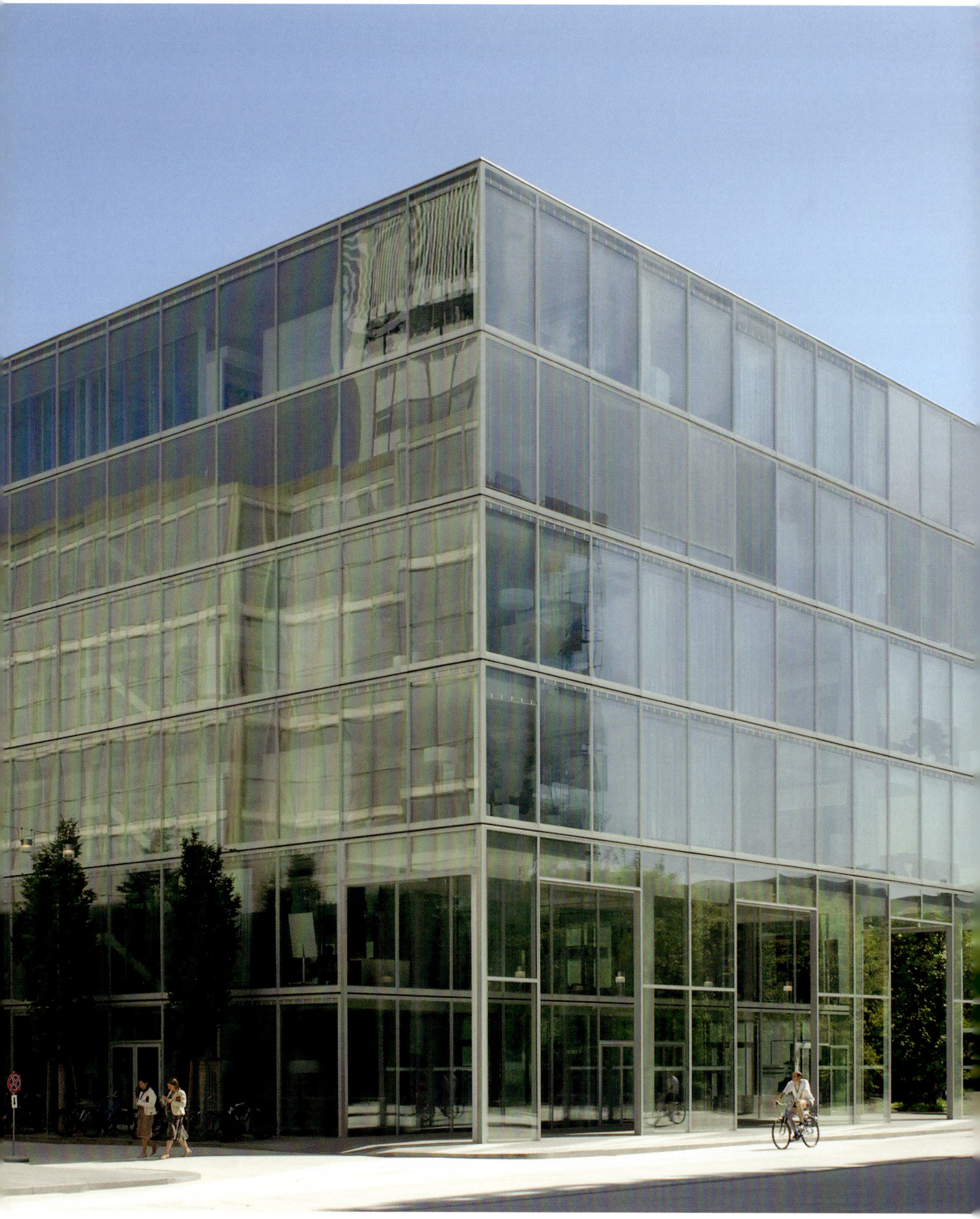

Sejima & Nishizawa (SANAA),
4 Fabrikstrasse, 2006

Left: Main façade on the Forum

Above: Interior view of the recreation room

Below: Façade detail, inner courtyard

Marco Serra, 2 Fabrikstrasse, 2007

Above: Reception building of the Novartis Campus

Above left: Reception of visitors

Left: View of the underground garage

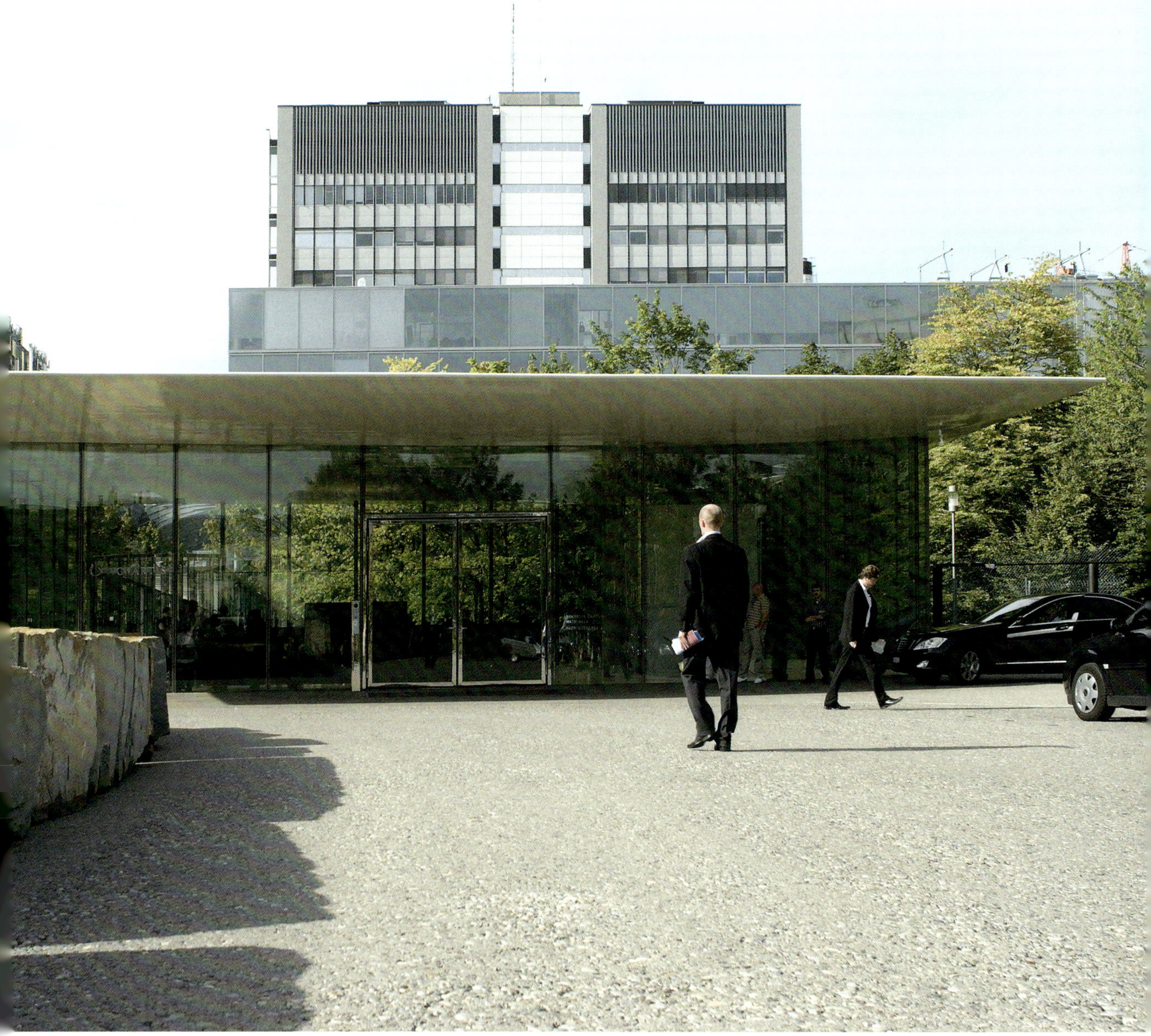

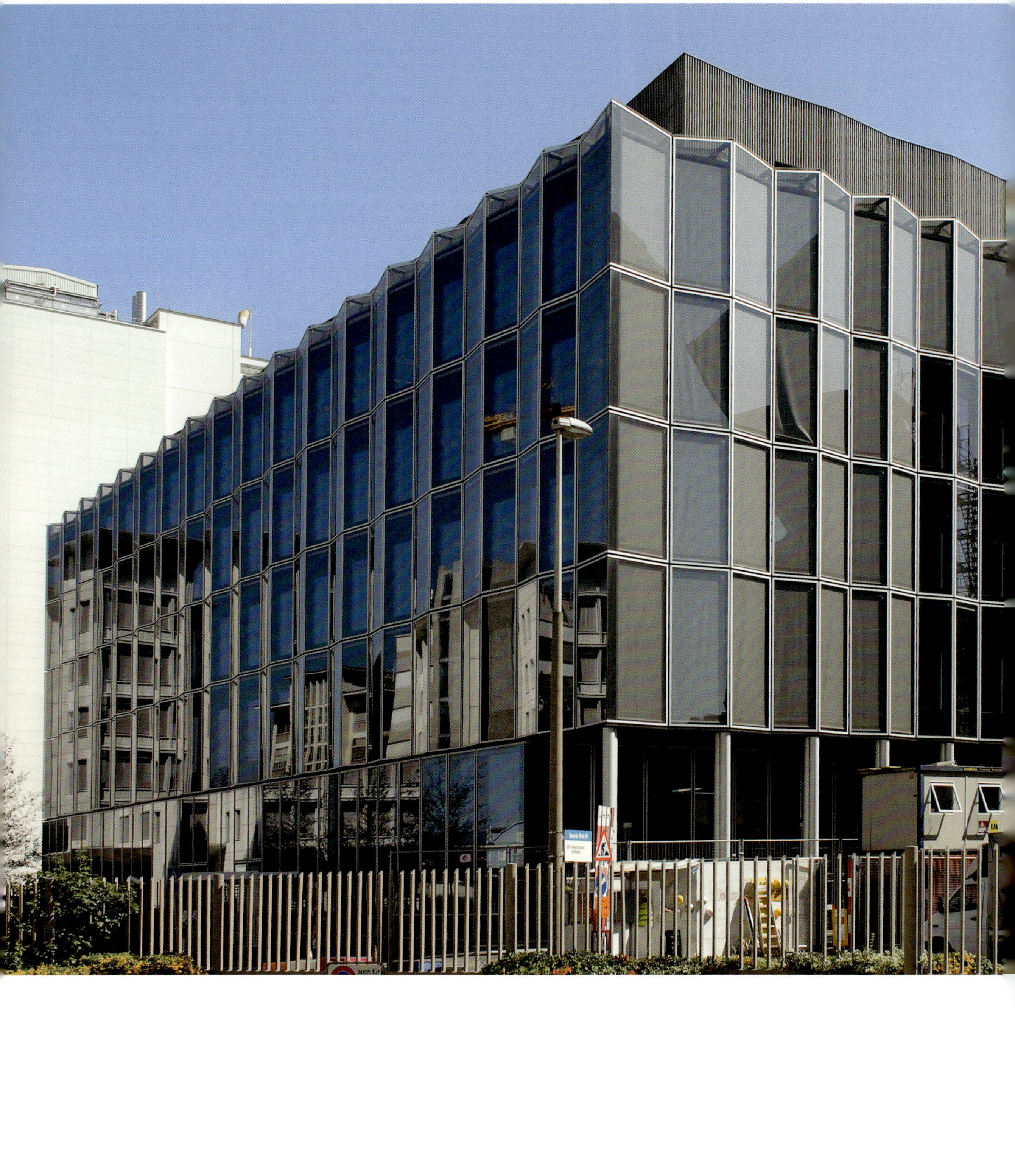

Adolf Krischanitz, 16 Fabrikstrasse, 2008

Left: Main façade at the corner of Hüningerstrasse and Fabrikstrasse

Above: Interior view of the stairwell

Below: View from the foyer into the offices

Studio di Architettura, 12 Fabrikstrasse, 2008

Right: Main façade on Fabrikstrasse

Above: Central stairwell

Below: Entrance lobby

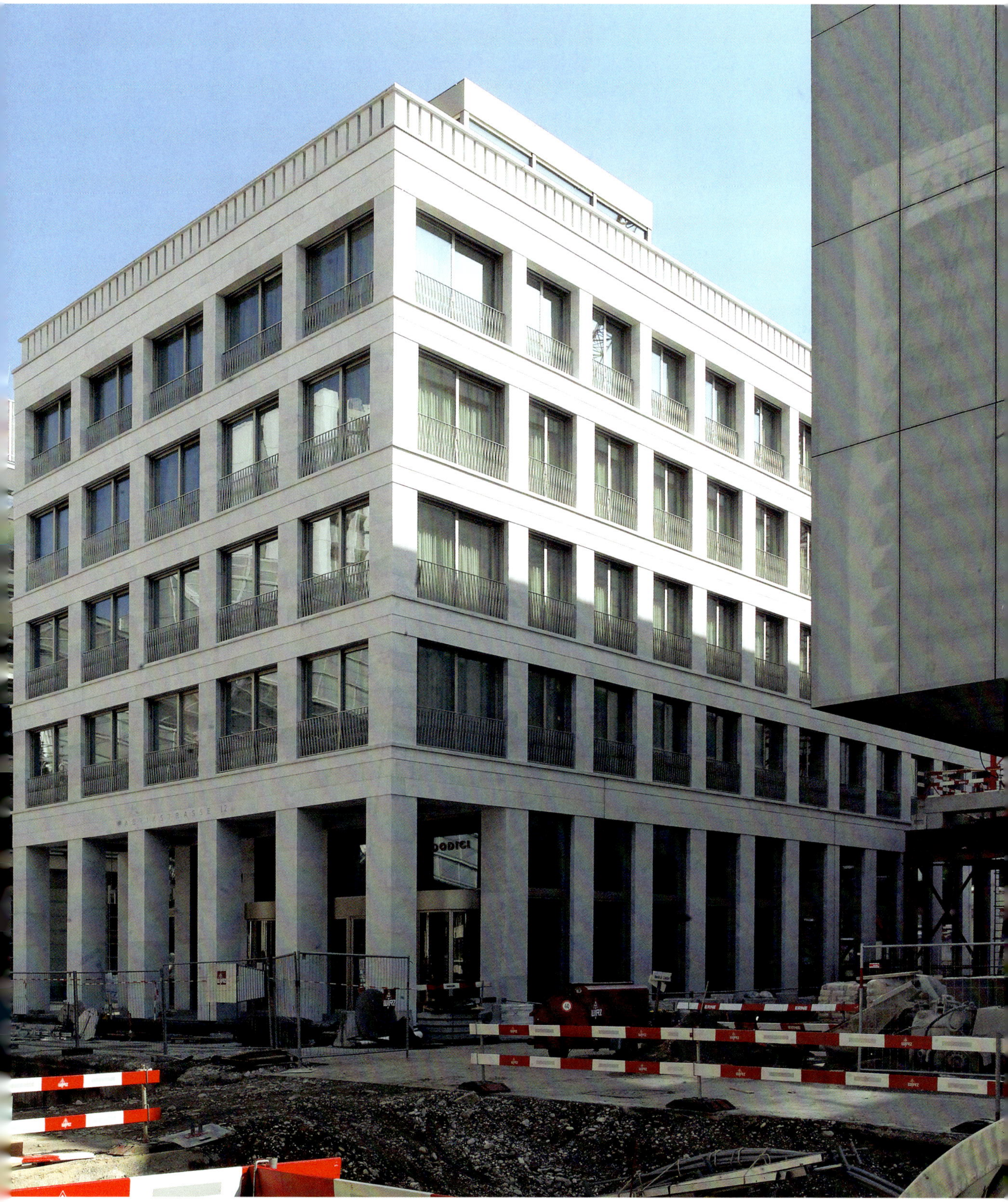

Rafael Moneo, 14 Fabrikstrasse (under construction), 2008: Main façade on Fabrikstrasse

Frank O. Gehry, 15 Fabrikstrasse (under construction), 2008

Left: Work on the complex structure of the glass façade

Below: Façade on the corner of Hüningerstrasse and Fabrikstrasse

Tadao Ando, 28 Fabrikstrasse (under construction), 2008

Fumihiko Maki, Square 4 (under construction), 2008

David Chipperfield, 22 Fabrikstrasse (under construction), 2008

Yoshio Taniguchi, 10 Fabrikstrasse (under construction), 2008: Main façade on Fabrikstrasse

Eduardo Souto de Moura, Physic
Garden 3 (under construction), 2008

Álvaro Siza, Virchow 6
(under construction), 2008

Urban Spaces: Requirements and Design Strategies

Vittorio Magnago Lampugnani

Planning and design work on the Novartis Campus focused on the open spaces from the very start. This was already implicit in the program—they necessarily have a central role in the scheme involving communicative work and intensive information exchange. In fact, the Master Plan was never conceived as involving the addition of more buildings between which spaces would then open up, but, on the contrary, as a system of spaces within which building areas would be located.

This spatial system is constructed sequentially: from the new entrance on Voltastrasse as far as the French border and to the crossing to the sports center, various spatial systems that are coordinated with each other appear in sequence along Fabrikstrasse. They offer a wide range of locations where people can linger or meet up with each other, and they invitingly offer a variety of possible uses. More spaces open to the east and west of Fabrikstrasse, in order to compensate for and soften the density of the Campus buildings. In principle, an attempt was made to provide a view of an open space from each individual building, whether it is a view of a park, a square, or a main road lined with trees.

However, the public spaces were defined not only geometrically and spatially, but above all in relation to their social function and the atmosphere they create. This definition was established both on the basis of hypothetical uses and also on the basis of archetypal situations in the history of city and landscape design. The result was a strategic arrangement of each individual public space on the Campus, based programmatically on its architectural design.

The Place of Knowledge

The Platz des Wissens, or Place of Knowledge, has a spatial reference to the Novartis Campus, but it actually belongs to the city of Basel. Its functional task consists of ingesting and distributing the traffic coming from both sides of Voltastrasse into Fabrikstrasse and thus into the Campus. However, the traffic also passes into the high-rise complex occupied by the University of Basel and the Swiss Federal Institute of Technology Zurich (ETH Zurich). In addition, it marks out a spatial separation between the bridge, with its ramps, and the new Voltastrasse boulevard. In 1929, Martin Wagner (then head of the municipal planning and building control office in Berlin) defined the large city square as a "traffic distribution point", the main purpose of which was to meet the needs of car drivers. Although the Place of Knowledge is actually a traffic point of this type, it is nevertheless by no means true that it only serves to regulate vehicular traffic. Its functioning is based on simplicity and neutrality. In this way, it forms a space that is also capable of accommodating pedestrians in a simple but friendly fashion.

Schematic representation of the open spaces of the Campus, Studio di Architettura, 2006: The built elements are shown in red, and the garden elements are shown in green. The sequence on Fabrikstrasse is in dark grey.

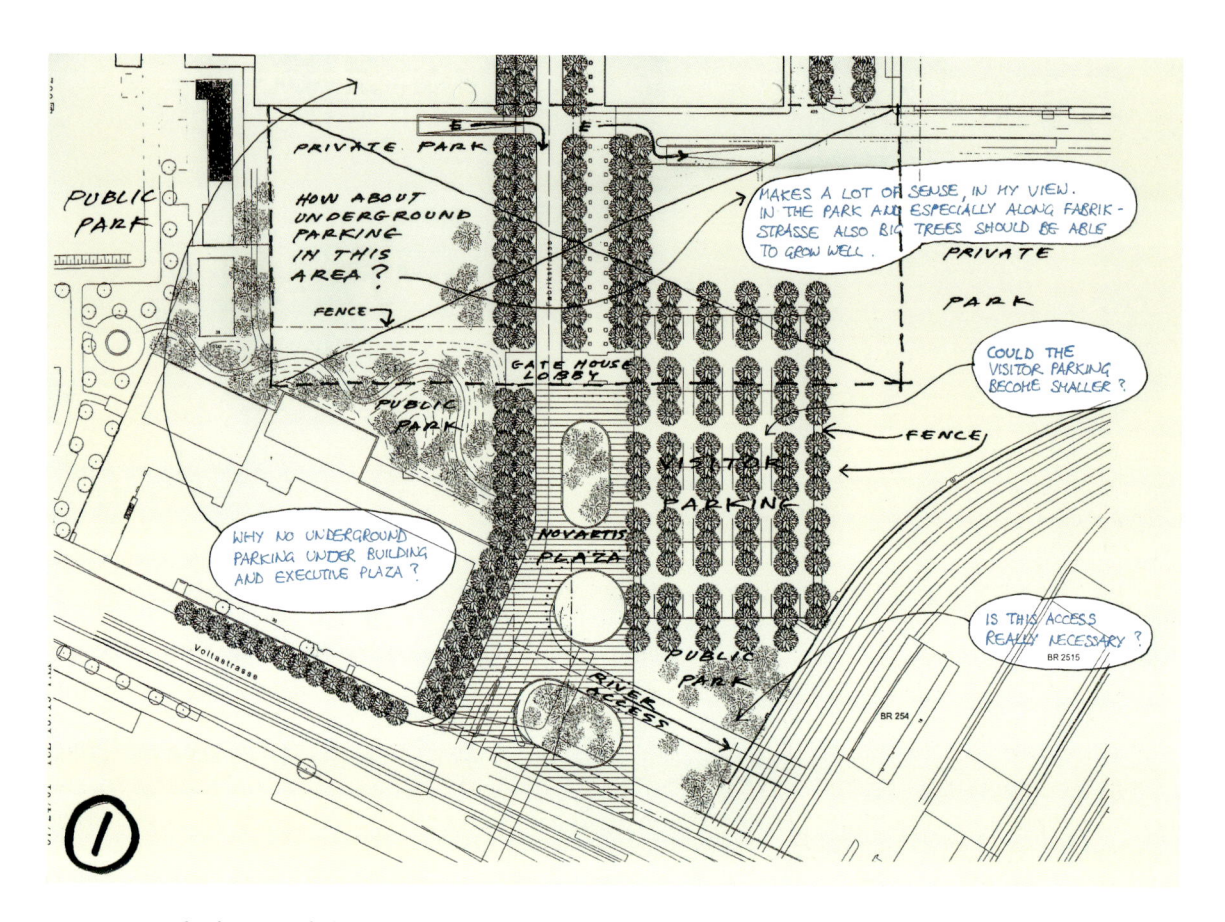

Comments on the design study for
Novartis Place, fax between Peter
Walker and Vittorio Magnago
Lampugnani, 2001

Novartis Place

This is a place that is accessible to the public, but nevertheless forms part of the Novartis Campus, and in particular part of the Novartis Park, a place that can be crossed by employees as well as visitors both easily and quickly and without any hindrance. A place on which taxis and other vehicles are able to wait without being in the way, and on which even a delivery truck will be able to turn if it happens to have lost its way, Novartis Place is a subordinate traffic node that is intended to look as little as possible like a traffic node and is meant to work more like a clearing in the park, or a crossing of pathways in a Baroque garden. It relates to the entrance pavilion and may possibly include a sculpture or a fountain as well. In comparison with the Place of Knowledge, it is more private, smaller, and designed more for pedestrians.

Novartis Place forms the entrance to the Campus—a kind of visiting card that already hints at the Campus's central qualities: functionality, elegance, and refinement.

The Park

For people arriving from the city, from the motorway and from Voltastrasse, the park provides a kind of surprising and friendly reception. You find yourself unexpectedly in a green oasis that creates a visual connection between the Voltamatte and the banks of the Rhine. But the Park is above all a place of contemplation in which you can stroll, wander about on your own or in groups, and chat with people quietly. Refreshments should be available nearby, but this is not what will define the principal usage of the Park. Nature—or rather a harnessed, exaggerated ideal of it—is what is meant to shape the park primarily. It is not a garden, but nor is it a forest. It is in the tradition of the picturesque English landscape garden of someone like William Kent or Capability Brown (whose real first name was actually Lancelot). It will provide lawns, trees, curving pathways, and pleasant, shadowy locations where people can rest on comfortable benches. A selected area could also be designed as a spacious meeting-place—an artificial clearing in the artificial forest, but a clearing of an unobtrusive size that will not create an effect of emptiness if no one happens to be there. Individual leisure activities and quiet thinking should take priority over group meetings and social exchanges. The Park will be a quiet, unusual location and will offer an alternative to the hectic life of the city.

Fabrikstrasse

Both from an urban planning point of view and from a social point of view, Fabrikstrasse represents the principal thoroughfare of the Campus. At the point where it crosses the park, it will give the impression of being an avenue. The Park is intended to extend into this area of Fabrikstrasse as closely as possible, so that it can be seen more clearly as one walks along the street. However, this should not mean that the Park is divided into two areas. At the point where Fabrikstrasse penetrates into the more densely built areas of the Novartis Campus, it becomes explicitly urban. It is still lined with trees, which define the street space as an architectural element. The recognizable elements in Fabrikstrasse, however, are its arcades, where all of the public facilities for employees and visitors to the Campus will be located. Fabrikstrasse is not just a main road, but also an extended complex of restaurants and cafés, a sort of stretched-out shopping mall. And it is also a general location for people to meet up and exchange information in a lively way. It is no accident that the three most striking spaces on the Campus—the Forum, the Green, and the Piazzetta—all open onto Fabrikstrasse and are accessed from it.

The Forum

This is the most important and also the most prestigious public space in the entire Campus complex. It not only forms a common atrium for Novartis International's historic main building, the new and colorful Forum 3 building, the equally new office building with its visitor center, the unusual Novartis Pharma building dating from the nineteen-fifties, and the no less unusual glass *campanile*—for Novartis, it also represents a symbolic location. In everyday life, the Forum does not fulfill any specific function, apart from being an impressive square linking the most important company management buildings and allowing the company's directors and important visitors to drive up to the entrance. Official company ceremonies and celebrations—such as new product presentations or meetings for important internal announcements which all of the employees are able to attend in an environment that is undramatic but formal—can also be held here. In addition, the Forum is a place where people can go for a walk, meet up, and sit together. In other words, the Forum represents the very heart of the company. The square is bright and elegantly paved, slightly shaded, and kept largely uncluttered.

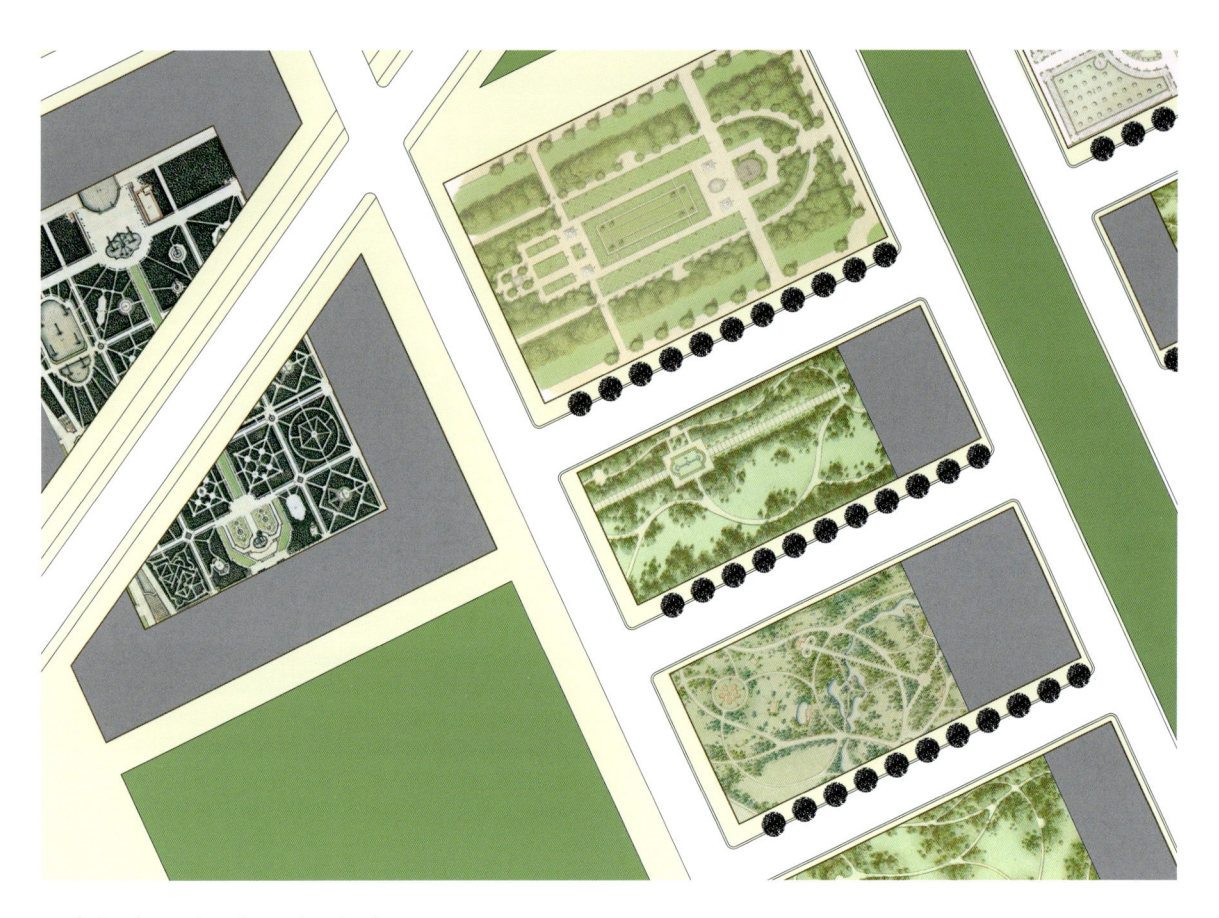

Study for the roof gardens, Alan Fletcher
and Studio di Architettura, 2003

The Green

The Green could be described as the exact opposite of the Forum, and it does, in fact, serve fundamentally different purposes. Employees can meet here on any occasion and sit together, have a drink, have a picnic, or have something to eat in the Italian café-bar or in the restaurant on the ground floor of the building designed by Frank O. Gehry. While the Forum forms the company's official heart, the Green is its unofficial heart. It belongs to the employees, in a sense—managers may be welcome, but mainly as guests. It will be designed as a park, an extended lawn on which a few large trees will offer shade and where people can sit down casually more or less anywhere in a relaxed atmosphere. In contrast to the Park, the Green is not a place for individual relaxation and recreation, but rather for sociability—a location where Novartis employees can get a feeling of belonging to a large, proud, and contented community.

From the point of view of urban space, the Green, like the Forum, represents an asymmetrically arranged extension of Fabrikstrasse that links the buildings on the square with each other and with the street itself.

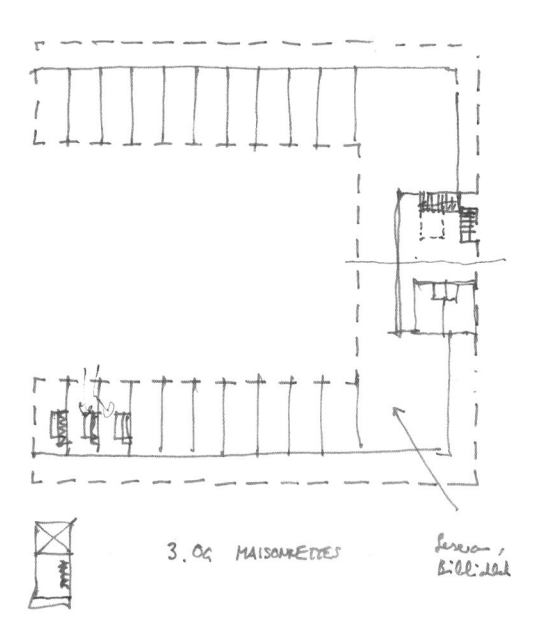

Study for the Piazzetta building,
Vittorio Magnago Lampugnani, 2001

The Piazzetta

The Piazzetta has the same functions as the Green, but with a completely different architectural design. The Piazzetta is also intended as an informal meeting-place that will provid an inviting location for people to chat, sit, eat, and drink. However, it is not planted with either trees or grass, but instead completely paved. It will therefore be a better place to be during bad weather, particularly thanks to its protective arcades, which partly form the boundaries of the square. The Piazzetta could also become a popular place for the evening, when the lights under the arcades and on the small square create a relaxing and inviting atmosphere.

Like the Forum and the Green, the Piazzetta forms an asymmetrical extension of Fabrikstrasse. In addition, it marks the point at which Fabrikstrasse is crossed at right angles by the Campus's second main thoroughfare. This spatial situation is emphasized above all by the square shape and the suggested potential extension of the Campus toward the west. Thus, while the Forum and the Green are spaces that arise from the tension between free-standing buildings, the Piazzetta forms a break in the urban planning structure, for three of its closed sides are defined by a single building. In the central area of this "urban" building, a passageway will create a discreet connection to the Arboretum.

The Novartis Campus, Forum, 2008

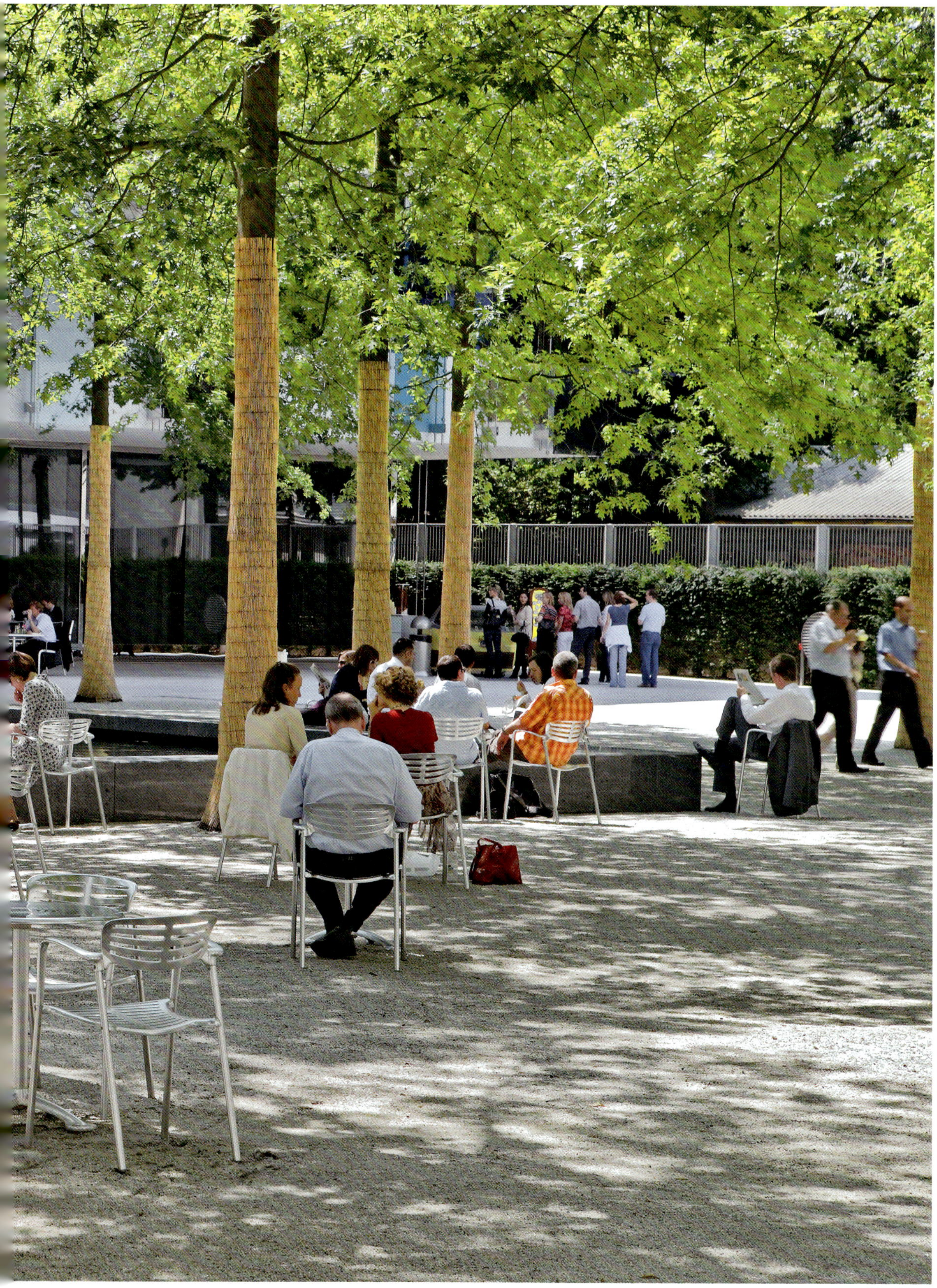

Swiss Place

This marks the end of Fabrikstrasse and the rear entrance to the Novartis Campus, although without giving the impression of being a rear entrance, even though it is designed less prestigiously than the main entrance on Novartis Square. Its task essentially consists of offering employees and visitors to the Campus an efficient and attractive entrance and exit by creating a transitional area between the Campus and the parking lots or sports facilities.

Swiss Place represents a symmetrical extension of Fabrikstrasse on a modest scale. It marks not only the boundary of the Novartis Campus, but also the border between Switzerland and France. The small square will become a fascinating and emblematic location in its interplay with Richard Serra's sculpture *Dirk's Pod,* which functions as a *point de vue* for Fabrikstrasse, and the two buildings by Tadao Ando, which at thirty-eight meters tower above the normal height of the buildings on the rest of the Campus.

The Quadrangle

From a functional point of view, this is a smaller counterpart to the Novartis Park. While the latter relates to the Campus, the quadrangle is connected with the extension of the Campus. It is both picturesquely designed and inviting, with generous open spaces for individual recreation and contemplation. People can meet here or simply sit or lie down for a rest. However, while Novartis Park is extroverted and opens onto another green space—the Voltamatte—and the Rhine, the Quadrangle is introverted and forms a spatial and social focus for the Campus's extension area. Defined by the adjoining high-rise buildings in a geometrically clear and almost dogmatic way, it is a miniature Central Park, but at the same time, as its name suggests, it is inspired by the grassy central courtyards of historic British and American colleges. The Quadrangle has a life of its own and at the same time provides space for people to stroll across from the neighboring cafés and restaurants.

The Atrium Plaza

As an extension and end point of Hüningerstrasse, the Atrium Plaza forms an opening in the urban Campus structure that is towered over by tall buildings and loosely connected with the Green. The square is above all a functional location that serves as a side entrance to the Campus and as a delivery point for the neighboring buildings—including the one by Frank O. Gehry—and the Green. It also mediates between the diagonal Hüningerstrasse and the Campus's rectangular grid. In addition, it welcomes people entering the Campus from Elsässerstrasse and provides the whole of the immediate neighborhood with an attractive urban space.

The Arboretum

The function of the arboretum is similar to that of the Park and the Quadrangle, although it is much smaller and unusually long. It is a place for walking, either alone or in groups, as well as for resting and thinking. There would also be no objection to people jogging here, of course, although the nearby sports complex would be much more suitable for that. The Arboretum is principally intended for reflection and contemplation. Despite its narrow shape, it will offer small, intimate places of refuge along a promenade. If Hüningerstrasse is preserved, the main function of the Arboretum will lie in the charming and natural way in which it connects the two halves of the Campus by allowing pedestrians and cyclists to cross the street without having to leave the Novartis complex. In addition, it provides the buildings opposite with a fine view of pleasant greenery, as well as quiet and fresh air.

As its name suggests, the Arboretum will be planted with a special collection of trees, which will make it an educational location—a museum of the natural elements of the plant world.

The Squares

Like the squares of London, these are small, intimate gardens, but in contrast to the squares on which they are modeled, they are accessible to everyone on the Campus. Not primarily conceived of as meeting-places, they are instead quiet, cozy oases in which people can walk, sit, talk, or even drink something and have a snack. The main function of the Squares consists of providing the Campus buildings with additional public space, and in general they serve as orientation points. As in the Arboretum, their greenery will ensure attractive views and fresh air. In contrast to the Arboretum, however, the buildings will open onto the green areas not with loggias and quiet workrooms or meeting rooms, but instead with entrance and reception rooms. This will give the Squares a more public quality.

The Hanging Gardens

These form the most important pivotal point between the Novartis Campus and the Rhine. The Park also opens towards the river, but here it is the buildings that are oriented towards the water. From a functional point of view, the Hanging Gardens do, in fact, represent extensions of the Campus buildings toward the bank of the Rhine. The area will be used for leisure activities, but also particularly for individual work and for group meetings in the open air. This function will be expressed by its prestigious quality, in contrast to the picturesque design of the other parks.

The Hanging Gardens, as the name suggests, are genuine garden complexes in the tradition of the Italian Renaissance. These decidedly (and visibly) artificial gardens will create an equally artificial, almost dramatized relationship to the water of the Rhine and to the opposite bank of the river. Separated from the lower-lying public promenade by a high and attractively designed natural stone wall, they will at the same time grow over a storage room for around a thousand bicycles and possibly other service rooms. The delicate structure of a pier café on the water, which will be accessible from the Campus, from the Promenade, and from the Rhine, will symbolize as a subtle architectural metaphor the point of convergence between the Campus, the river, and the city.

Gap between the roadway and the sidewalk, Studio di Architettura, 2005: This standard detail is binding for all Campus streets, but is adapted to the geometry of each respective building.

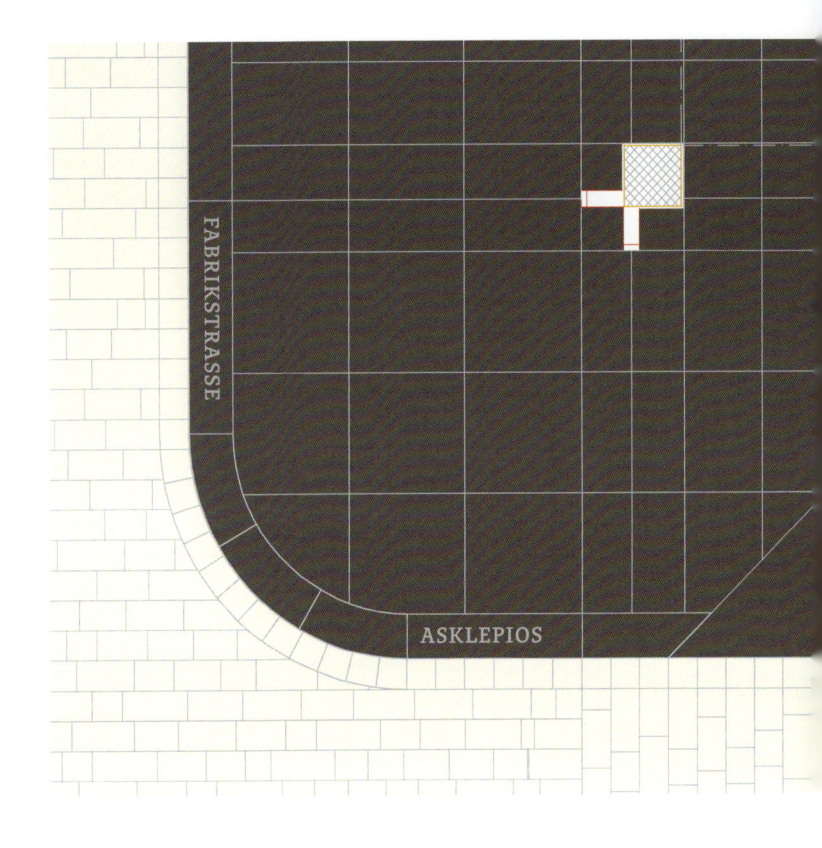

FABRIKSTRASSE

ASKLEPIOS

The Streets

The Campus's public spaces also include the streets, of course. In addition to their access function, they also have many other tasks, which are entirely in the tradition of the European city—not least that of being places to meet and spend time in. The prerequisite for this was the decision to keep the whole Campus free of road traffic as a matter of principle. Only taxis, small delivery trucks, and limousines belonging to the company management and official visitors will be permitted. This will keep to a minimum the potential dangers represented by motor vehicles for cyclists and above all for pedestrians.

The prerequisite for this privileged usage of the streets is that they should be carefully designed. They are divided into main streets and side streets, with different designs to correspond to the types. The main streets will have symmetrically arranged pavements, side drainage, and, if they are running from east to west, double rows of trees, while the side streets will have asymmetrically arranged pavements, central drainage, and, again only when running from east to west, a single row of trees on the north side. Particular attention has been given to the streets' surfaces. Asphalt was ruled out from the start, to avoid the impression of streets designed for cars. Instead, cobblestones were chosen. However, this involved numerous functional requirements: it had to be suitable for delivery truck traffic, but it also needed to be comfortable for cyclists, for people with walking difficulties, and for women with high-heeled shoes. After numerous experiments, the lanes were laid with twelve-centimeter-thick slabs of white Moncini granite, the edges of which are cut in one direction and broken in the other; the walking surface was cut with a saw. The bright color has a light and friendly effect even in bad weather. In contrast to this, a dark grey Negro Grapesa granite was used for the curbs and pavements. Again in contrast to the streets, large-format slabs were used here, with the joints being cut to correspond to the geometry of each building.

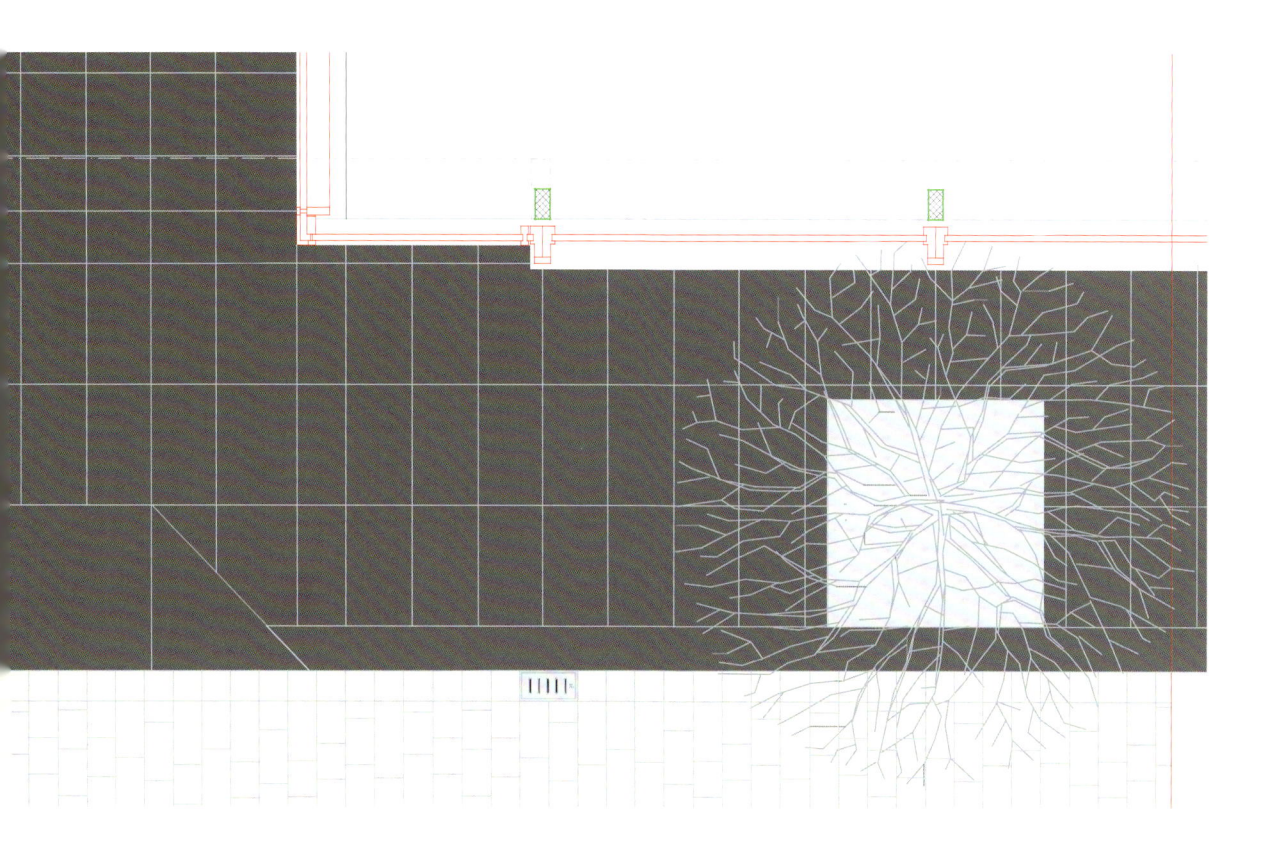

The streets on the Campus do in fact have an important aesthetic role, in addition to their functional and social tasks. They are the uniform, continuous element that holds together the different appearances of the (deliberately) heterogeneous Campus buildings. In other words, while the buildings express the individual element, the streets symbolize the community element. The arcade space forms a special area that has a mediating function: its paving is also of Negro Grapesa granite, but with an option for each architect to vary the cutting of the joint and to incorporate elements from his or her own building.

Above: Stone and surface patterns for the sidewalk and roadway, 2001–04

Right: Curbstone and gully of a Campus street, 2006

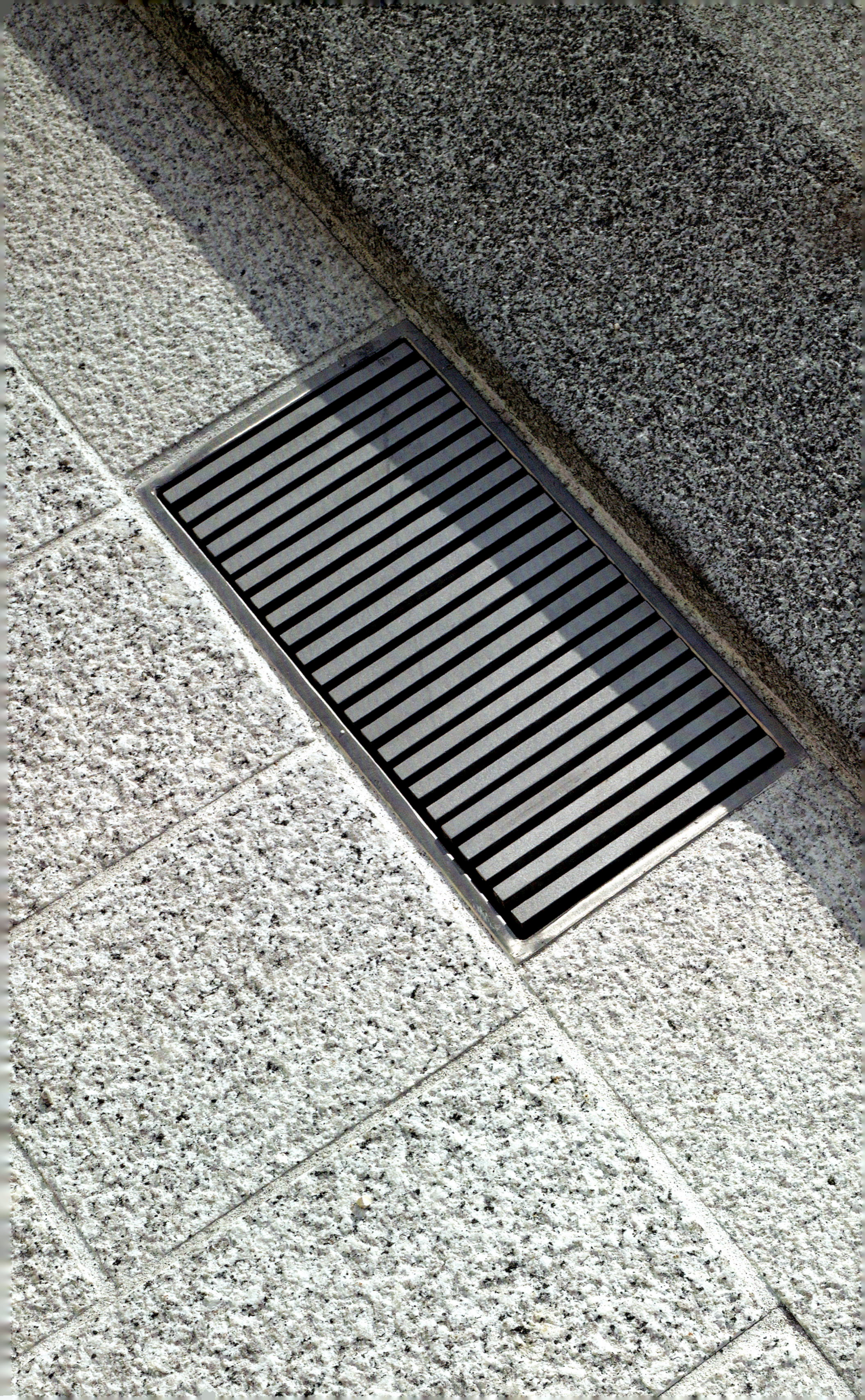

Landscape Architecture: Streets and Squares
Peter Walker

Peter Walker and Partners has participated in the development of the site landscape of today's Novartis Campus since the beginning, setting in motion a series of remarkable events that have begun the transformation of the old fifty-one-acre industrial plant located roughly halfway between the city center of Basel and the Basel airport. Although beautifully located along the Rhine, the site was largely a paved industrial landscape, crisscrossed with train tracks that contained only sparse and separated bits of landscape with few important trees. The task was to transform the site into a modern research and administrative campus with a pedestrian-friendly ambience of trees, benches, greens, parks, and squares. In addition to the design of the open spaces, the landscape plan dealt with an extensive existing network of underground vaults and basements.

The Master Plan, which was developed in 2001 by Vittorio Magnago Lampugnani, called for an urban composition of mid-rise buildings set in a grid of major and minor streets animated with greens, plazas, and pedestrian throughways. A large park proposed for the Campus entrance was intended to contrast with the intense urban fabric of the buildings and set the stage for the future development of open public spaces between the Novartis Campus and the river's edge.

After the urban design plan was adopted, an interdisciplinary committee developed guidelines for the Campus. Continuing workshops assured that the guidelines address such interrelated issues of Campus growth as the selection of street and plaza materials, wayfaring, street and open-space lighting, security and fire protection, pedestrian movement, public assembly, landscape accessibility, the incorporation of water, recreation, bicycle parking, and the acquisition and placement of major outdoor art. Within the overall direction of the urban design plan, several of the architectural competitions have been completed with attendant collaboration on landscape design and art acquisition. As directed by the Workshop and the steering committee, a series of landscape projects has been completed and a development plan for infrastructure and site landscape has been initiated.

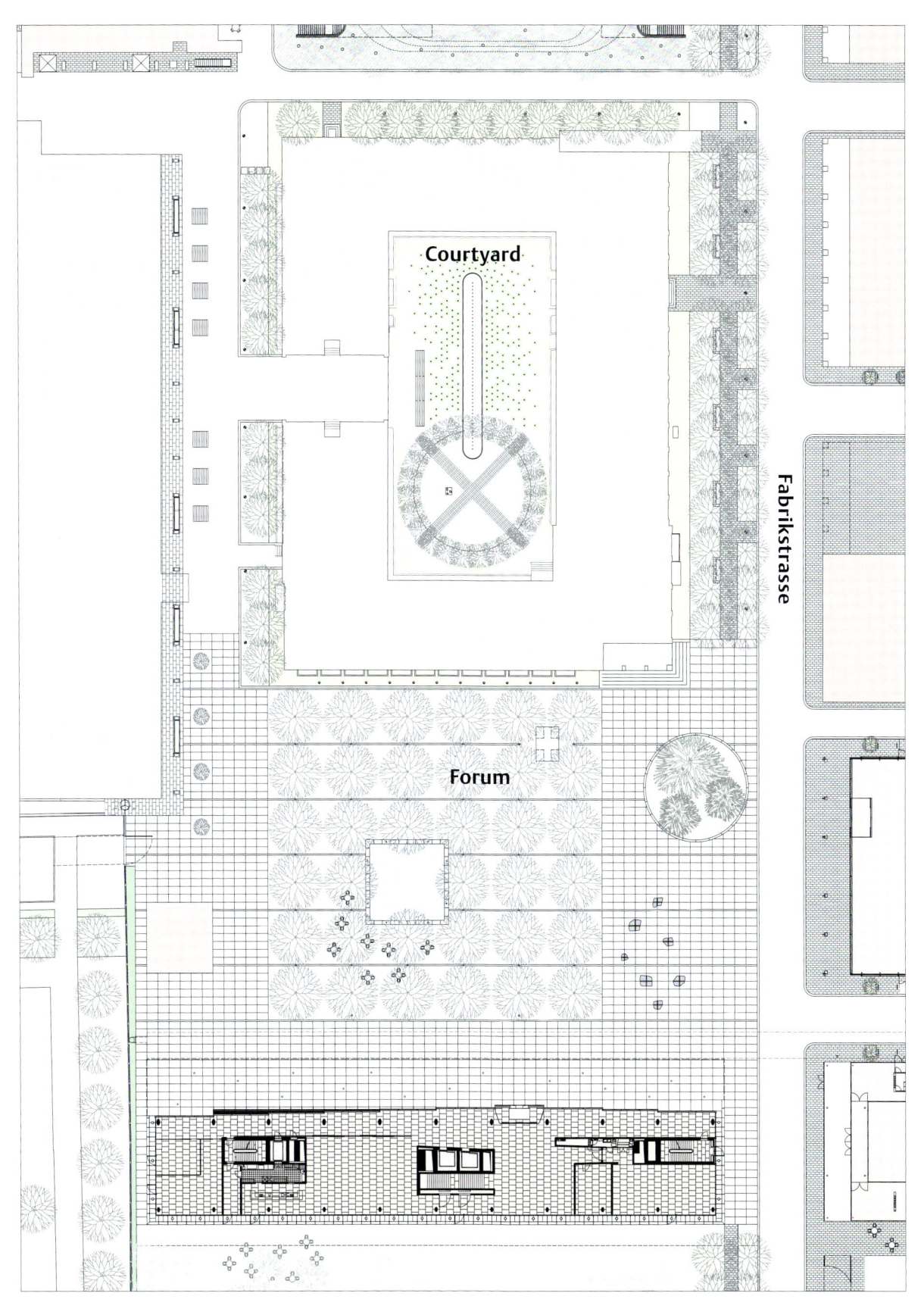

Forum and immediately adjacent open spaces, inner courtyard of the historic administration building, Peter Walker and Partners, 2005: The design shown here of the Forum (which was actually realized) is the result of the interdisciplinary work of the Workshop and the distillation of the sometimes extremely heated discussions of its members.

The Forum

Between the administration building and the first new building designed by Diener & Diener, Forum 3, a stone plaza has been designed and constructed. Named the Forum, it is made of large blocks of White Moncini granite. Toward the administration building, a cutout paved with decomposed granite contains a grid of thirty-five carefully matched *Quercus palustris* (pin oaks). Diagonally south in the oak grove is a polished granite pool containing water lilies and koi. Beneath the cantilevered entry of the Diener building, tables and chairs spill out from a restaurant onto the plaza. Two major sculptures by Ulrich Rückriem form a symbolic table of Bleu-de-Vire stone and a loose grouping of White Moncini boulders cut to reflect the joints in the White Moncini pavement. It is possible that on the west side of the Forum a campanile by Vittorio Magnago Lampugnani will be erected, which would be on axis with a newly completed linear pedestrian plaza with benches and plantings along the west side of Building 200 (Forum 1). The Plaza adjoins the remodeled Building 202 (Forum 2) and leads north to a green that will be designed by the office of Günther Vogt to face the Frank O. Gehry building now under construction.

Courtyard of the Historic Administration Building

A new internal courtyard for the administration building removed a temporary archives building and a defunct and overgrown garden. In their place, a new circular lawn surrounded by twenty-four ironwood trees forms a space used for outdoor celebrations and formal parties, and a grove of slender white birch sheltering informal tables and chairs can be used in good weather for lunches and coffee. Joining the two new garden spaces is a linear reflecting pool, which can be lit for evening activities by fixtures that reflect seasonal and celebratory transitions through changing colors. The lawn is crossed by a series of white marble paths that reference both Switzerland and the medical activities of Novartis. A monumental bronze artwork by Alicia Penalba has been set between the paths.

Fabrikstrasse and Side Streets

At the heart of the urban design plan is the reconstructed historic street of Fabrikstrasse. This pedestrian and service street flows from the main entry of the Campus on Voltastrasse through the park and then north to the French border and the major employee parking lot beyond. The Fabrikstrasse roadbed is made of White Moncini granite with Negro Grapesa curbs and sidewalks. The west side of Fabrikstrasse is planted with single or double rows of *Liriodendron tulipifera* (tulip trees). The east side is a continuous covered pedestrian arcade built into the buildings as they are designed and containing shops, public spaces, restaurants, and cafés. Running east and west off of Fabrikstrasse are a series of narrow service and pedestrian streets planted with *Carpinus betulus 'Fastigata'* (columnar hornbeam).

Swiss Place and the Pedestrian Underpass

At the north end of Fabrikstrasse is a plaza, also of White Moncini granite, containing the five monumental Corten steel artworks by the artist Richard Serra named *Dirk's Pod.* The plaza is connected beneath the existing train tracks to the parking area by a newly designed pedestrian underpass made of steps of poured concrete and stone with stainless steel and glass fittings. After entering through security within the underpass, one climbs up the stairs to a magnificent rising view of the sculptures.

The Park

At the entrance pavilion on Voltastrasse one passes over a newly built underground parking garage covered by a major park designed by the office of Günther Vogt. The park is an eco-revelatory naturalistic design referencing the rocky watershed toward the Rhine and planted to look like a natural forest. In the future the park will be extended east to the river's edge, joining a linear park planned by the city. At the main entry the stone elegance of Fabrikstrasse gives way to the soft naturalism of the park so that one goes through "nature" and then continues north through the series of new urban spaces.

Future plans include an urban piazza, a linear botanic garden (arboretum), a square, a medicinal garden, and a "village green."

With its elegant infrastructure and open spaces the Campus is perhaps the most ambitious corporate campus since the General Motors Technical Center, built in Detroit in 1956. It has been a pleasure and honor to have worked on the Campus landscape and with the Workshop and Novartis staff.

Above: Inner courtyard of Forum 1, water basin, 2006

Right: Inner courtyard of Forum 1, beech trees, 2007

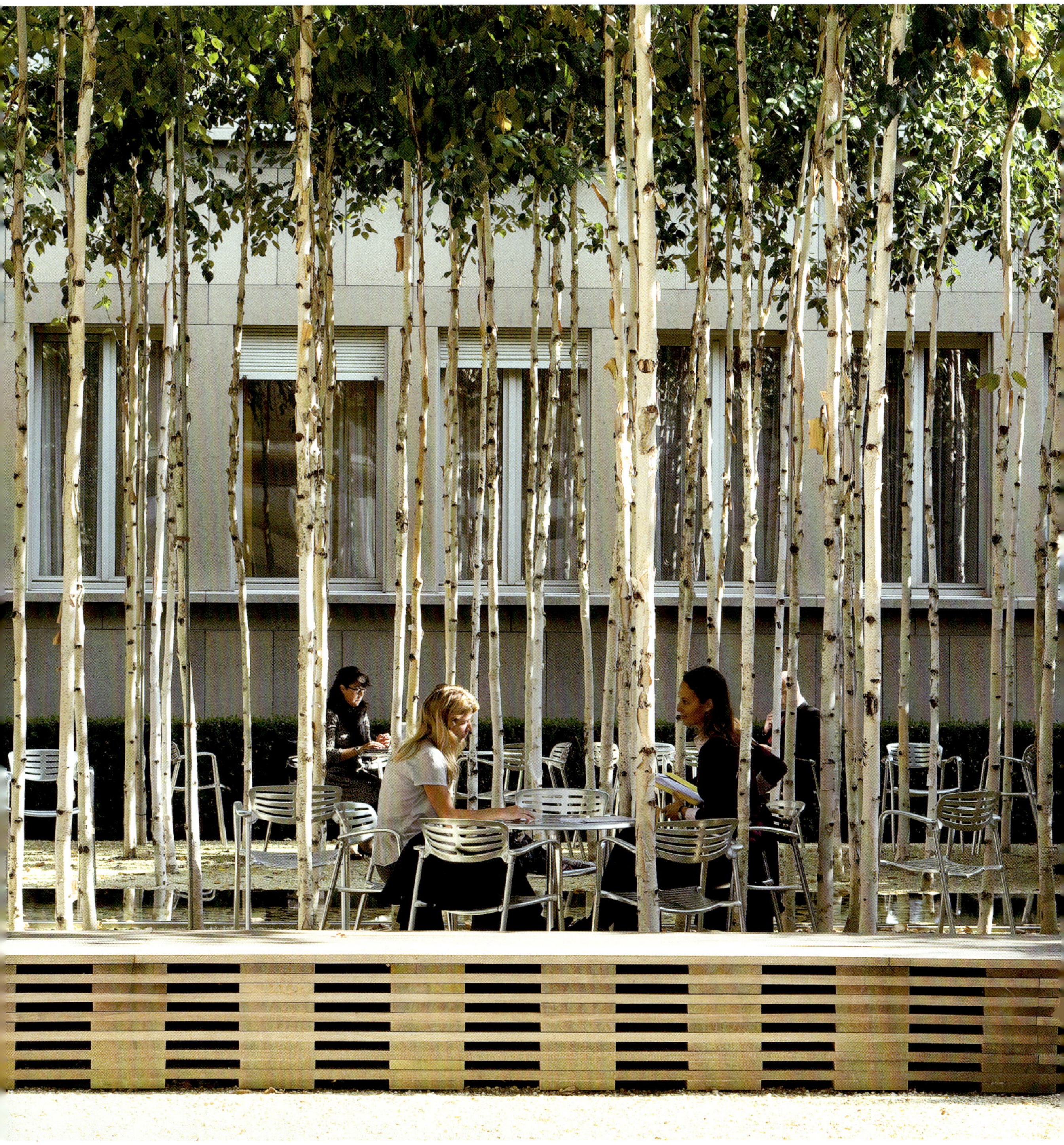

Above and right:
Pedestrian underpass
at Swiss Place at the
north end of Fabrik-
strasse, 2005

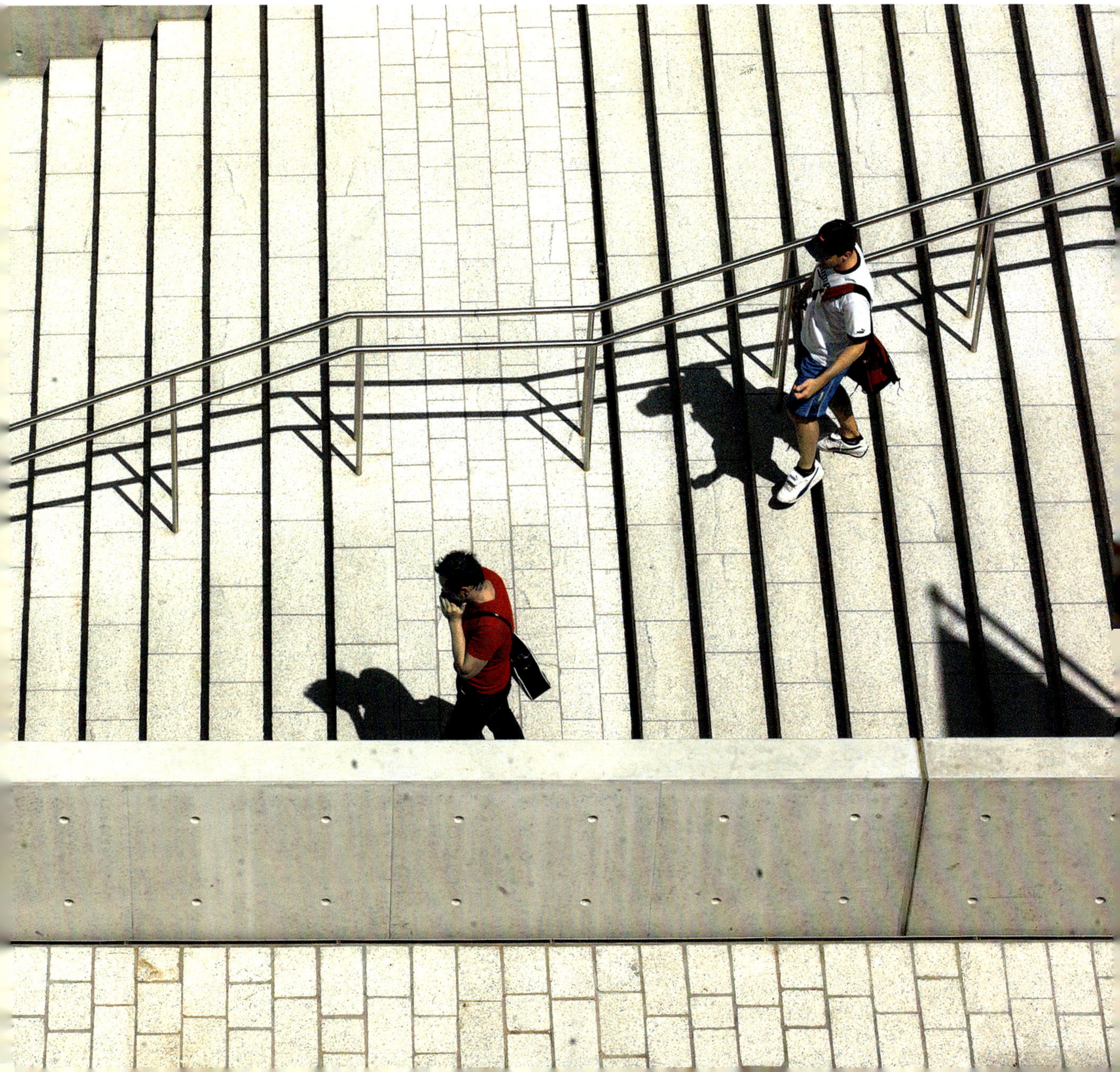

Nature under Laboratory Conditions: The Open Spaces of Vogt Landschaftsarchitekten

Alice Foxley, Silke Schmeing, and Günther Vogt

Just as pharmacology is rooted in phytotherapy, so the first forms of settlement can be seen as the basis of urban construction. And just as it would not be just to view the multifaceted research of Novartis as a linear extension of phytotherapy, so the Novartis Campus is much more than a city in a city. Ways of thinking drawing on a much wider spectrum, and not just urban developmental aspects, have influenced and continue to influence its planning.

The structure of the Campus may at first glance remind one of urban developmental principles from earlier times, but the area requires a second, more differentiated inspection. Instead of a wall, there is a partly transparent fence surrounding the Campus park, the largest contiguous green surface on the grounds. What appears to be exclusive from outside actually has a connective effect when viewed from the inside. The Campus gathers together where there is potential for synergies: the limiting of access to the space creates encounters among kindred spirits.

Several thousand highly trained employees in the fields of economics, science, marketing, management, and other disciplines are to be seen on the grounds; on the other hand, the through traffic remains outside and vehicles are parked in front of the Campus and in the underground garage beneath it. Aside from the squares and green areas, the center of the Campus is densely built-up. The courtyards offer more individual outdoor space, for instance, for personal meetings. In both execution and details, it becomes clear that modern planning and design are behind the apparently traditional urban structure. Set within a matrix of imposing buildings that have received a great amount of publicity, the parks, courtyards, and squares are reserved for the exclusive use of the Campus's employees and visitors. Open space is the luxury of the cities of today, and on Campus its design should be of a high quality, establish an identity, and be innovative. The position and function of the outdoor spaces are delineated in the Master Plan with descriptors like "the heart of the Campus" or "space for rest and relaxation." The projects by Vogt Landschaftsarchitekten are based on the differentiated reflection and realization of these core statements. The inner courtyard of the transparent SANAA building, a subdued, geometric design of sandstone and water, is intended as an abstraction of the basic elements of the Rhine—water, fog,

A park as a greened roof, Vogt Landschaftsarchitekten, 2006: The Campus Park is located at the entrance to the grounds on top of the underground garage.

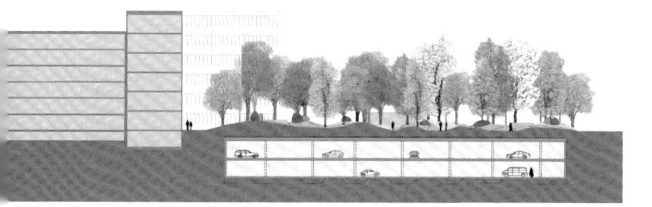

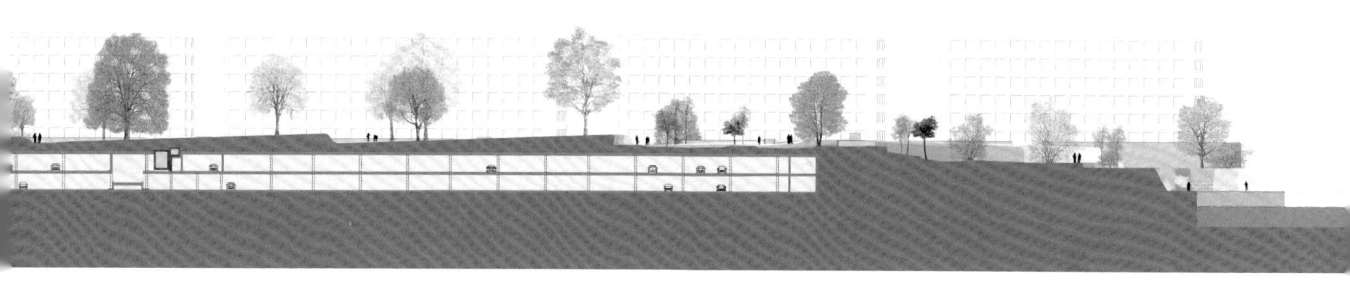

stone, and riverbank vegetation. The Green is a classic square located in the center of Campus in front of Frank O. Gehry's building, whose design recalls aspects of an Alpine karst landscape such as the Silberen in the Muotatal, which are typical rain channels washed out from the limestone in this porous landscape. These hollows find their urban expression in the subterranean lecture halls located beneath the surface of the Green.

The Park is a good example of the role of the green areas on the Novartis Campus grounds. It is the uppermost layer of the most intensive surface use in the vertical sense: in and of itself an oversized roof garden, the Park is located at the entrance of the Campus as a roof layer on top of the subterranean architecture of the underground garage. Two hectares of cast concrete separate the Park from this underground world. Not unlike natural stone, this manmade layer of geological crust has its own appeal, and the concept of the "urban crust" became the starting point for the Park's concept. From the beginning, the design of the Park was connected with the idea of delving into the depths of Earth's history—and thus into the history of the ground beneath the garage in order to rediscover the hidden landscape. The construction work on Campus furnished witnesses in great quantities of the hidden landscape of the Rhine: the ground on which the city and the Campus are located harbors a great variety of different stones, which can also be seen on the medieval, cobblestoned streets of Basel—ochre and carmine-red cobblestones shaded with juniper

Section of the Park with paths,
clay brick walls, lawns, and trees as
a 1:1 mock-up on the still exposed
concrete surface, 2007

About 1,500 trees were planted in the Campus Park, some as densely as in a forest. A special lava-based substrate was used. It is light enough for the load-bearing capacity of the underground garage but still provides the plants enough root space, 2007.

Frozen landslide, 2007: A tilted forest and a system of paths that winds around the trees as if they were boulders in a landslide characterize the upper section of the Park.

greens and violet reds. The history of these stones began long before the last Ice Age. They arrived in Basel with the debris of the Rhine and its tributaries. The Rhine gathered up the multicolored mixture from different regions of the Alps and deposited a part of the stones on its riverbed on its way to the sea in Basel. This slow process of erosion and sedimentation is as old as the Rhine itself. The current topographical structure of Basel's Rhine valley is in contrast relatively young. It arose less than a million years ago at the end of the last Ice Age. The traces of the creation of this landscape appear in the geological map of Basel: the oxbow lakes of the postglacial river system have developed into the marshlands of the Petite Camargue. The parallel running gullies created by glacier runoff end in a system of alluvial fans. They make up the backbone of the landscape today and are reminders of the masses of water which once swept over the landscape bearing their heavy load. The marked, gently ascending lower terraces to the east and west of Basel tell the story of the water's retreat. Most of these basic landscape elements today lie buried under human settlement.

The clear differentiation of elements derived from the urban and natural contexts is a centrale element of the Master Plan. But how does the Park fit into the "urban crust"? In the field of tension existing between these two elements an autonomous attitude of design had to be developed. The design concept considers the Rhine as a determining factor in the natural history of the location, as a counterweight to the autonomy of the Master Plan. Therefore, the design proposed widening the perimeter of the Campus to St. Johann harbor, which was in any case to be decommissioned. "To the Rhine" became the name of and the concept for a park which celebrated its geological context. The concept of geology and vegetation, which because of the architectonic parameters could not be derived directly from the Park's grounds, was imported from the immediate vicinity. The Park's design drew the hidden Rhine valley landscape in the form of a composition of geomorphologic and vegetative phenomena. The Park grounds descend from the higher-lying terraces down to the Rhine. As in the naturally occurring, surrounding landscape of the Rhine terraces, the natural phenomena of this landscape are recreated on a small scale in their natural array and fit together with the artifice of design into the atmospheric landscape of the Park.

In this way, the Park tells a story and can itself be told as a story. As used to happen with seventeenth-century cabinets of curiosities, the unusual details of the Park on the Novartis Campus will be what is noticed first. The effect of the whole will only become apparent to those who have experienced and walked through the Park themselves. The perception of the whole is then retained as the personal, subjective cosmos of the individual.

Compressed geological array, 2008: The park displays different geological phenomena of the Rhine valley and the different stages of the occupation of the surfaces by plants. The history of the landscape becomes the subject of the Park's design.

134

The park visitor who does not stop to sit down on the lawn or at a café table will experience a series of different situations on their stroll. At first they will notice the density of trees, which is unusual for a park. In the first phase of construction, about 1,500 trees were placed, in order to create the atmosphere of a forest landscape. If our imaginary strollers are familiar with northern European flora, they will experience a recognizable forest scene of oaks, beech, cherry, birch, and hedge and Norway maples. The image seems to be of a moment of destruction that has been frozen; as if in a steep mountain terrain after the spring snow melt, the lindens, with their trunks buried sixty centimeter beneath the debris, had been tipped over every which way by the force of the boulders. It is an homogenous, grey-brown landscape that reveals the splendor of the colors of Basel's geology in the rain. The trained eye will discover wonderful treasures underneath the stones, because the material originates from the vicinity of Allschwil, where a tributary of the Rhine deposited stone formed during the Pleistocene. The large, random blocks hidden beneath the underbrush come from the same aggregate, and are slowly becoming overgrown by the young hornbeams.

If the visitor leaves this raw terrain and risks a further sally in the forest landscape, the scenery develops differently in every direction. Here mature birch trees offer pools of shadows in which fern, grasses, bulbs, and perennials flourish; there the young birch and cherry trees stand closely together. As with natural ruderal areas, some will die over time and make room for others to grow. Since they are not removed by the Park maintenance, they will slowly deteriorate into humus, overgrown by moss and fungi.

At Fabrikstrasse, the point of contact for different sections of the Park, the different species and typologies meet up with each other. The constructed forest landscape ends and the structure of the landscape changes fundamentally. East of the street, the ground steadily ascends and defines the horizon at a certain distance, before descending to the Rhine in terraces. The path, continuing on at its original height, cuts deeper and deeper into the rising landscape and soon disappears as a hollow between the embankments. Those who know Basel's country surroundings associate the term "hollow" with a very specific image: a sunken, narrow path in the landscape, frequently created by a dried-up streambed. Constricted to a tunnel by densely packed bushes, it either radiates wild luxuriance or evokes the bleak mood of aging forests in the twilight depending on the season, the time of day, and the constitution of the observer.

This is the goal that is strived for in the hollows of the Campus Park. While the meadows on the terrace are mowed regularly, in a few years the species in the hollows should develop into a densely rambling riot of vegetation consisting of apple, quince, autumn fire Japanese maple, fragrant wintersweet, and spindle trees that appeal to all the senses. But the sunken paths offer yet another image. Their richly structured, layered walls of gravel, trass lime, clay, and loam cut almost geometrically into the terrain and make visible what distinguishes the Campus Park from the traditional landscape parks of our cities: here, growth, decay, and change are part and parcel of the design concept, whereas in the traditional approach the image of a landscape is built and maintained by constant human intervention.

If the stroller follows the hollow in the direction of the terraces, the contrast between the landscape opening up to the Rhine and the narrow path could not be greater. This pertains to the status of the Park today as well as to the planned final state. There will be a typical alluvial area with terraced gravel banks leading down to the Rhine at the point where the Park devolves into unused grounds. Here and there loose groups of poplar and birch break through the

Gravel of varying granulation, trass lime, clay, and loam form the walls of the hollows constructed by the loam specialist, Martin Rauch, 2007: The almost geometrical appearance of the structure immediately after construction will, over the course of time and with the growth of plants, develop into overgrown hollows.

horizon of the meadows of sedge and grass-leaved iris which are native to this landscape and which accompany visitors to the boundary of the Campus area on the bank of the Rhine. A rotation of 360 degrees at this point will reveal the clash of two fundamentally different concepts of landscape perception. With a glance at the river and its background, the panorama is like those recorded by eighteenth-century painters. The diorama, becomes visible with a glance at the Park: a stage of nature for the park visitors of the twenty-first century.

Behind the natural scenery of the Park is a highly artificial construct. Like the workings of a stage, the mechanics behind this "natural play" can be discovered as they were built into the landscape. If the ground suddenly crunches beneath the feet, it is the little balls of lava making the sound. Eighty-five percent lava is mixed with 7.5 percent humus and 7.5 percent topsoil for a substratum specifically suited to the Park. By digging a little, at a depth of 120 centimeters one would run up against a steel net to which the root balls are fastened with Nylon belts. Further down one would meet up with the base of the mechanically shaped topography: the roof of the underground garage. The lava substratum already indicates the limited load capacity of the subsoil. The monumental ventilation shafts made of concrete and the stairs for the emergency exits make it clear that visitors are moving about on top of a subterranean architectural world.

What does this mean for the many hundreds of mature trees on the grounds? The common oak, a slow-growing deep rooter which only flourishes in well-developed areas, can be found in the Park just as easily as the birch, an undemanding pioneer tree. A specialist in biological succession can read the vegetation of the Rhine valley like a map and draw conclusions about the geological substrate and its age. He or she would not be surprised to find dense, old forest on the upper terraces, somewhat younger, agriculturally influenced vegetation on the middle terraces, and pioneer plants on the alluvial levels. In spite of the presence of a difficult substratum in some places, planting according to the principles of succession allowed the use of demanding species in the Campus Park—an interaction of scientific knowledge and artistic freedom.

The "natural theater" in the Park represents a special challenge for the gardeners: that of "laissez-vivre." Accustomed as they are to always restoring the changing vegetation to the desired appearance, here they must become accustomed to allowing change to occur, as long as it does not hinder use of the Park. The Park is just as artificial as the models created in the workshops of landscape architects, but its components are very much alive. And with each cycle of growth and decay, the opportunity arises to cover up the Park construct with another layer of nature as part of the "urban crust."

The Art Program: A Sketch
Harald Szeemann

Harald Szeemann (1933–2005) wrote the following text in 2001, when he began his work at the Novartis Campus in the capacities of art critic, curator, and innovative and unorthodox thinker. Written for no specific publication, the text laid the groundwork for the very first program aimed at integrating visual art into the planning of the Novartis Campus.

Although not all of his suggestions were realized, the strategy Szeemann outlined was followed, and it proved to be both farsighted and successful. Therefore, in order to honor one of the most important men who shaped the adventure of the Novartis Campus's design, we will let him speak for himself. V. M. L.

The Master Plan provides for a number of urban-style parks and squares on the Campus. Another important consideration is the overview of the approach by way of Voltastrasse. A conceivable solution would be four different types of street furnishings for the public areas (benches, lighting, garbage cans, pavements) alongside individual objects and sculptures.

Artists of the second twentieth-century revolution tend to be best suited to this task, along with the "pure" sculptors of the postwar period.

Cooperation: Art and Architecture, Contrasted and Integrated

In particular, Fabrikstrasse, with its pedestrian zone, arcades, and building entrances, suggests a number of possibilities for getting artists of the middle and younger generations interested in an integration along these lines. But one might also consider an integrated design of the roof gardens along Fabrikstrasse.

Environments Integrated into the City Plan

For this purpose, individual buildings are envisaged, or they can be seen through display windows on Fabrikstrasse. We should be thinking in terms of parallel phenomena of interest to the pharmaceutical industry. Specifically, I would suggest the following interventions.

The Courtyard of the Novartis International Headquarters Building

As the design by Peter Walker and Partners has now been definitively adopted, I would suggest a reconsideration of the disposition of sculpture and furniture. The proposed sculpture site seems to me to be very much relegated "to one side." A conceivable solution would be to set up here the already existing sculpture by the Argentinean artist Alicia Penalba (1913–1982). For the benches, cooperation with Jenny Holzer (*1950) would be beneficial. As the courtyard otherwise offers virtually no opportunities—the design of the pools, hedges, and birches is comprehensive—the question arises of a possible intervention on the façades of the courtyard (e.g., Rémy Zaugg (1943–2005), who has great experience with such assignments).

The Forum

Here the design is still completely open, and I should like to propose quite specifically Chris Burden's (*1946) work *The Flying Steamroller*. It requires, however, a shelter measuring twenty-two meters in diameter, which could also be octagonal. The twenty-two meters result from the flight path of the yellow steamroller, and the height, of at least nine and a half meters, from the electric power supply via the axis of rotation. It seems to me that this work is in keeping with the site: the creation of a place of innovation. The work is spectacular, powerful, and innovative.

Fabrikstrasse

For one of the shops behind the arcade, I suggest an absolutely unique project, the life's work of the farmer Emery Blagdon (1907–1986). In a hut in the Sandhills region in the north of the state of Nebraska, he integrated more than six hundred sculptures of wire, copper, and wood, along with eighty paintings, into a gesamtkunstwerk that, in his opinion, was able to cure diseases such as cancer with the "electromagnetic field" it generated. After Blagdon's death, Dan Dryd, a North Platte pharmacist turned musician, and his friend, the painter Don Christensen, acquired the complete project at auction, after the work had been reconstructed for the first time at the 1997 Lyons Biennale. A second showing, for which I was also responsible, took place in the context of the 1998 American Outsiders exhibition at the Philadelphia Museum of Art. The two owners are now prepared to sell the entire fragile work, as only a permanent site could protect it from damage and general wear and tear. I would regard the work as a positive enrichment for the Campus.

The Green

For a freestanding sculpture on one of the planned "turf mounds," a work by Eduardo Chillida (1924–2002) might be considered.

The Life Sciences Park

Here, too, there is no shortage of possible sites for freestanding sculptures and artists' environments, but consideration might also be given to enlivening the place through illumination (Jenny Holzer).

The End of Fabrikstrasse

A dynamic, powerful sculpture would be ideal for what is a vanishing point for the eye from the viewpoint of the gatehouse and a "center of distribution" for all those coming from the parking lot. There is only one sculptor today who fits the bill: Richard Serra (*1939). I am not thinking in terms of an open structure, such as the one in the Theaterplatz in Basel, but rather of a closed form, such as the one which was on view at the Gagosian Gallery at the end of 2001.

The Fabrikstrasse Road Surface

Here, too, an artistic solution is conceivable. On the square between the two Deichtor Halls in Hamburg, Lawrence Weiner has integrated his verbal creations into the existing surface. "Cobblestones" are precisely what he finds to be an interesting material.

The Entrance Pavilions

An artist/architect collaboration (e.g., involving Vito Acconci; *1940) would surely be more innovative than a purely functional building.

Für MARCO SERRA
von SZ.

NOVARTIS

ZUR KUNST
Typologisch heute

I. Grosse Entscheidungen
   Endpunkt Fabrikstrasse: Richard Serra
   Eingangssituation: Chris Burden

II. Vorschläge Workshop
   Forum: Chillida
   Hof 200: Alicia Penalba (früherer Ankauf)
   Märkli: Jenny Holzer (Fassade)
           Steiner/Lenzlinger (Innenhof)

   202: Edi Rama
   Cafeteria: Gursky (Ankauf o.k.)
              Tozoni (in situ)

   Restaurant: Delmorini (Ankauf)
   Eingangstor: Ulrich Rückriem (ev. auch Georg)
   Passage: Eva Schlegel
   Garage: Zoderer
   Fence: Olaf Nicolai

III. Vorschläge Architekten
   Diener a Diener: Helmut Federle
   Krischanitz: Gilbert Brettenbauer
   Saana: Walter Niedermayer
          Toko Sakamoto

IV. Schwebende Verfahren
   Serge Spitzer
   Blagdon Project

Alicia Penalba, *La grande cathédrale*, bronze, 4.5 x 1.5 x 1.5 m, 1969–71: The sculpture found a location in the inner courtyard of the historical administration building (Forum 1) as suggested by Harald Szeemann.

Left: "Concerning art," handwritten fax communication from Harald Szeemann to Marco Serra, March 25, 2004

Left, top to bottom: Bending the steel plates for Richard Serra's *Dirk's Pod* at Pickhan Umformtechnik in Siegen, 2003; transportation of the steel plates on the Rhine, 2004

Richard Serra, *Dirk's Pod* on Fabrikstrasse at the north entrance, 2004: The ten torus-shaped elements made of weatherproof steel are each 5 meters high and 13.2 meters long, with a thickness of 5 centimeters and a weight of approximately 29 tons each. There are a total of five sculptural structures, each consisting of two of these steel elements.

The Detour Art Offers Is Worth Taking
Jacqueline Burckhardt

The profound transformation of the former St. Johann Works grounds into Novartis's "Campus of Knowledge" is underway. The forces of innovation and creativity are at work. When such terms are heard, then art cannot be far away, for the business of artists is innovation and creativity.

Even if today art is found mostly in museums, galleries, and collections, it has in fact always belonged in the public and private spaces that were not at first considered appropriate for it; the same is true of the Campus, where something else is the main concern. Art should appear where sponsors and artists consider it proper.

In the museum, "Do not touch" is posted in order to protect the works of art. This stern commandment serves at the same time to create a reverential distance between viewer and work. At the beginning of the twentieth century the avant-garde wanted to break that taboo, as do most of the young artists of today. They want to address society with their works in the midst of life. This can happen on the Novartis Campus. The opportunity of direct confrontation is possible here, as is physical contact with works of art, for instance, at the Main Gate, where chairs by Franz West (b. 1947 in Vienna) can be seen. The seven chairs belong to the series *Onkel-Stühle,* which since 2003 West has had built from metal, always covering them with a different fabric. Every one is unique. If one sits on a chair, one becomes part of the work of art, and art and life merge with one another.

With a day-to-day opportunity to become acquainted with works of art on the Campus, the straining for an answer to the question "What is behind the work?" can be relaxed into a more playful kind of inquiry that can be very productive: What is actually going on between me and the work of art? What is going on in this moment for me as a viewer? What does the work of art trigger in me in terms of feelings and thoughts? Viewing art is perpetually a small act within a broader freedom. Every person should encounter the works with their own associative network of knowledge and personal interpretation or fantasy. A non-professional can perhaps have an easier time giving free rein to his or her thoughts when confronted by a work of art.

The Novartis Campus is set up in such a way that everyone can strike a personal balance between a strictly business mode and a more contemplative mood. One is literally encouraged to wander the Campus's streets and parks and plazas from time to time, in order not to take the shortest route to work. Detours create distance, and what is important here is the distance one needs to find solutions for the problems one is trying to address. The detour via art is always one that pays, and the work of art is an ideal object with which one can whet one's thoughts. Art is an interlocutor with much to say, one who is always there.

There are many surprise locations on the Campus that display artworks, which were, in fact, understood from the beginning as an integral part of the overall complex. Even before the first building was dedicated on the Campus on May 25, 2004, Richard Serra's (b. 1939 in San Francisco) monumental sculpture *Dirk's Pod* was unveiled. The work's title suggests the association of five steel sculptures with a group of whales, and in deference to this dynamic, the group is not mounted on a common base like a traditional sculpture, but rather consciously incorporates the ground and its surroundings.[1] It is worth the effort to take in the changing spatial volumes from different perspectives and to follow the play of changing silhouettes. If one listens closely to the voices and noises in the interstices of the individual steel structures, one even notices acoustic phenomena. For a short moment one slips into a suggestive sluice of perception—one can succumb entirely to the situation and afterwards be in another register, as if one would wish to pace blindly off the Fabrikstrasse as straight as an arrow.

Art Between the Blocks of Disciplines

Wagging tongues like to remonstrate that art in a corporate context is just a thin cultural coating, an expensive status symbol, the fruit of advertising strategy. In the case of the Novartis Campus, these cliché-laden ideas miss the point. The interest in art that is so obvious on Campus originates much more from a contemporary interest in the idea of a humanist education, which teaches that exactly where the fight to survive is fought, it is urgent to step out of specialized roles and to think more comprehensively. Art can do this because it likes to nestle in the interstices of the disciplinary blocks, where it can stimulate communication and freedom of thought. In addition, the creation of art arises from the urge to experiment and the tendency to cross borders—both of which are characteristics that belong to the set of tools wielded by artists and researchers alike.

In the entry hall of the lab building built by Adolf Krischanitz, the mural developed by Sigmar Polke (b. 1941 in Lower Saxony), an alchemist par excellence among artists, is a symbol for this interface. It is a careful composition in which Polke has floated 365 pyrite "suns" discretely mounted in brass over a flat, black strip of wall. Inspired by his science studies, Polke went one step further in transforming natural material into a cultural product, as he has done with agate, uranium, or what is perhaps the most expensive dye in the world, the secretion of the purple snail. The pyrite was extracted from mines in Illinois, where, in the geological stratum that had evolved at an unimaginably slow rate into a slatelike bedrock, the pyrite suns were transformed under heat and pressure from a biological material into the mineral substance of iron sulphide.

In the Campus laboratory building, biologists, crystallographers, and chemists are looking for new medications, and are therefore aiming at similar kinds of transformations. To be fair, however, while the broad expanse of time needed for the process of the pyrite suns' creation is governed in nature by the god of time, Aion, the researchers in the laboratory buildings urgently seek the favor of Kairos, the god of serendipity.

---

[1] The tradition of sculpture without a pedestal began with Auguste Rodin's *Burghers of Calais*, which the artist wanted to place on the ground in 1895 in the square in front of the town hall in Calais, in order for the work to be able to come into direct contact with the people. He did not succeed, however, because society was not ready for what at the time was an unusual concept.

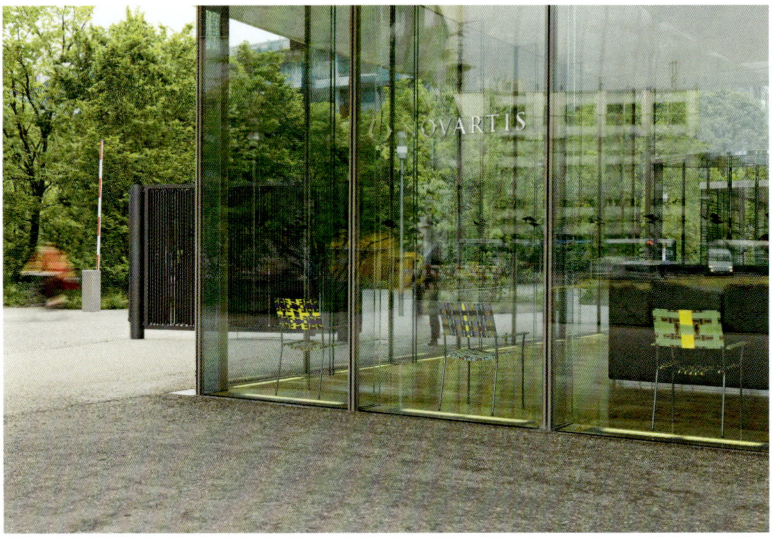
OVARTIS
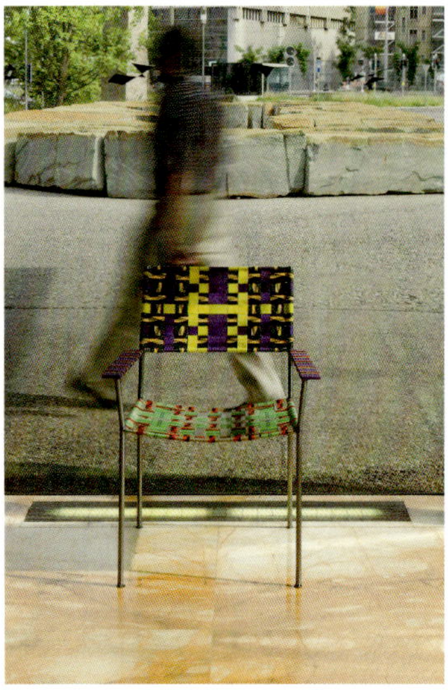
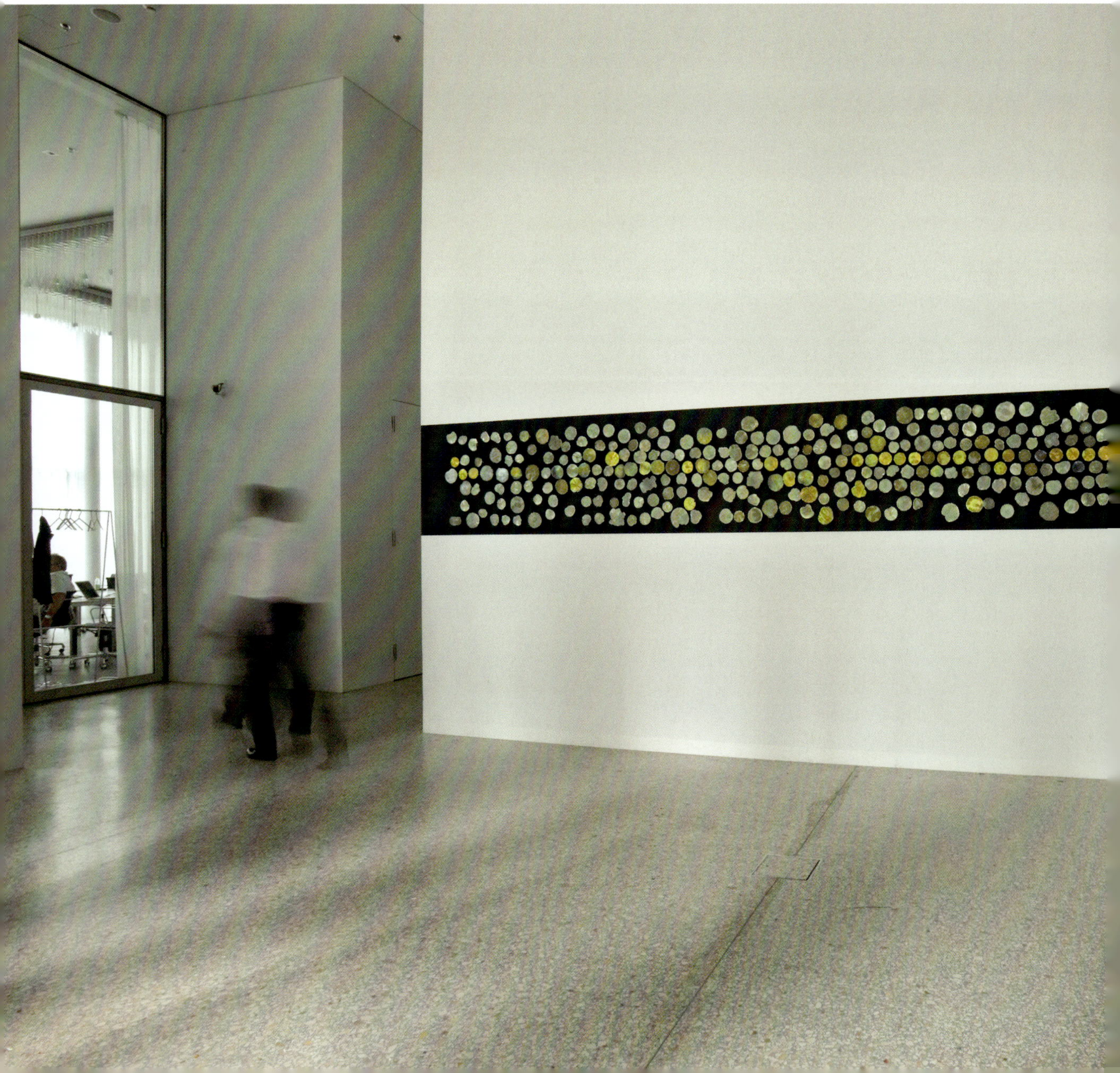

Left: Franz West, seven chairs from the *Onkel-Stühle*-Serie, which the Austrian artist has been creating since 2003. Each chair is handmade and furnished with a different cloth netting. Displayed in the entrance pavilion of the Campus, 2008

Sigmar Polke, *365 Pyrit-Sonnen*, 2008, ca. 250 million years old, on a black frieze, 0.85 x 6 m, hung in the laboratory building at 16 Fabrikstrasse

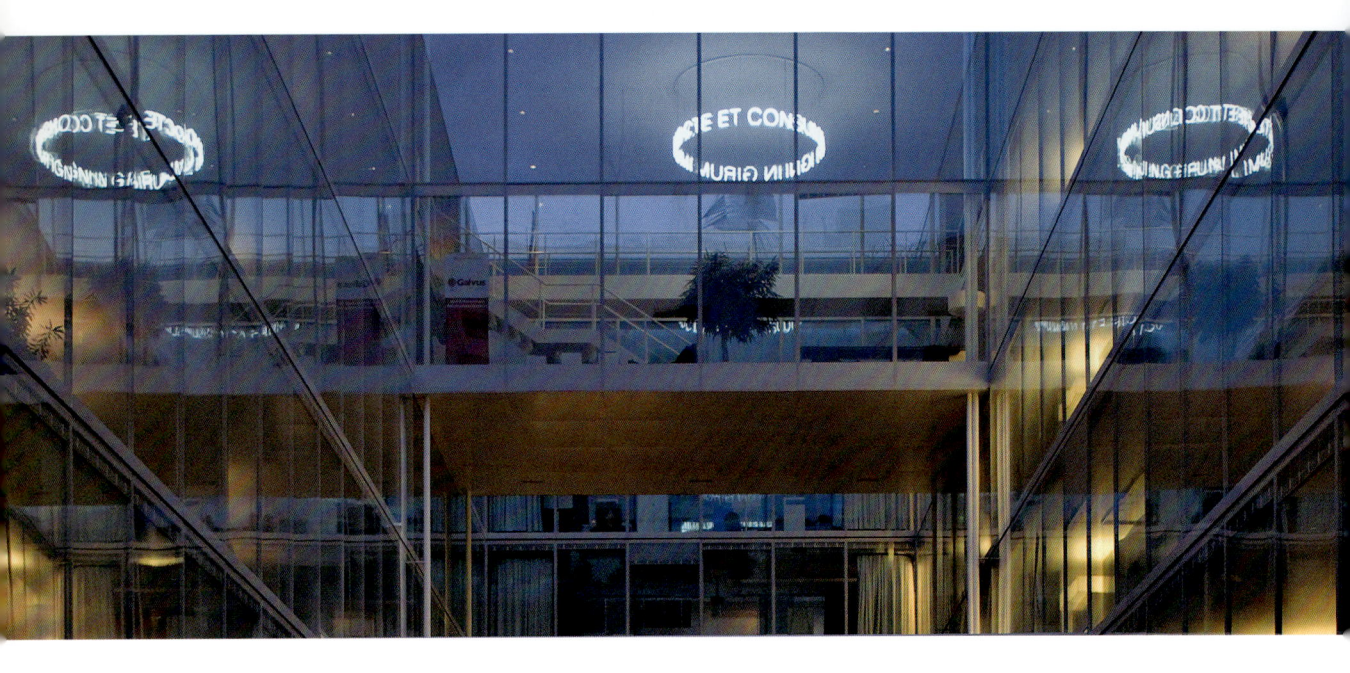

Cerith Wyn Evans, *In girum imus nocte et consumimur igni*, 2007, neon letters, 0.3 x 3 m, hung in the offices at 4 Fabrikstrasse

Demands for Quality and Place Specificity

Those who are active as advisors in the Novartis System as Harald Szeemann once was, and as I am today, work with criteria of quality and want non-professionals to have the confidence not to have to get involved with coincidental or meaningless things or risk having to confront feeble artwork. Everything that Novartis strives for must be of the utmost quality, so this also pertains to the on-site art—in spite of the difficulties associated with the definition of "high-quality" contemporary art. Qualifications like "innovative" and "creative" are only useful to a limited extent, and systems of criteria fail, as does the attempt to pin down the definition of the term "art."

One often hears the truism "De gustibus non est disputandum," or "one can not argue with taste," which means that what really counts in the final analysis is any individual's preference, and that is the end of the matter. But this attitude opens the door to arbitrariness, which can never be a good strategy. The Campus's art should develop along loosely gathered strands of direction. Therefore, the art must be suggested with professional caution and a sure hand and presented with great respect for the people working on Campus.

Place specificity plays an important role in the selection of Campus artworks, so that the works selected can take part in a manifold way in a dialogue with their individual locations.

The circular light installation by Cerith Wyn Evans (b. 1958 in Wales) in the SANAA building is a floating, almost entirely immaterial work of art that accentuates the ease and transparency of the structure in which it is viewed. One can read clockwise and counterclockwise in neon letters the poetic content of the Latin palindrome "In girum imus nocte et consumimur igni" (We ramble through the night and are consumed by fire).

With his sculptures in the Campus's public spaces, Ulrich Rückriem (b. 1938 in Düsseldorf) has devoted his attention since the 1970s to the relationship between works of art and their locations. He is represented on the Campus with four large works that run in a sequence from outside in front of the south portal to inside in front of the administration building. His *Stele* stands at the Campus entrance from Voltastrasse. It gives a vertical signal and marks its location like a kind of giant boundary stone.[2] Stone is the decisive work material for Rückriem—heavy, dense stone from different quarries, granite or perhaps dolomite. The forms of his sculptures are elemental, archetypal. Rückriem splits or cuts the stone, horizontally, vertically, or sometimes diagonally. He lets the stone be in its nature, so that it never has to represent anything but itself.

Rückriem's *Wellenbrecher* (Wave Breaker) functions as an anachronistic traffic island with an irregular, empty form inside. In a way, it plays the role of the ancestral traffic island, standing self-consciously and imperturbably in stark contrast to the highly developed world of the limousines which drive around it daily. In contrast to *Stele,* which statically and vertically marks its location, *Wellenbrecher* has a horizontal, supine form, and thereby breaks up the traffic flow dynamic.

Rückriem's third work on the way to the administration building is *7 Steine* (7 Stones). In the local Campus jargon it has acquired the additional title of "Seven Mountains," which harbors a charming interpretation: apparently one associates a Japanese Zen garden, with its miniature mountain landscape lacking green plants, with the stone settings. But the vertical cuts in the raw blocks of stone reveal another context. They connect the seven stones to the pavement slabs, which came from the same Sardinian quarry. They are cut flat on the bottom so that they fit precisely on the slabs. The vertical cross cuts, which divide the blocks in four, correspond exactly with the floor pattern of slab joints. They thereby create a distracting play with the slabs, breaking up their organization purely optically and enlivening the square.

Ulrich Rückriem's *Tisch* (Table) is a gigantic, cubic granite monolith that is divided into three equally thick horizontal layers according to precise arithmetic relations and reassembled on the Forum. A cross form was cut out of the middle layer—about five ninths of the mass—so that only the "table legs" remain, while the bottom layer is flush with the ground. With this sculpture, Rückriem shows how he can coax the most gentle and powerful sounds from the stone, how he uses the marks left behind by the tools as design elements and brings the colored nuances of the natural patina or the rough to finely treated surfaces into play.

[2] Ulrich Rückriem gave the *Stele* to the Novartis Campus as a gift after he received the contract for the other three works.

Right: Ulrich Rückriem, *Wellenbrecher*, 2007, Anroechter dolomite stone, composed from connected pieces of broken stone, 1.1 x 28 x 8 m. It is displayed in Novartis Square.

Ulrich Rückriem, *Stele*, 2006, from a single block of pink Porrino granite, split in one place at a height of 1.2 m, creating a plinth and the actual pillar, 1.2 x 1.2 x 6.36 m, donated by the artist in 2006. It is displayed between the Place of Knowledge and Novartis Place.

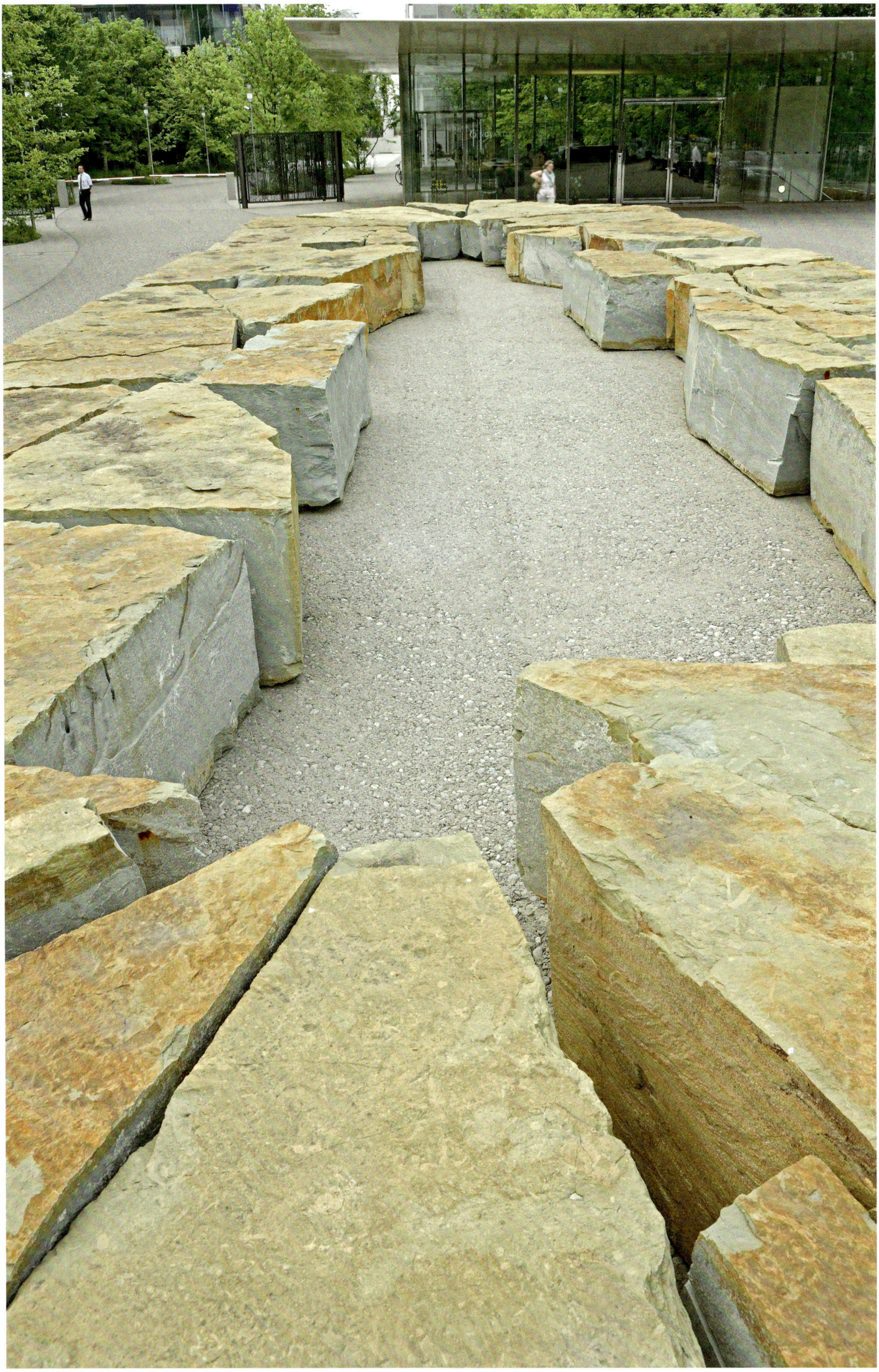

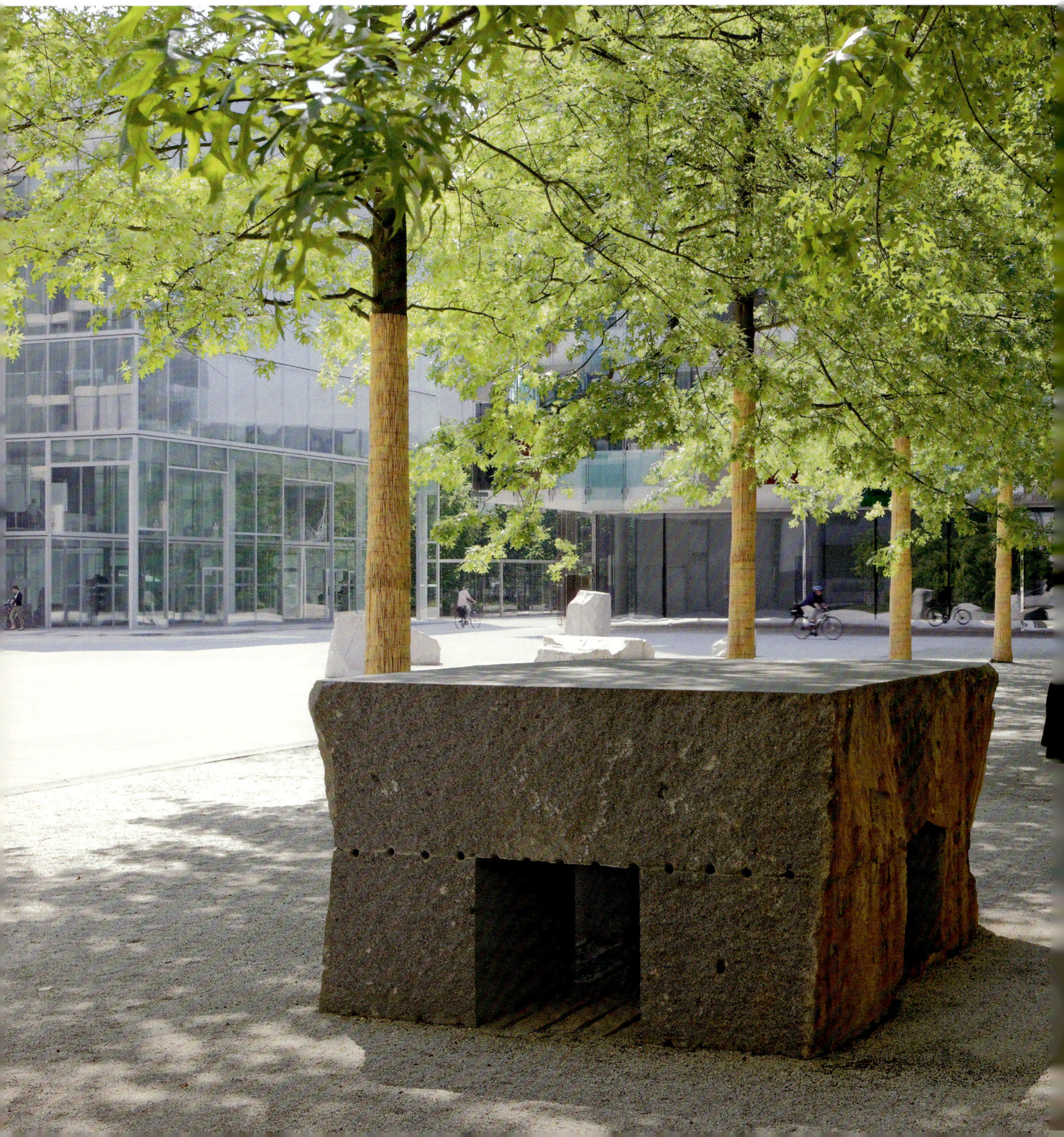

Above: Ulrich Rückriem, 7 *Steine*, 2007 (idea from 1970), White Moncini granite from Sardinia: The unfinished blocks were cut with crosses and set on the joints of the pavement slabs of the Forum.

Left: Ulrich Rückriem, *Tisch*, 2006, Bleu de Vire granite from Normandy, 2.1 x 2 x 3 m: The monolith was split in three equal sections with a cross-shaped cutout. One part is embedded in the earth in the Forum.

Jenny Holzer, *1,000 Sayings*, 2006, LED scroll, 3 m high: This work comprised of sayings and aphorisms from around the world is entirely integrated into the architecture of Peter Märkli (office building at 6 Fabrikstrasse).

Whoever turns his gaze from Rückriem's *Tisch* to the façade of Peter Märkli's Visitor Center instantaneously makes the journey through time from the primordial past to the urban modernity of a twenty-first-century metropolis. The façade literally speaks to us, because the texts by Jenny Holzer (b. 1950 in Ohio) are flashing over the surface of its arcades on an electronic fleece of white light diodes. The texts are short and concise and touch on social subjects. There are instructions, aphorisms, truisms, and irritating political and philosophical insights. Some work like slogans, little poetical messages, or riddles. The architect and the artist collaborated closely on the work so that Holzer's piece would be entirely integrated into the architectonic structure and not merely applied as an unrelated afterthought. The architecture thereby became a double content provider. As a pedestrian on the Novartis Campus, one can now exploit the wonderfully stimulating opportunity to seize upon one of the short texts on the Visitor Center façade as a source of mental inspiration for the day ahead. However, the visibility of these texts is entirely dependent on the weather and the time of day, that is, the light conditions, a fact which also has its charm.

The glass façades of the Forum 1 building by Roger Diener (b. 1950 in Basel) also reveal themselves variably with changing weather and light conditions. Diener conceptualized them in collaboration with the artist Helmut Federle (b. 1944 in Solothurn) and the architect Gerold Wiederin (b. 1961 in Vorarlberg; d. 2006 in Vienna). Here again architecture and art are inseparable, engaged in an interplay with one another. Glass panels of different colors and sizes are fastened at varying distances on a grid system. One can sometimes see through them, but at other times they reflect back their surroundings, lending the architecture an infatuating ease.

Eva Schlegel, *Walkway*, 2007, steel and 43 glass panels with blurred silkscreened text, 47.7 x 3.5 x 3 m

Among the works of art on the Campus, Eva Schlegel's (b. 1960 in the Tirol) *Walkway* is one that also fulfills a function. Schlegel's intervention in the Park consists of three elements: one passage, two car ramps, and four pedestrian stairwells that lead to the underground garage. The approximately forty-eight-meter-long, two-and-a-half-meter-wide, and three-meter-high *Walkway*, which protects visitors from the rain on their way from the south portal through the Park to the inner Campus area, was inspired by Japanese pavilions. Transparency, ease, and a lively rhythm created by the irregular intervals of the glass panels on the sides, which alternately overlap or leave access to the Park like sliding doors, were her guidelines for a virtuoso solution to the static and technical characteristics of the project. Pages of text blurred to the point of illegibility are printed with a silkscreen process on the glass panels. By means of their formal structure, each viewer can associate possible content based on his or her own experience.

Schlegel also designed a dizzying canopy for the two car ramps leading to the underground garage that rest only on two points. She vapor-deposited circular mirrors ten meters in diameter on the glass side walls in the stairwells, so that daylight and reflections of nature can penetrate two stories down into the basement.

Dan Graham, sketches of two versions of the *Two-Way Mirror Pavilion "Curve and Straight Line,"* 2007: The version on the left was selected.

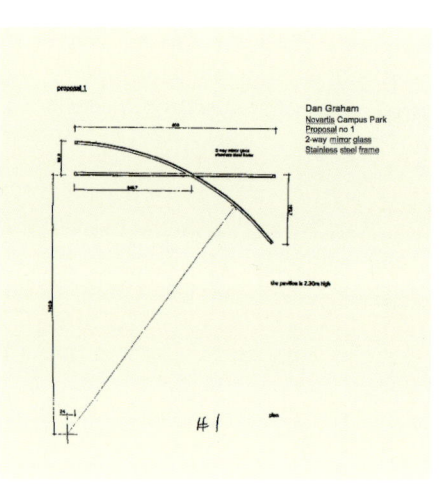

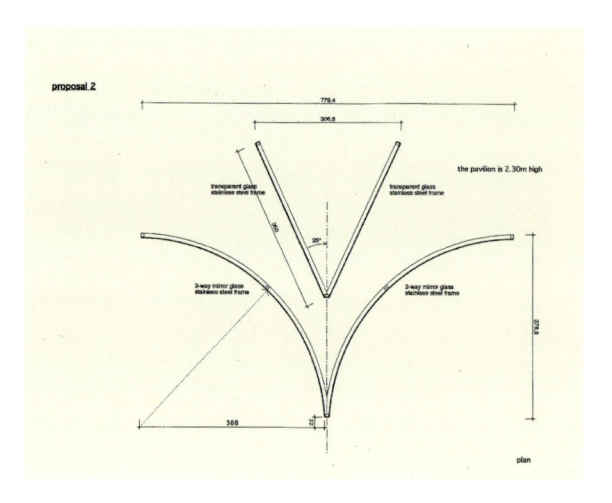

158

Dan Graham, *Two-Way Mirror Pavilion "Curve and Straight Line,"* 2008, steel and glass, 6 x 2.3 m

Above: The assembly

Below: The pavilion at its definitive location in the park

In front of the SANAA building, the *Two-Way Mirror Pavilion* by Dan Graham (b. 1942 in Illinois) stands on the meadow in a finely balanced position. In multiple cross-fades, the people and the surroundings melt together in the half-transparent mirrored glass. Those who attempt to decipher all the levels of reality of the reflections and deformations and discern those seen beyond the glass while observing themselves in the act of perception and being perceived will stay baffled. Graham's pavilion thereby takes its place in the tradition of the follies once devised for historical pleasure gardens.

In Praise of Passionate Understanding

Not everyone on the Novartis Campus must stand before every work of art with the same will to accept it. One should be able to choose for oneself, and leave open the possibility that this choice can always change again. But sometimes the irritation itself constitutes a challenge to penetrate different unknown universes and other worlds and, thereby, to soften up the tendency to one-sidedness conditioned by the factors of time, energy, and economy. If one is open and involved and tunes all of the senses and keeps a passionate understanding at the ready, then looking at art will be a pleasure.

Notes on the Appearance of and Communication on the Campus
Alan Fletcher

Like Harald Szeemann, Alan Fletcher (1931–2006) also guided the planning of the Novartis Campus from the very beginning. In order to outline his work, he wrote the text reproduced here in 2001. He represents the seedbed, so to speak, of the absolutely explosive intellectual productivity that shaped far more than just the graphic design of the Campus. When Alan passed away two years ago, the Campus team lost not only a source of inspiration, but also a man who helped to integrate and bring together the team. In 2007, the London Design Museum honored Alan's work for the Novartis Campus, as well as his many other pursuits.
V. M. L.

These remarks are initial thoughts and reflections about the graphic design of the description of the Novartis company grounds. The plan is to represent a typical Campus appearance. It should include the entrance gates, signs, visitor ID's, vehicles et cetera. The Novartis corporate identity will become manifest inside the offices, the buildings and on the areas used by the company.

Signage

The street plan of the Novartis Campus is a grid with wide avenues and narrow cross streets: it is a small town. Although this pattern enables routes to be simply labeled, the program will also need to address other issues:

1. We are starting from scratch.
2. There is a Master Plan, but the site still has to be developed.
3. The area is enclosed for security and is only accessible through a few entries.
4. The buildings (with few exceptions) will be new.
5. Each building will be designed by a different architect.
6. Although there will be a variety of architectural styles, the buildings will be designed within given dimensions.
7. The public areas and streets of the Campus require a sign system to identify, direct, locate, and inform.
8. There is (hopefully) no obligation for signs to conform to local urban regulations and ordinances.
9. The sign system must be flexible and have longevity, as it will be applied while the Campus is developed over a thirty-year period.
10. The intention is to create street graphics that will exceed their purpose and practical utility. They must also be appropriate, attractive, friendly, and an asset to the environment.

Handwritten notes on sketch:

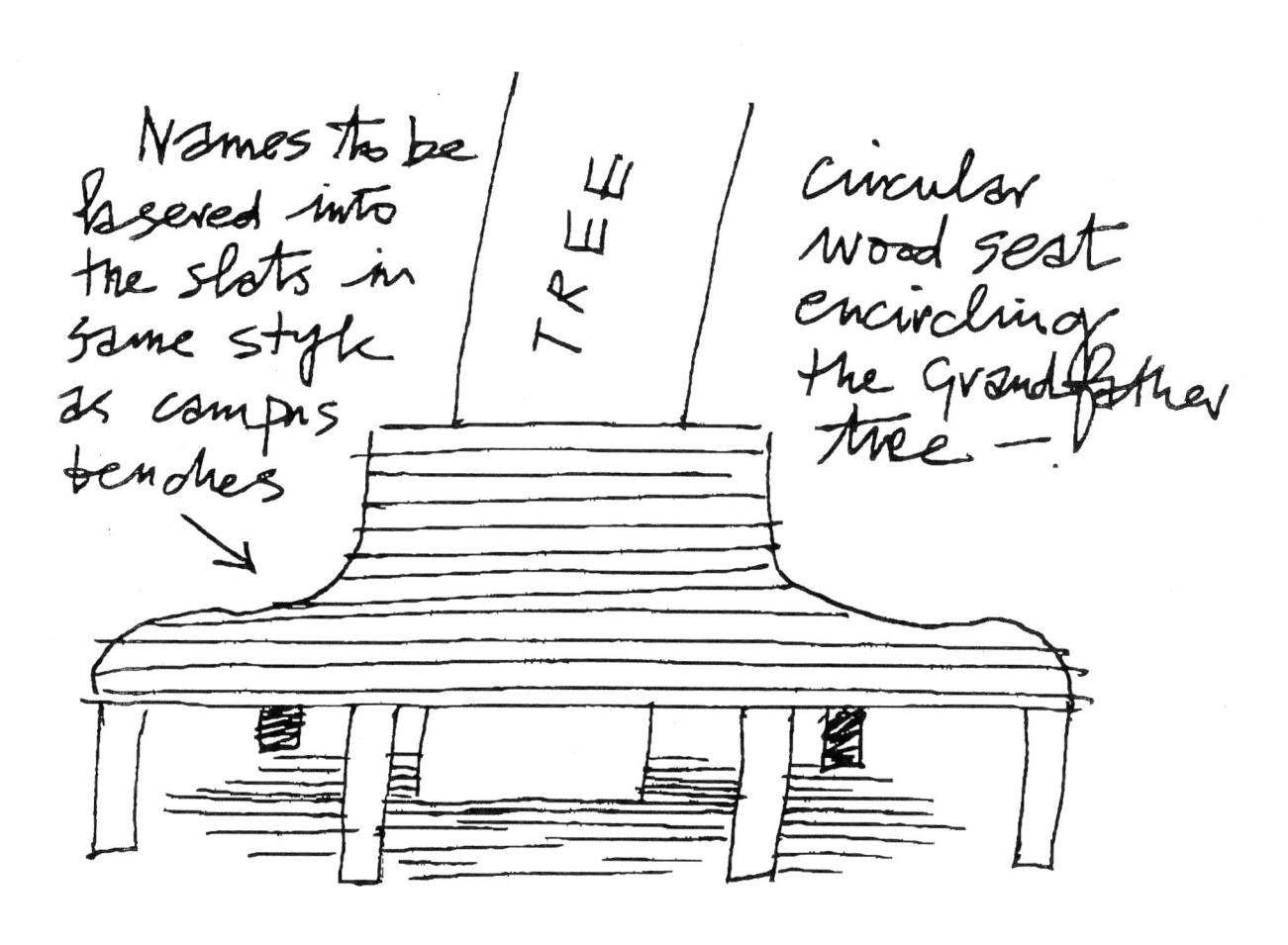

Names to be lasered into the slots in same style as campus benches →

TREE

circular wood seat encircling the Grandfather tree.

"The Grandfather Tree," fax from Alan Fletcher to Kaspar Schmid, May 2005

"The Grandfathers" – Influential Figures for Novartis

Bindschedler, Robert
Böniger, Melchior
Brodbeck-Sandreuter, Jacques
Clavel, Alexandre
Dollfus, Gaspard
Dunant, Yves
Durand, Louis
Engi, Gadient
Flückiger, Edward Werner
Geigy-Gemuseus, Johann Rudolf
Geigy-Merian, Johann Rudolf
Geigy-Schlumberger, J. Rudolf
Gnehm, Robert
Hartmann, Max
Hofmann, Albert
Huguenin, Daniel Edouard
Jacottet, Carl Maurice
Käppeli, Robert
Kern, Alfred
Koechlin-Vischer, Carl
Krauer, Alex
Leemann, Hans
Miescher, Karl
Moret, Marc
Müller, Paul Hermann
Müller-Pack, Johann Jakob
Mylius, Albert
Passavant, Emanuel
Planta, Louis von
Ritter, Oscar
Rothlin, Ernst
Ryhiner, Carl
Dandmeyer, Traugott
Sandoz, Aurèle
Sandoz, Edouard
Schmid, Jakob
Schuster, Johann Jakob
Simonius, Alphons
Speiser, Paul
Stoll, Arthur
Staehelin, Max
Wettstein, Albert

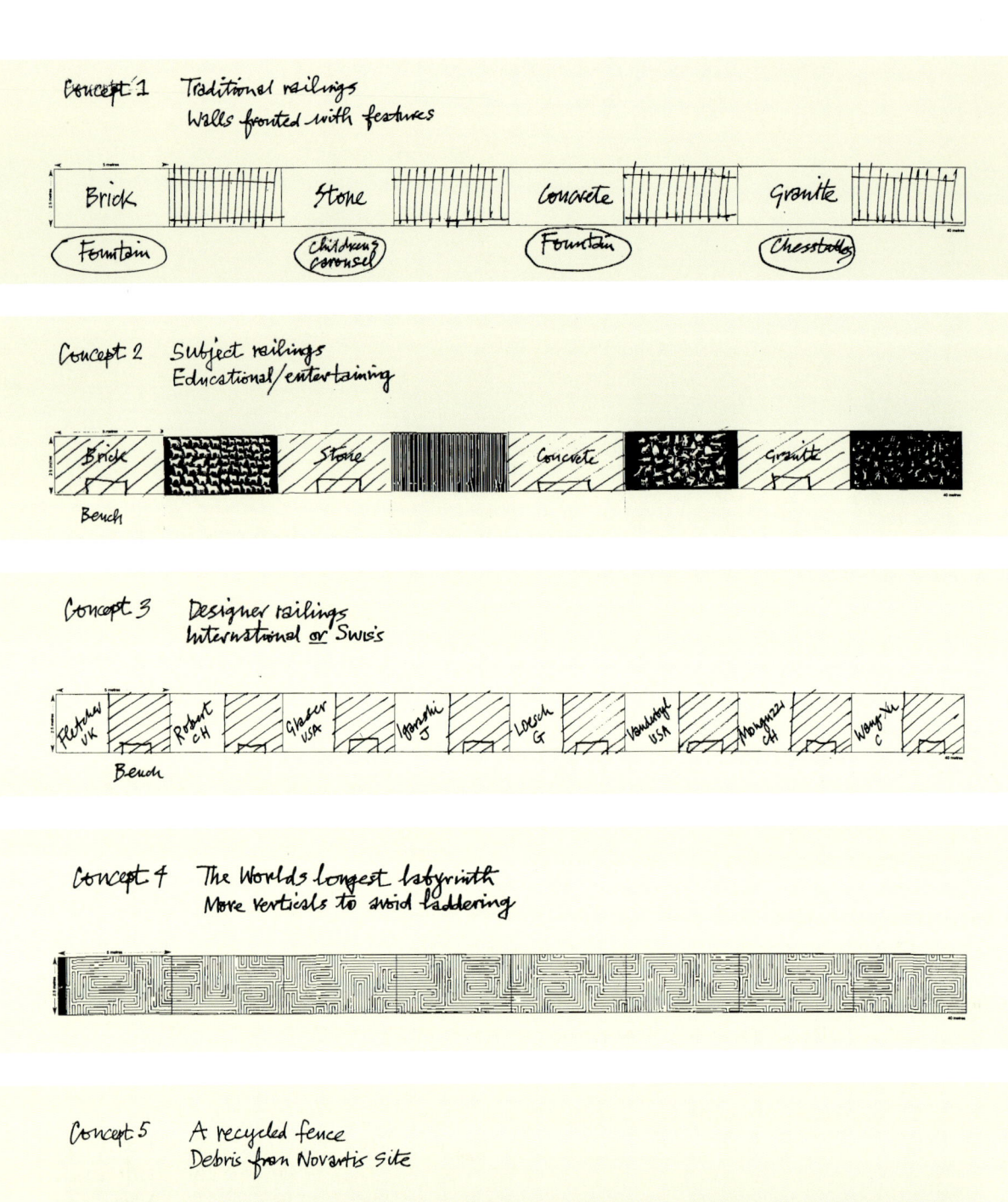

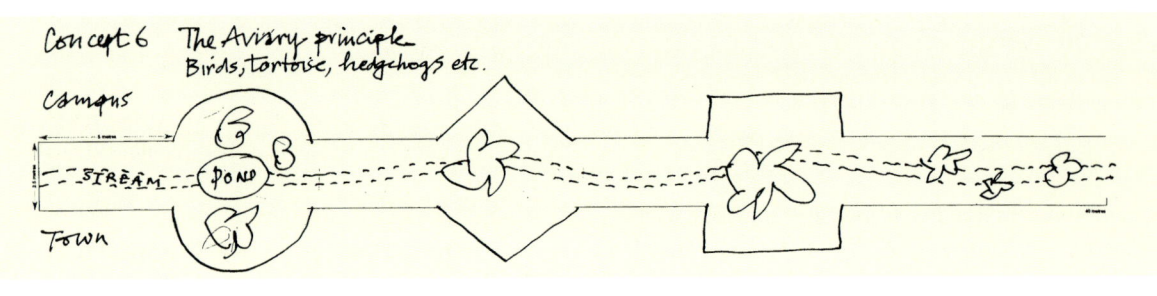

Suggestions for the design of the
fences, Alan Fletcher, sketches, 2003

The Names

For signs, the names are the starting point. A simple option is to name the streets 1, 2, 3, etc., and the avenues A, B, C, and so on. I feel this is too clinical, more appropriate to a penitentiary than a campus. A more evocative notion is borrowing names of scientists associated with the life sciences to label the streets: Pasteur and Fleming, for example. This would create a memorable profile for the Campus, honor those relevant to Novartis, and reflect the activities of the company. One method of selection might be to use names of individuals awarded the Nobel Prize, or some other acknowledged criteria. Names applied in alphabetical order to thoroughfares (Arber, Bloch, Crick) would aid orientation and location. The buildings could be numbered as well as named.

The Lettering

The choice of alphabet and style is important. For example, the signs must avoid being bland and characterless yet avoid the authoritarian flavor of signs in airport terminals.

The Street Signs

External signs for buildings, such as the library, present a problem. Should they follow company or Campus style? There may be a need for directional signs around the Campus indicating routes to important buildings—or visitors could be given maps with their entry badges.

Street Markings

Street surface markings for traffic—arrows, bicycle routes, pedestrian crossings, and other indications—should probably follow the standard (and familiar) local Swiss ordinances.

Advertising / Information Billboards

The subject of advertising billboards has not yet emerged. Public information and consumer advertising is not necessarily environmentally detrimental. This point still needs to be addressed. Advertising could, for example, be restricted to posters promoting and announcing cultural events. Examples such as theater posters would enliven the ambience.

Commercial Signs

Signs for retail spaces and amenities pose a separate issue. Experience demonstrates that regulations enforcing styles, alphabets, façades, and illuminations in renovated areas often emasculate rather than enhance. Nevertheless, a degree of control needs to be established, perhaps basic rules regarding projecting signs and illuminations and a requirement to submit proposed commercial signs to the steering committee for approval.

Cultivating Visual Identity
Lize Mifflin and Kaspar Schmid

Renowned British graphic designer Alan Fletcher was invited to join the Novartis Campus Workshop team as Visual Identity Consultant. Under his leadership, a distinctive attitude towards signage and imagery in the corporate landscape emerged on the Campus. We had the good fortune to be asked by Alan to serve as his local design team and we were able to collaborate with him closely for over four years, helping him to realize the Novartis Campus Workshop's decisions. Alan has since departed from this world, but not without leaving a number of wonderful marks on the Campus.

Standard Corporate Design in a Non-standard Context

Novartis International's corporate design standards normally determine the graphics for products, communications, and signage worldwide, but the singular nature of the Novartis Campus demanded singular visual solutions for such things as street signage and way-finding.

The Campus was to launch a new approach to scientific research and collaboration. Gone were the cubicles in which scientists had formerly squirreled themselves away in competitive solitude. Instead, the Campus was being structured to engender vivid, interdepartmental knowledge-sharing. Flexible open workspaces were introduced to accommodate changing projects and teams. People were encouraged to leave their offices, encounter others, and exchange ideas. Old buildings vanished at an astonishing pace, replaced by equally astonishing new ones. This new operational attitude demanded an alternative to the standard corporate design treatments applied elsewhere, and before it was visible to everyone else, Alan recognized the need for not only highly innovative visual solutions, but also collegial and colloquial ones that would impart an attitude of shared enjoyment and company pride—a sort of Campus spirit. The projects below illustrate the unique intellectual vitality Alan's suggestions contributed to the Campus.

Naming the Streets

Decisions about the Campus have been driven from the outset by the desire to create a living celebration of scientific accomplishment. The most immediate manifestation of this ambition can be found in the street names. On the Novartis Campus, the very pavements themselves pay homage to noteworthy pioneers who laid the groundwork for contemporary scientific research in medicine. In an alphabetical grid, the name of a historic scientist is attributed to each street with A (Asklepios) to N (Nightingale) providing the south-north axis, and O to W (Osler to Waksman) the west-east axis. Only Fabrikstrasse, itself a historic player in company lineage, has kept its original name.

Curbstone Street Signage

Always pursuing originality in standard decision making, Alan proposed placing the street names not on standard corner posts, but in the curbstones instead, effectively making the scientists' names the very groundwork on which new scientific developments would be founded. However unconventional, the orientation system is quite logical for the pedestrian, non-automotive Campus environment. Cyclists and pedestrians traversing the Campus look to the scientists of the past for orientation in the present and find them right there at their feet.

A special type font was developed for the curbstone street signage. Designed by London-based Swiss typographer Bruno Maag, the "Campus Font" is a typeface unique to Novartis's Basel site. Its unusual application requirements determined its form. Each letterform is precision-cut into the Negro Grapesa granite curbstone by water jet, creating the grooves into which individual stainless-steel letters are then inlaid and secured. Applied only in stonework, the type can also be seen along the ring of stone at the base of the tradition-rich magnolia known as "The Bonus Tree," where it tells the tree's story.

"Biodata Benches"

Recognition of the great forerunners of research is further expressed in biographical data on the Campus's benches. Employees and guests strolling the streets can appreciate the accomplishments of each scientist by reading the biographies carved into the benches' wooden slats.

The Lettergate

The Campus entrance gate is a typographic curio. At first glance, we see a classic wicket gate with tall, narrow metal rails. A second glance, however, reveals something unusual. A conventional gate is a protective device, as this one is, but unlike conventional gates, this one's railings spell out "CAMPUS OF INNOVATION KNOWLEDGE ENCOUNTER" in letters that have been elongated and compressed to suit the frame. This way, the Campus motto greets everyone arriving at the gate.

The Wonderwall

Illustration, not typography, is the engaging graphic feature of a stretch of fence separating the Campus grounds from the public at Voltamatte Park on the southwest corner of the Campus. Alan asked British illustrator Andrew Davidson to create over 1,000 images for the Wonderwall, each of which has been lasered out of ten-millimeter-thick steel sheet. The Wonderwall is a series of five 2.6-by-2.1-meter steel panels elaborately decorated with lyrical motifs. A galloping cowboy with an arrow through his hat takes aim at a witch on a broomstick, and both are dwarfed by the silhouette of a large hammer. Scenes like this seem to mingle and move among other motifs, and shift from panel to panel. Alan envisioned grandparents with their grandchildren in Voltamatte Park elaborating stories based on the two children leap-frogging over each other in one panel, and monkey-rolling through another. In a gracious way, he managed to mark a boundary without communicating the less gracious "Keep out."

...OF MAN SEEING IN A ... A KNOWLEDGEABLE

Alan Fletcher with Mifflin-Schmid Design, the magnolia story found in the Forum, 2006

Left: Detail

Below: View of the tree and the inscription

In the newly created Campus, Fletcher endeavored to preserve cultural heritage by embedding it in the groundwork.

THIS MAGNOLIA TREE (MAGNOLIA DENUDATA) WAS KNOWN TO SANDOZ STAFF AS THE "BONUS TREE." STANDING BEFORE THE EXECUTIVE ENTRANCE TO THE ADMINISTRATION BUILDING, IT IS THOUGHT TO HAVE BEEN PLANTED AT THE INITIATIVE OF HANS LEEMANN, A KNOWLEDGEABLE NATURE LOVER AND CHAIRMAN OF THE BOARD AT SANDOZ FROM 1952 TO 1963. THE BLOSSOMING OF THE TREE IN THE FIRST OR SECOND WEEK OF APRIL WAS TO COINCIDE WITH THE TIMING OF THE SANDOZ ANNUAL GENERAL MEETING, WHICH TRADITIONALLY ENDED WITH THE COMPANY'S MANAGEMENT PERSONALLY DISTRIBUTING BONUSES TO THE WORKFORCE. HENCE THE TREE'S NICKNAME.

ABCDEFGHIJKLMNOPQRSTUVWXYZ
0123456789 ÄÀÁÂÃÅÇÈÉÊÎÌÍ
ÏÑÖÕÜÛÚÙŸÆŒ?!&
- ` ´ ˆ ˜ ¸ . ; : " " « » ‹ › ' ' — * ¸ °

Above: Alan Fletcher, *The Lettergate,* multisection entrance gate, installed in August 2007, welded steel frame with aluminum letters, 2008: Detail, frontal view at entrance

The gate literally embodies the Campus philosophy and presents it to the visitor upon entrance: CAMPUS OF INNOVATION KNOWLEDGE ENCOUNTER

Left: Alan Fletcher and Bruno Maag, "The Campus Font" and three applications of it, 2008

Pedestrians navigating Campus streets find no conventional street signage; instead, street names are found in the curbstones at their feet.

Following double page: Alan Fletcher, *The Wonderwall,* 2008: The lasered steel wall element, and the motif in black and white on paper

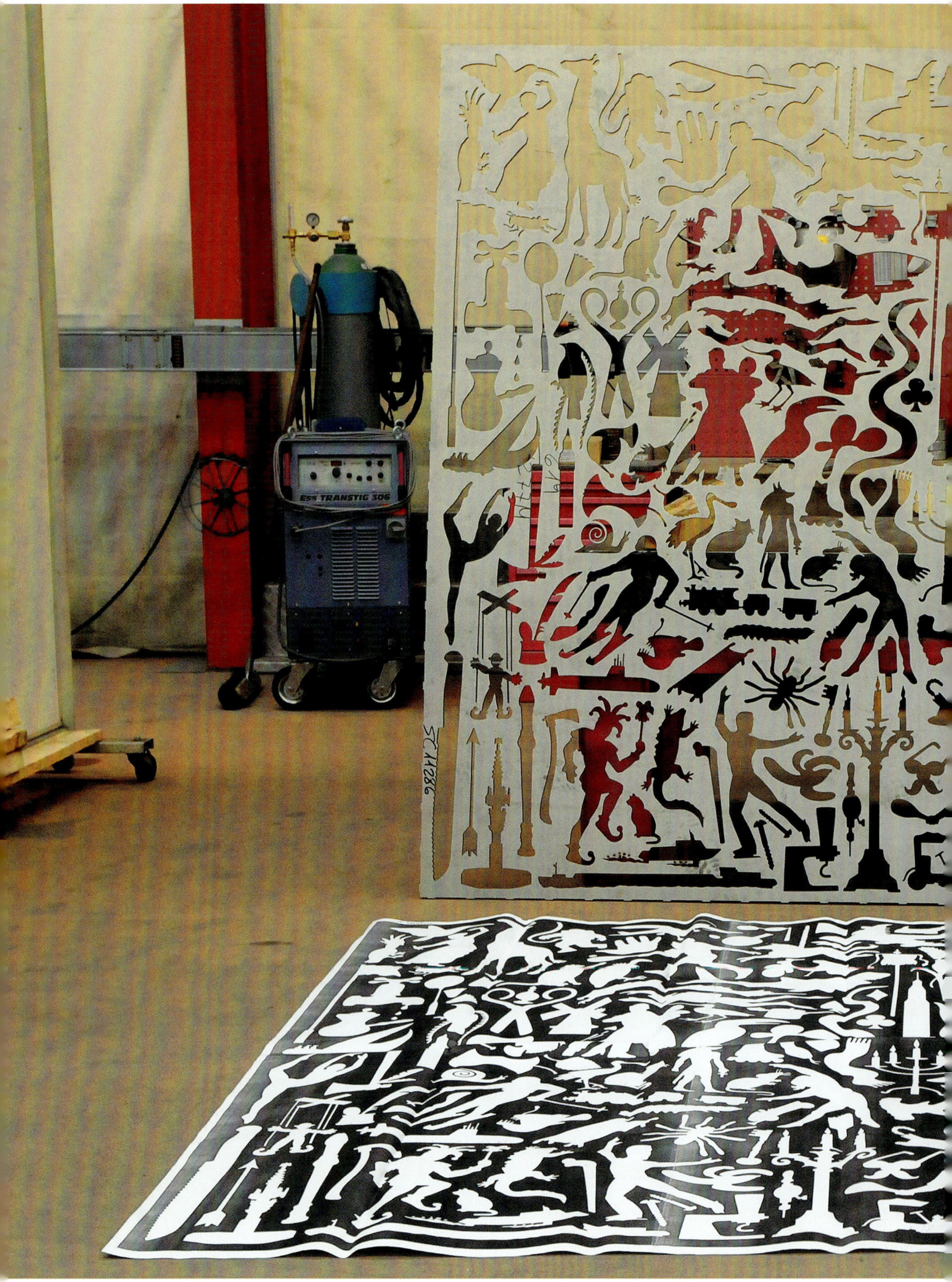
TRANSTIG 306

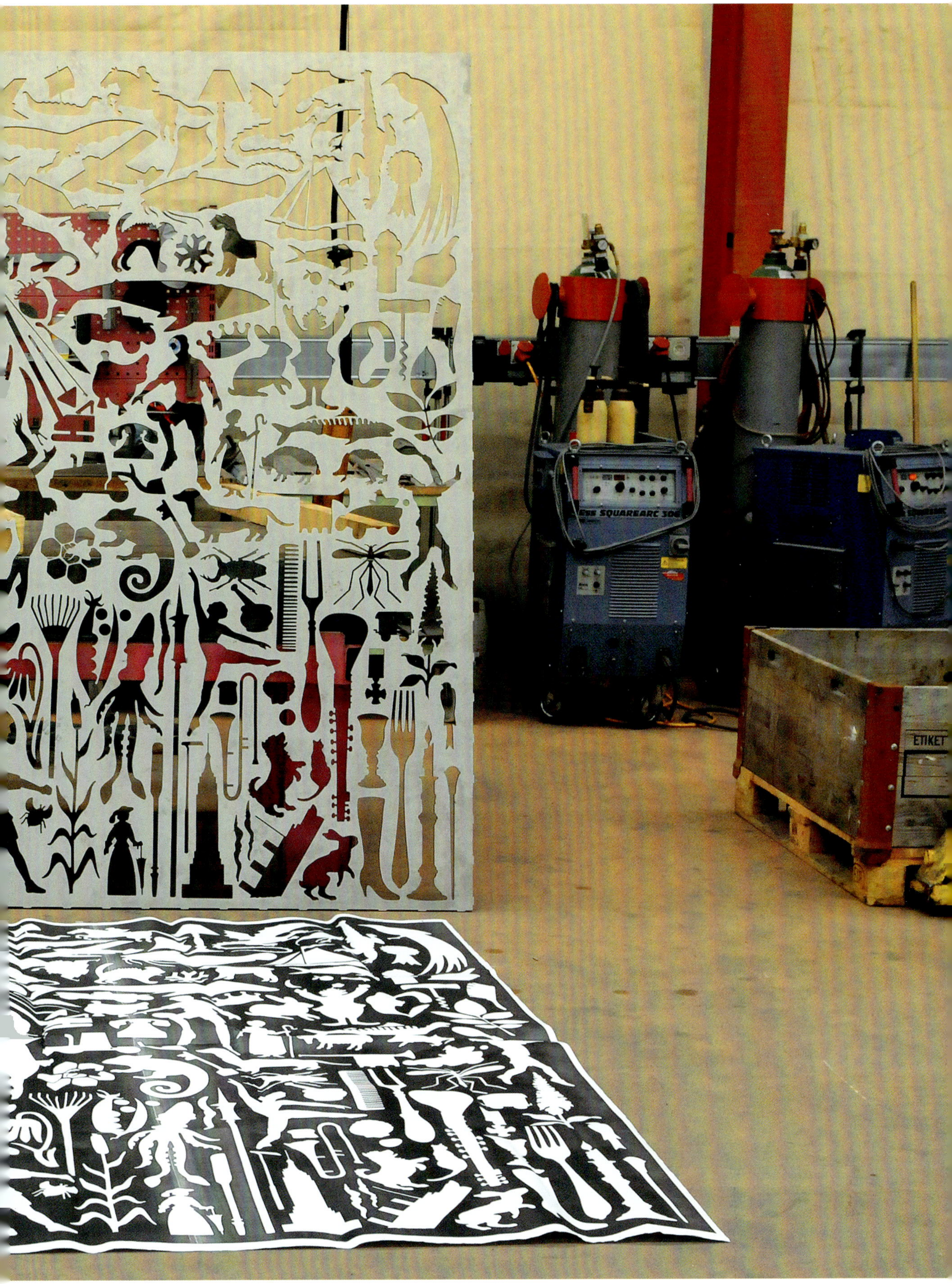
ETIKET

Alan Fletcher, *The Wonderwall*, installed in August 2008

Above: Separating Novartis Campus and Voltamatte Park

Right: Detail
For park visitors the *Wonderwall* offers playful storytellers lively material. More than 1,000 motifs were lasered out of five ten-millimeter-thick steel slabs to create the wall series.

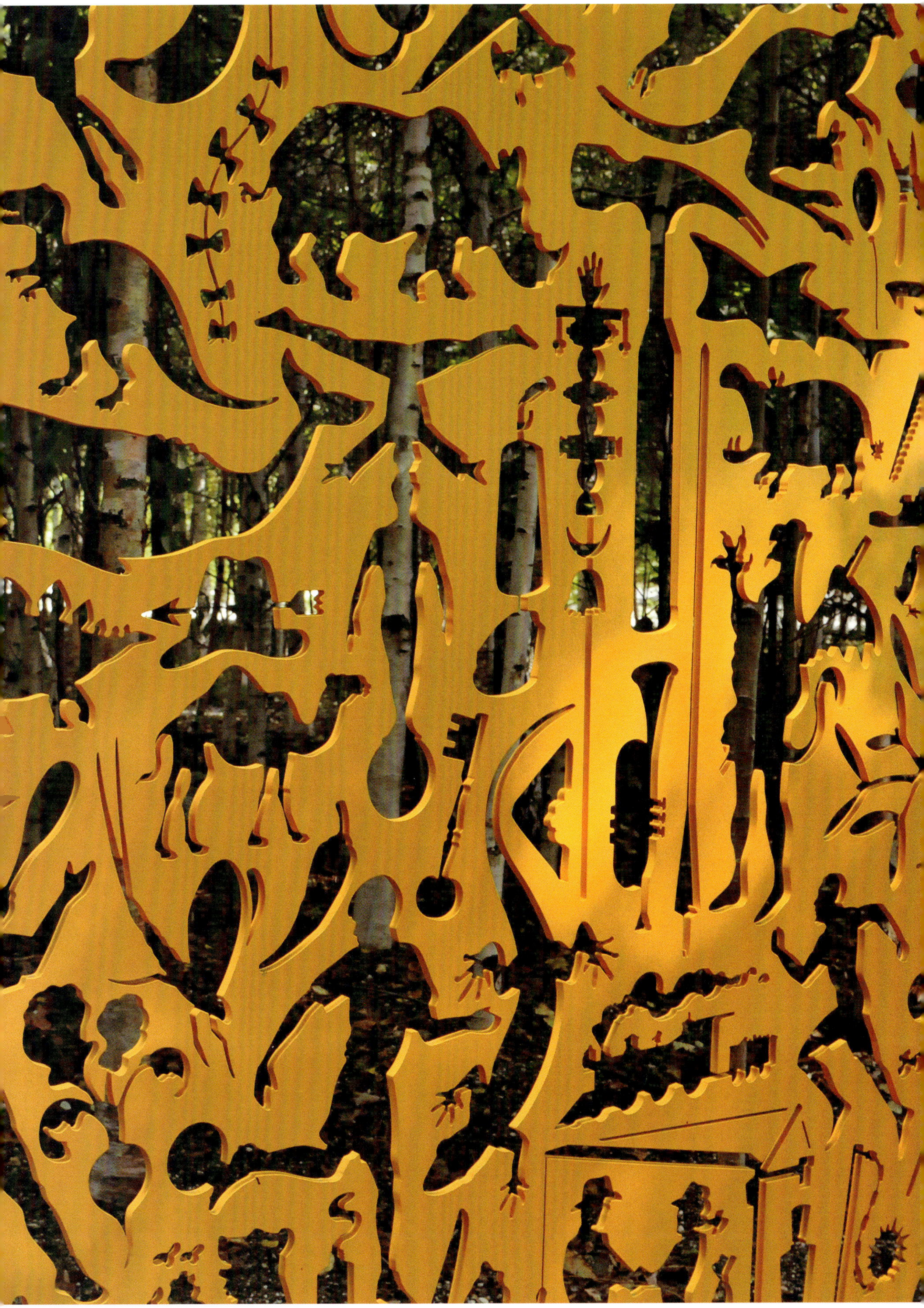

"The Physic Garden"

Physic Gardens originated in the sixteenth century and were formally designed gardens used by teachers, students, and practitioners of the use of medicinal herbs in healing, hence the term "physician." The gardens were first used as convenient plant supplies, but they soon came to be indispensable as sources of properly identified, dependable ingredients. The plants in the Physic Garden were more reliable than those picked in the wild or purchased from "herb women." In the twentieth century, the term "Physic Garden" evolved into "Healing Garden," reflecting the belief that tending and even simply being in such gardens was healing in and of itself. This further evolved into the "Sensory Garden," which was designed to excite acute sensory experiences through color, fragrance, and spatial composition. Given the Physic Garden's association with healing, producing medicinal substances, and the use of aesthetics to enhance health, what could suit the Novartis Campus better?

The Novartis Campus's new laboratory building, which was designed by Portuguese architect Souto de Moura, faces the Physic Garden, and its street address will therefore be "Physic Garden 3." That this modern laboratory will be labeled with the name of its historic forerunner is precisely the kind of dialogue between the old and the new that sparks the lively dynamic that characterizes the Campus.

Cultural Poster Walls

Not everyone working on the Novartis Campus was provided with an inspiring vision of what the Campus was to become, and many might have considered the idea of working in the middle of a construction site as anything but inspirational. Alan had an idea, though: plaster the standard, bright yellow construction walls with posters promoting contemporary cultural events from all over Switzerland. Construction-site life was instantly more enjoyable, informative, and entertaining.

"Living Archive" Posters

Motivated by the desire to engage the external community in the transformation process, Novartis accepted Alan's proposal of contacting the local Hochschule für Gestaltung und Kunst. People from the school jumped at the chance to photograph, sketch, videotape, and produce collages of emerging developments and changes on Campus. We created a poster series to showcase their work. "The Living Archive" series was added to the Cultural Poster Walls, complimenting off-site cultural activities with artists' reflections about on-site changes.

Rooftop Gardens

In collaboration with Peter Walker and the rest of the Workshop group, Alan took a bird's-eye view of the strict original layout of the Master Plan, which placed a "ceiling" on building heights. They discussed the concept of rooftop greening, something which would play nicely into the Campus ideal of encouraging the use of outdoor spaces for the exchange of thoughts, protecting nature, and generally fostering an innovative corporate campus culture. The idea was to restore to some degree the natural habitats appropriated by the Campus grounds.

One idea was to initiate rooftop apiaries by planting nectar sources such as lavender hedges and wildflowers, thereby inviting bees to set up shop above the buzz of human activity taking place in the buildings below. As it turned out, bees laden with pollen would not manage the height climb, so this idea never got off the ground. Other rooftop greening plans did take root, however. Many of the new buildings have specific garden rooftops planned, and most of the rest are spread with a bed of gravel conducive to snatching wild seeds from the wind and enabling them to take root there. Building by building, the ground space occupied by the structures is being reclaimed by nature on their rooftops.

Campus Signage Work

Aside from helping Alan, we were invited to design the building signage for the Diener building (Forum 3), the SANAA building, and Marco Serra's garage and main gate complex. Providing signage for these three heterogeneous buildings served as an excellent context for framing the question of whether a standardized Novartis corporate signage should be applied uniformly on all of the buildings to follow. The answer was no. Besides the obvious fact that each building has a different function, the architects who work on the Novartis Campus are given license to express extremes of individuality in their use of materials, light, and space. The initial Novartis Campus Building Signage Guidelines thereby served a valuable inaugural function: legitimizing individualized signage building by building, rather than applying a standardized corporate signage. The Guidelines champion individual signage design in accordance with architectural authorship while ruling on Campus-wide issues such as consistency in language usage and official safety regulations.

Retail Signage Guidelines

We were also asked to develop guidelines for the signage of the public spaces along the arcade for the new stores, cafés, and restaurants. These guidelines, too, champion lively, individualized signage over a standardized corporate design. They provide parameters encouraging an inspiring attitude towards concept and materiality while ensuring that official safety and environmental standards are met. Most importantly, they safeguard the visual integrity of the arcade that is so important to the overall Master Plan. Nothing is to disrupt its visual rhythm. At the time that this essay was written, signage solutions for restaurants, cafés, retail stores, and services such as dry cleaners and florists are all waiting for the future to catch up with them.

Standardized Signage

In addition to consistent safety standards, there was some demand for standardized signage inside Campus buildings for particular things. One of these was the use of a codified visual vocabulary on laboratory doors to communicate lab-specific information, warnings, restrictions, and important emergency information to scientists and lab technicians. We developed a flexible system to label laboratories according to project. The system establishes a single meaning code that is recognizable and shared in labs across Campus.

Another signage requirement that favored Campus-wide standardization rather than individualization by building was the waste disposal pictograms that would appear in almost every building. Used for sorting and recycling common waste materials ranging from Styrofoam to coffee grounds, there would be no need to have these redesigned each time a new building went up—and every reason to standardize them. What existed in buildings company-wide was a graphic chaos of signs and symbols. We therefore had the pictograms redrawn in a consistent, pleasing visual style for application everywhere.

In Conclusion

We would like to end this essay with a comment on the nature of our collaboration with Alan Fletcher on the Novartis Campus, one which is also necessarily a comment on Alan's leadership style.

Alan was a person whose ingenuity could be measured in wit, and his abundant wit was matched in equal measure by charm. Add to these his generous and engaging leadership style and you begin to get an idea of what a pleasure it was to work with him. Extraordinarily inclusive, he brought on board every contact possible, from his neighbor the potter in Notting Hill, to ex-Pentagrammers he had met twenty years earlier in New York City, to students studying at the Basel School of Art whom he had never met. The guiding purpose behind his engaging leadership style was more than professional collegiality. We opened this essay with a description of how the new Novartis Campus was different: "Gone were the cubicles in which scientists had formerly squirreled themselves away in competitive solitude. Instead, the Campus was being structured to engender vivid, interdepartmental knowledge-sharing." Alan was the embodiment of this work style in the design world, and this made him perfectly suited to the Novartis Campus project. Its goals matched his design leadership instincts.

In an environment whose architectural heritage would be demolished and whose habitual professional behaviors would be transformed, design was to be used to foster a lively, collegial spirit on Campus. Alan recognized that creating a "brave new world" risked eliminating meaningful cultural heritage, and with it the foundations for genuine corporate collegiality. He listened acutely for anecdotal details of shared heritage in order to find ways to visualize, celebrate, and conserve them as cornerstones of the Campus's "corporate identity" in the best sense of the term. Visualizing shared heritage by designing it into the Campus was one of the ways he helped to jump-start Novartis Campus culture.

Evidence can be seen in the elements described above, such as the anecdote ringing the old "Bonus Tree," science's forefathers coming back to life on the Campus's streets, and the Living Archive Posters bringing local Basel commentary onto the Campus. These and many additional examples bear witness to Alan Fletcher's design leadership style and its unique influence on the Novartis Campus's "corporate identity."

living archive
NOVARTIS

living archive
NOVARTIS

WATER
living archive
NOVARTIS

living archive
NOVARTIS

living archive
NOVARTIS

living archive
NOVARTIS

living archive
NOVARTIS

living archive
NOVARTIS

living archive
NOVARTIS

living archive
NOVARTIS
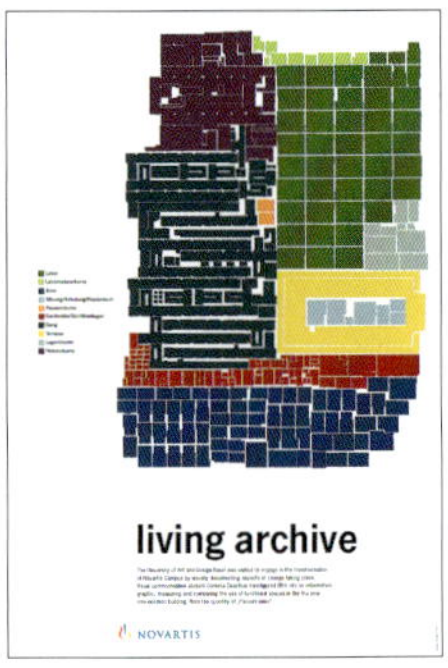
living archive
NOVARTIS
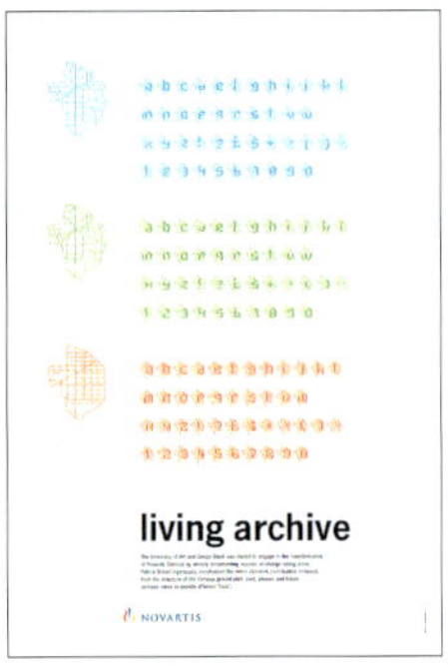
living archive
NOVARTIS

living archive
NOVARTIS
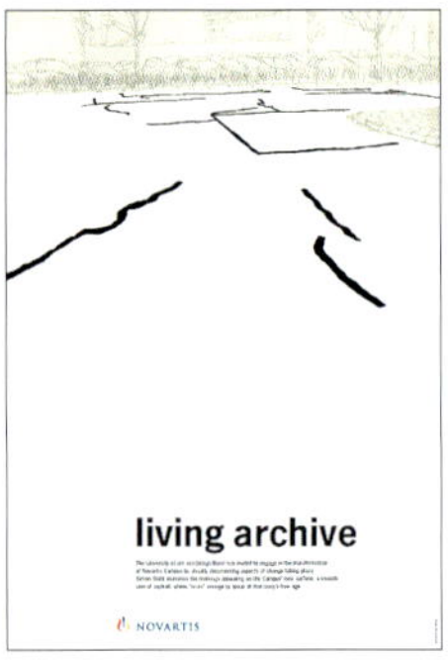
living archive
NOVARTIS

WAS
WAR
living archive
NOVARTIS
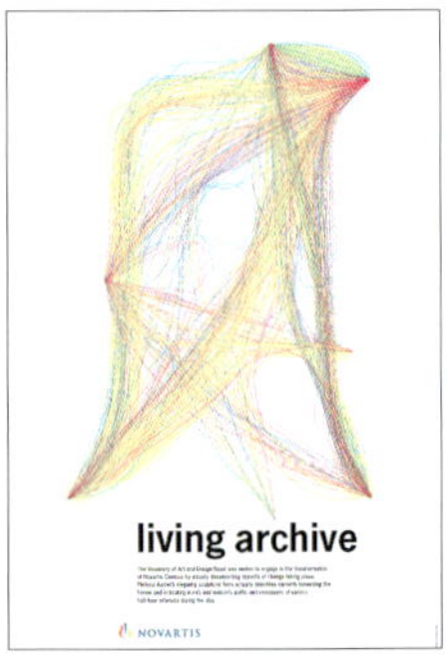
living archive
NOVARTIS
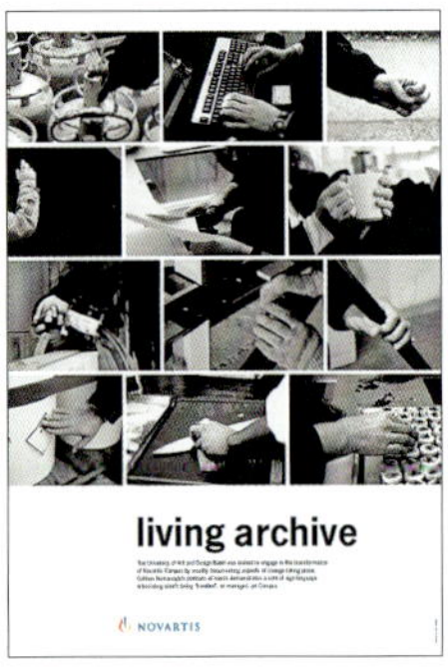
living archive
NOVARTIS
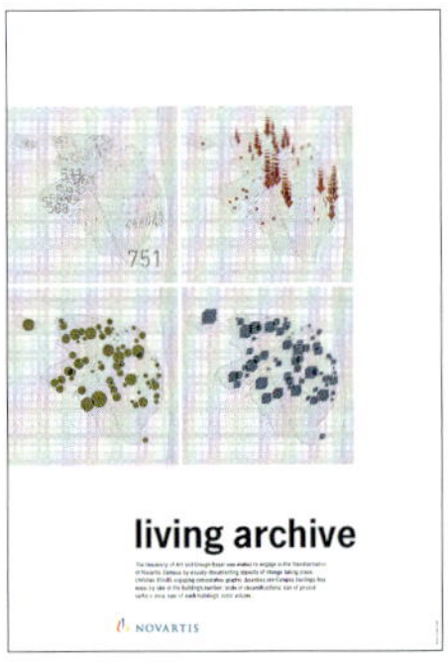
living archive
NOVARTIS
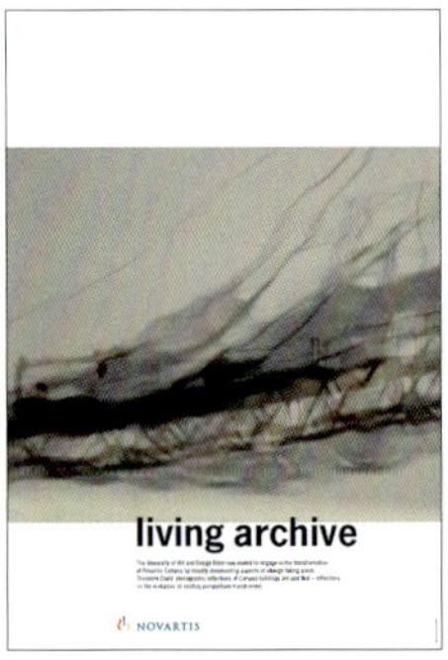
living archive
NOVARTIS

living archive
NOVARTIS

living archive
NOVARTIS

living archive
NOVARTIS

living archive
NOVARTIS

living archive
NOVARTIS

living archive
NOVARTIS

Mifflin-Schmid Design and Hochschule für Gestaltung und Kunst, "Living Archive" poster series

Left: "Living Archive" poster series overview

Above: The posters placed on construction site walls. The artworks document facets of transformations observed on Campus.

Below and right: Mifflin-Schmid Design, building inscription on the Campus: The experiences from the building identification for the first new buildings (Forum 3 and the underground garage and reception building) served as the basis for the basic decision that individual concepts are to be preferred to standardized corporate design solutions.

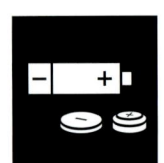

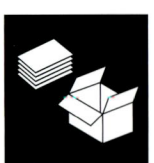

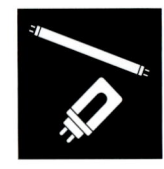

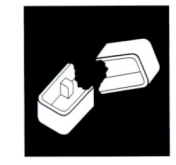

Mifflin-Schmid Design and Anne-Christine Krämer: From styrofoam to coffee capsules, a unified pictogram vocabulary gracefully consistent the chaos of waste disposal imagery found in buildings across the Campus.

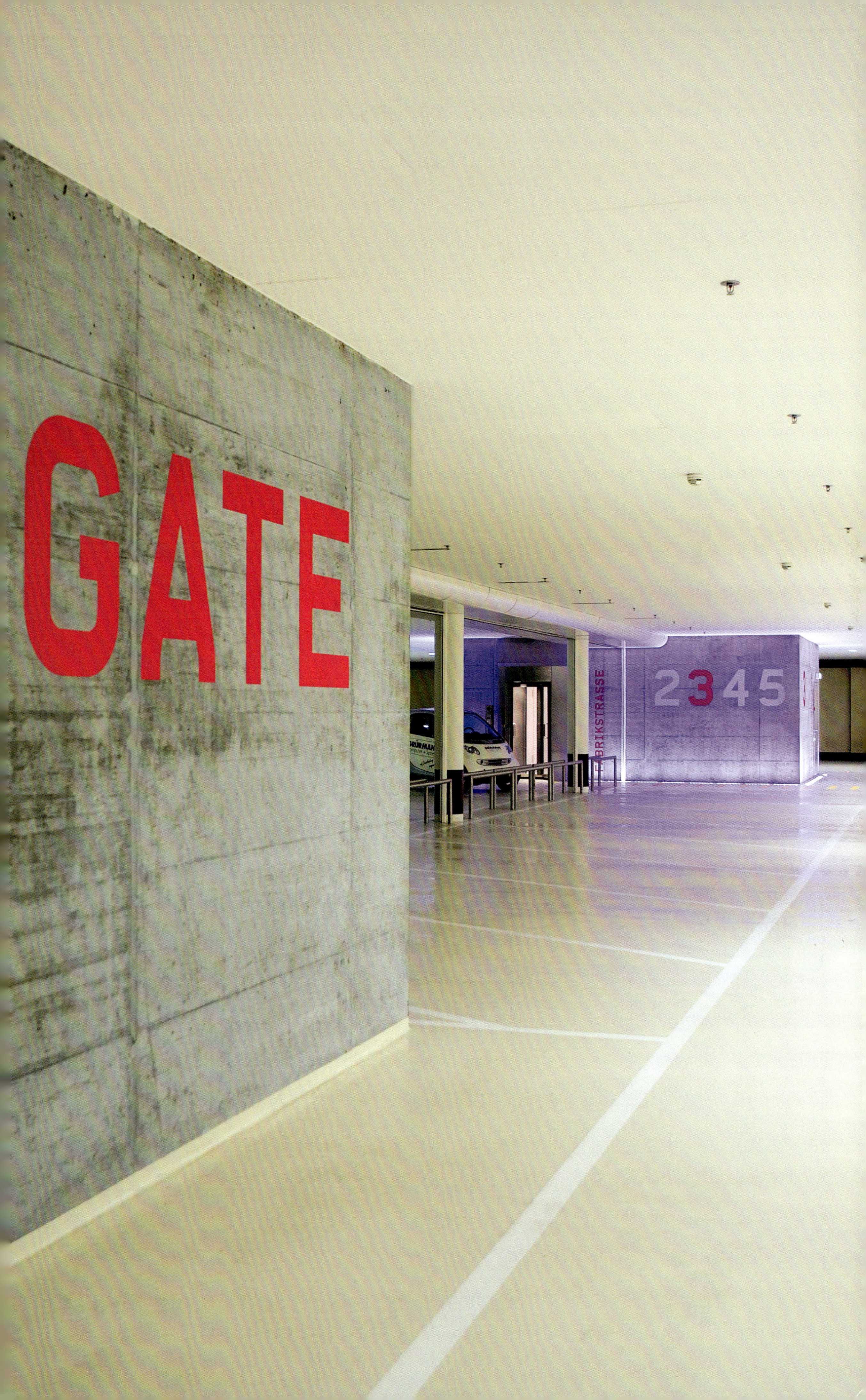
GATE
2345
BRIKSTRASSE

Lighting Orchestration: Between Technology and Atmosphere

Andreas Schulz

The visionary quality of an urban ensemble on the scale of a city district comprised of first-class architectural works and designed as a campus in the middle of a former manufacturing site offers a unique opportunity for lighting design.

Although a sensitization to the subject of light and lighting also occurs in the public sphere, the implementation of carefully developed concepts and ideas is only conceivable and possible with great effort and under fortunate circumstances, for instance, the reworking of several contingent areas within a city district or zone. Such concepts are, however, then subject to the restraints of the relevant norms and regulations arising from past planning decisions which specify the types of lighting instruments and systems to be used within cities and communities.

In the case of the lighting for the Campus, the project began with an attitude, in the sense of a vision, that was to be developed: the Campus's light levels were to emulate the atmosphere of a small northern Italian town and yet avoid excessive uniformity—in essence, a kind of "wave effect" created by alternating illuminated areas with less illuminated ones, something which expresses the exact difference between an "on the move" metropolis and a more manageable city in which one can more easily imagine being able to live.

Given that the campus concept also implies that people from all over the world will work on the site, sometimes only temporarily, an important further goal of the "city lighting" was to provide a certain feeling of security and easy orientation.

The street system of New York is a model for this idea. There, the north-south routes are emphasized by series of softly glowing, lantern-shaped glass forms. In contrast, in the narrower side streets running east-west, "hanging lamps" strung from cables stretched between the façades serve to illuminate the lateral direction. Both types of lighting are arranged so that they make possible a clear directional orientation. Thus, in the north-south direction visitors can only see the lanterns; if they look directly down a side street, they can orient themselves by recognizing the lamps hanging from the cables. The same principle applies to the side streets: visitors walking along these will not see another lantern until they encounter another north-south street with this type of lighting.

Refraining from additional city furnishings in the narrow side streets is not the only aspect of the success of the Campus's lighting system. Others include the structure that emerged from the concept of lanterns and cable-hung lamps and the hierarchical ordering of the Campus according to the Master Plan.

After the main thoroughfares, side streets, and the third zone of the Campus, the next item of interest is the illumination of the arcades. At this point in the planning of the lighting design, the question of which "lamp family" could be used in these areas in order to reconcile the municipal planning principle with the overall design concept was posed.

All three lamp types—lanterns, cable-hung lamps, and arcade lamps—work according to the same principle: a light source consisting of a reflector with a directed, highly efficient metal-vapor halogen bulb is located in the upper part of the lamp. The partially sanitized glass cylinder of the lamp transmits a part of the emitted light in a diffuse fashion, while the other, directed component directs the light downwards in order to fulfill the basic task of illumination.

The desired side effect of this kind of light generation is the gentle illumination of the immediate vicinity of the light fixtures. In this way, the lanterns and the cable-hung lamps create a more self-evident

Different models of the pendant lamps, Licht Kunst Licht, 2008

illumination of their surroundings. In the case of the façades, the level of illumination is always the same, but the effect varies because of the different materials used in the surfaces of the façades.

The precise sequence of the arcade lamps facilitates their effect, especially at night. The upper region of the arcade becomes recognizable thanks to the diffuse part of the light emitted by the suspended lamps while the precisely targeted, direct components react with each of the carefully selected surfaces of the arcade pavement. The effect that the richly varied sequence of arcade entrances—from the façade structure to the entrance areas, the entrance to a restaurant or a laboratory building—has on pedestrians is similar to the lighting atmosphere in cities such as Milan, Paris, Bern, or Bolzano.

At the beginning of this process of searching for a lighting concept for the Campus, there was an initial discussion about the design of the lamps and lighting elements. The Workshop team members expressed the wish to discover design elements that would allow the independent effects of the exceptional and varied architectural façades to be shown on the one hand, but would be reserved enough in order to avoid the appearance of a distinct, autarkic layer in the space of the street on the other.

The already completed streets and squares show very well that this wish was fulfilled for everyone involved, including the architects working on the Campus, who have since been able to identify with the overall lighting design and its individual elements.

Different ideas emerged for the illumination of green areas and the Park. In these areas, a more casual arrangement of the lanterns in relationship to the groupings of trees in the entry zone in front of the gate generates a playful and also spacious impression, while at the same time the light generated by it provides a suitably grand illumination of the gate designed by Marco Serra.

The western part of the Park is gently illuminated from the level of the planted areas, while in the eastern part of the Park there is no lighting at all.

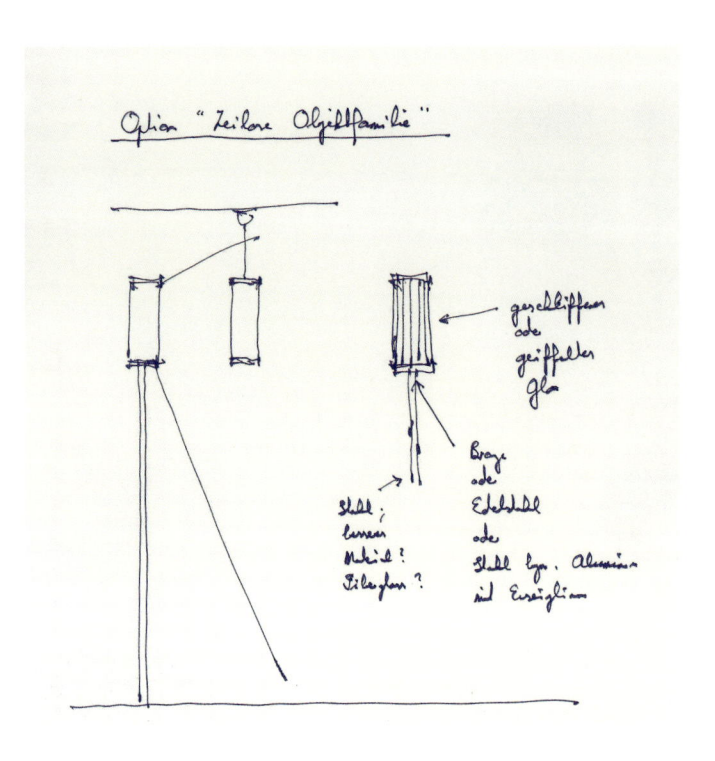

Above: Study for the design of a lighting fixture, Vittorio Magnago Lampugnani, 2002

Right: Pole-mounted lamps, 2008

Above: Arcade lamps, 2008

Center: Arcade lamps and pendant lamps, Licht Kunst Licht, 2002

Below: Pole-mounted lamps and arcade lamps, Licht Kunst Licht, 2002

A Culture of Dining and Communication

Andreas U. Fürst

In tandem with the development of Novartis, the opportunities to eat at the company's various work locations—in the Klybeck area and at the St. Johann Works—have gradually changed. Originally, the joint dining facility was the centerpiece. The primary concern of the former catering service was to serve a variety of healthy foods to the employees for their midday meal.

Contemporary forms of catering and a variety of menus have developed in response to the continually changing needs of Novartis's younger generations of employees of diverse nationalities. In what follows, the focus of the discussion will be the revamping of the dining facilities on the Novartis Campus.

One of the first important decisions concerning the future planning of the dining opportunities on the Campus was made in January 2004. On the basis of the projected increase of the number of employees at the St. Johann Works from 4,500 in 2005 to almost 8,000 in 2010, the question of how to provide appropriate service for the employees in the future was put squarely "on the table." In response, two options were developed, tested, and suggested. The first envisioned a central production with decentralized restaurant and café facilities, which would be run by a single operator. The other proposed decentralized production with restaurant and café facilities run by different operators on the ground floor of every building.

In the end, the decision was made in favor of the second option. In each new building the necessary space for restaurant and retail facilities would be made available on the ground floor. The planned seating capacity of approximately 2,800 seats in different restaurants and cafés could thereby be guaranteed for the Campus's approximately 8,000 employees.

The main goal of the new dining facilities is to provide innovative and spatially differentiated places in which to dine on Campus that respond to the needs of today. Interaction and communication among the employees can also be assisted by these facilities. A comfortable, functional, and aesthetically pleasing atmosphere facilitates dialogue and social exchange, and the well-being of the employees thus achieved in turn helps to encourage the efficiency of their work. The goods and services connected with food and beverages, based on surveys of the employees, contribute greatly to the perception of the Novartis Campus as an attractive workplace. The concept of, as well as the guidelines for, the provision of food and beverages on Campus was described in the corresponding customer requirement specifications of the projects, in order to bring them to the attention of the project participants.

The various forms of food and beverage operations range from self-service restaurants to restaurants with service and guest restaurants, including a variety of cafés and bars. In addition, catering for on-site occasions is available, and areas for taking breaks in the buildings are equipped with vending machines. Stands with take-out food complete the range of food and beverage options on the Campus.

So-called social amenities have gained in significance in the last few years. They once consisted primarily of the employee shops, in which company medicines were sold. In the future, the product range will be expanded substantially. In addition, the employees will also be offered time-saving, complementary services on the Campus. For instance, the fitness center has been operating since 2000, and other sport and leisure-time offerings, the dry cleaner, and the Healthy Snack Corner have been in operation since 2003. The Campus post office, bank branch, florist, garage, and other retail businesses will open in 2009.

2008

2015

Development of the choice
of restaurants and the
complementary services,
2008

■ Choice of restaurants
■ Services

2030

Workshop, Alan Fletcher, drawing, Locarno, June 21, 2004

A few of the new, already operating gastronomy facilities include the Italian café-bar, which is equipped with seating for forty outdoors and twenty indoors. This bar was the first gastronomic facility on the Campus that was realized as a pilot project beyond the possibilities first offered in 2003. Initial reservations expressed by the employees that "the boss might see us during our coffee break" are no longer to be heard. The Italian café-bar formula was very well received and enjoys ongoing popularity, thus encouraging the management to continue their efforts to expand the Campus's restaurant offerings further.

The Tapas Mundial Lounge & Bar has space for seventy patrons outdoors as well as indoors. The concept is based on the Spanish tapas bar, in which a constantly changing menu of snacklike meals are offered. The tapas bar went into operation in October 2005. In the summer of 2008 the terrace will be opened to expand the bar's seating capacity.

Nozomi, with seating for sixty indoors and the same number outdoors, is based on the concept of the Japanese noodle bar. The restaurant's noodle and ramen soup offerings are complemented by a large selection of sushi. Japanese salads, bento boxes in the summer, and other Asian dishes rotate through the menu. Nozomi went into operation in October 2006. The garden adjoining the SANAA building is also used in the summer for outdoor service.

The Visitors' Café with indoor seating for sixty is based on the model of the local Basel candy shop. These shops change their menu from week to week. Light meals, sandwiches, sweets, and chocolates are available for consumption on the premises or as take-away. The Café opened for business in October 2006.

Italian café-bar, 2008

Nozomi Restaurant, 2007

The manifold cuisines available on the Novartis Campus do not just satisfy the culinary needs of the employees and the visitors. They also provide a suitable framework for planned, unplanned, or leisurely meetings, which can be conducted either inside or in outdoor areas. Many of the food services are concentrated on the ground floor of Fabrikstrasse.

In the future, the gastronomic offerings available to the employees of the Campus will be even more tailored to their needs. A high level of flexibility, attuned to changing eating and consumption behavior, is one of the Campus's stated goals. The ability to execute fast changes in the Campus's food services requires a close collaboration with the architects designing its buildings. The functionality, aesthetics, and design of the buildings, as well as the furniture, the acoustics, the operating costs, and other factors must be taken into consideration. Good solutions that have been satisfying to all involved have been found thus far. But the process is by no means complete; in fact, the opposite is the case. It will remain a great challenge in the future to develop further gastronomic offerings that on the one hand respond to the different needs of the employees and on the other open up possibilities for various operators to realize their own ideas. This concerns not least the individual bidding for the various gastronomy facilities, about which decisions are made in close consultation with the architects and the project team. The management is dedicated to continuing to work on this in the future with continuing success.

Above: Tapas Mundial Lounge & Bar, 2008

Below: Visitors' Café, 2007

Implementation and Management Strategies

Albert Buchmüller, Robert A. Ettlin,
Gaby Keuerleber-Burk, Martin Kieser,
Roger Müller, Reto Naef, Markus Oser,
and René Rebmann

The following text is based on interviews conducted with the heads of several departments.

The Novartis Campus on the grounds of St. Johann in Basel is designed as a modern work environment. The idea associated with the Campus of a workplace which approaches the ideal as closely as possible is not just reflected in the implementation of the building. It is also expressed in the organizational and communication structures which make sure that the existing operation, as well as that which is coming on line, runs smoothly at all levels. The successive realization of the Master Plan for the Novartis Campus requires the bringing together of many forces that, working together, help control and manage the project.

Organization

For the implementation of the Campus project, an organization was selected that—very generally—operates on two levels: the first addresses long-term strategies, while the second is devoted to the practical realization of the project's construction.

The Campus Steering Committee establishes the strategic parameters for the development of the Campus. It initiates the project proposals and defines their business policy parameters. The Steering Committee also establishes the costs, schedules, and uses of the buildings and selects the architects who are to be involved. The Campus Implementation Management Team, which is composed of specialists in construction, energy, building services, and logistics among other things, functions as connecting link between strategy and implementation. Representatives of the Implementation Management Team ensure that the strategic decisions of the higher-ranking committees are fed directly into the projects and controlled. In addition, the Implementation Management Team sees to it that the necessary standards and guidelines are worked up and then implemented. The management of the schedule and cost also falls within its purview. The Campus Core Project Team is responsible for the coordination of the project participants—research, development, marketing, administration, area planning, etc.—and forms the organizational interface with the Steering Committee. In the Campus Workshop, conceptual suggestions are developed and then passed on to the Steering Committee. The Workshop involves experts in the areas of architecture, municipal planning, landscape design, art, and lighting. All necessary project-specific decisions during the planning and realization phases are made by building-specific Leadership Teams.

The Novartis Campus, Fabrikstrasse, 2008: The entrance area up to the Forum is finished. Behind it the Campus is still a construction site. In the foreground the members of the Steering Committee and the Workshop can be seen.

For instance, among other ideas, this is where the interior design and architectural concepts, as well as the material and color concepts, are established.

There is a project manager responsible for each project. He or she sets time and budget parameters, guarantees the quality and functionality of the building, and coordinates and controls the construction activities. The large number of projects underway on Campus requires a coordination of the building logistics on both the overall and project-specific levels. This involves ensuring the normal operation of business next to the construction sites: the management of the delivery of materials and on Campus traffic, and the coordination of the roughly six hundred construction workers who work on the grounds each day.

The coordination of construction site logistics is organized to a great extent via the Internet. As far as the construction activity goes, the Campus project is now running at top speed; work on eight large construction sites is currently underway.

2.18.2005

5.2.2006

5.30.2006

7.10.2006

10.6.2006

10.20.2006

1.31.2007

3.2.2007

3.20.2007

The transformation of the central areas of the Campus at the intersection of Fabrikstrasse and Hüningerstrasse, 2005–08

4.26.2007

6.5.2007

7.30.2007

8.14.2007

9.17.2007

12.6.2007

3.10.2008

4.29.2008

7.29.2008

Zoning

The demolition of obsolete production and infrastructure buildings, which has been going on since 1999, has been freeing up large areas of space upon which to build, thus creating the unique opportunity to reorganize the structure of the property.

The Campus Master Plan is characterized by a clear division of the road axes. The new building layout takes the old factory plan into account by reusing preexisting streets and axes as much as possible. This decision is important both functionally and economically, because it allows much of the extensive underground infrastructure for supply and waste removal to be maintained. In the southern area of the Campus, the administration buildings from the 1930s and '60s west of Fabrikstrasse as well as the high-rise have been retained and are being upgraded by embedding them within a broadly redesigned neighborhood. The main headquarters of Novartis International management and the pharmaceutical company, as well as other administrative functions, are located in this area.

In addition to the municipal planning and functional architectural criteria, the internal communications processes on the Campus are crucial, in order to be able to locate the future workplaces as precisely as possible. It is an explicit wish of management that the workplaces should optimally support project work, that is, the close collaboration of research and development through the proximity of their corresponding work spaces. Work is conducted in the new buildings, as well as in part of the old buildings, according to this principle. An extensive inquiry was made into how communication ought to work on Campus more generally and within the individual buildings more specifically, which is where exchanges take place regularly and synergies arise. The traditional, rigid division of work areas according to function is being consciously abandoned.

In addition to the workplaces for the employees, the support areas of the Campus's operation—for instance, those dedicated to supply, waste disposal, and storage—must be considered in the zoning plan.

Access and Traffic

In the last decades, two streets ran through the grounds of St. Johann. The north-south Fabrikstrasse, which runs almost parallel to the Rhine, divided the old historic paint and chemical buildings in the east from the administration buildings in the west, which were added to the core area in the 1930s. In contrast the public, east-west Hüningerstrasse divided the old factory grounds to the south from the first pharmaceutical research and production buildings built roughly at the same time to the north. The flow of personnel as well as materials was always interrupted by these alternating areas of private and public property and the gates and control points that they necessitated. In spite of this, Fabrikstrasse had already come to represent the site's backbone, becoming the indispensable connection axis for human and freight traffic because it was the only connection to Hüningerstrasse. Pedestrians and vehicles gained access to the St. Johann grounds via the main gates at the intersection of Fabrikstrasse and Hüningerstrasse. The grounds were completely fenced in only in the 1970s.

Today the main entrance to the Novartis Campus grounds is still on Fabrikstrasse, towards the south at Voltastrasse and near to public transportation, such as the tram and the bus, as well as to the Basel-Mulhouse EuroAirport and the autobahn headed in the direction of Germany, France, and central Switzerland. An underground parking garage has been added for visitors and employees. In the north, Fabrikstrasse terminates in a pedestrian underpass, which provides access to the second-largest employee parking lot.

In order to be able to offer both employees and visitors the most attractive working environment equipped with various points of encounter, the Campus was developed as a pedestrian and bicycle zone. In this way, Fabrikstrasse's arcades, restaurants, and other facilities have become an ideal place for meeting and exchange. Cars are only admitted on an exceptional basis, and so traffic signs are almost completely absent from the Campus, even if its overall organization and layout is compatible with the usual infrastructure of public transportation. An important exception to the rule is an internal company bus shuttle, which travels back and forth between the Campus and the Klybeck plant every ten minutes.

Among the different kinds of traffic that exist on Campus, the pedestrian enjoys absolute priority over the bicyclist. This is obvious from the details at the street level. For instance, the street names are set into the curb stones, thus being literally at pedestrians' feet. For the many bicycles on the Campus, many of which are internal company bicycles, there are covered areas for parking them (which will total three thousand places in the future, thus providing for about thirty percent of the Campus's employees) as well as uncovered parking areas for shorter stops.

In terms of the design and organization of other kinds of traffic, many ideas were considered and a variety of experiments were carried out on the grounds. For instance, the question of the necessary turning radius of the curb for the fire department vehicles and eighteen-ton, eleven-meter-long three-axel trucks had to be addressed. After several experiments, which were filmed and subsequently evaluated, it was determined that the desired road width of 6.6 meters with a curb radius of 1.5 meters provided an adequate turning radius for these larger vehicles. In addition, the street corners have been built up and reinforced so that forty-ton trucks can also pass through Campus if the need arises.

Every building on Campus has a delivery location where it can receive extensive freight deliveries. Freight deliveries are generally made via the north gate, while smaller deliveries are received in the central incoming goods department and distributed with the aid of a courier service. Larger deliveries are brought directly to the buildings where they are needed.

The whole Campus is also conceived to accommodate people with impaired mobility. The visually impaired must be accompanied. The approximately one hundred thousand annual visitors to the Campus are welcomed on the periphery of the Campus grounds at the main entrance; guests are intended to reach the Campus on foot. Excursion buses also arrive at the main entrance, where the visitors are received, undergo an identity check, and are then brought to the Visitor Center, from where they are also picked up at the end of their visit.

It has already become apparent that the Campus's employees have quickly become accustomed to the new traffic situation and are enjoying their new freedoms.

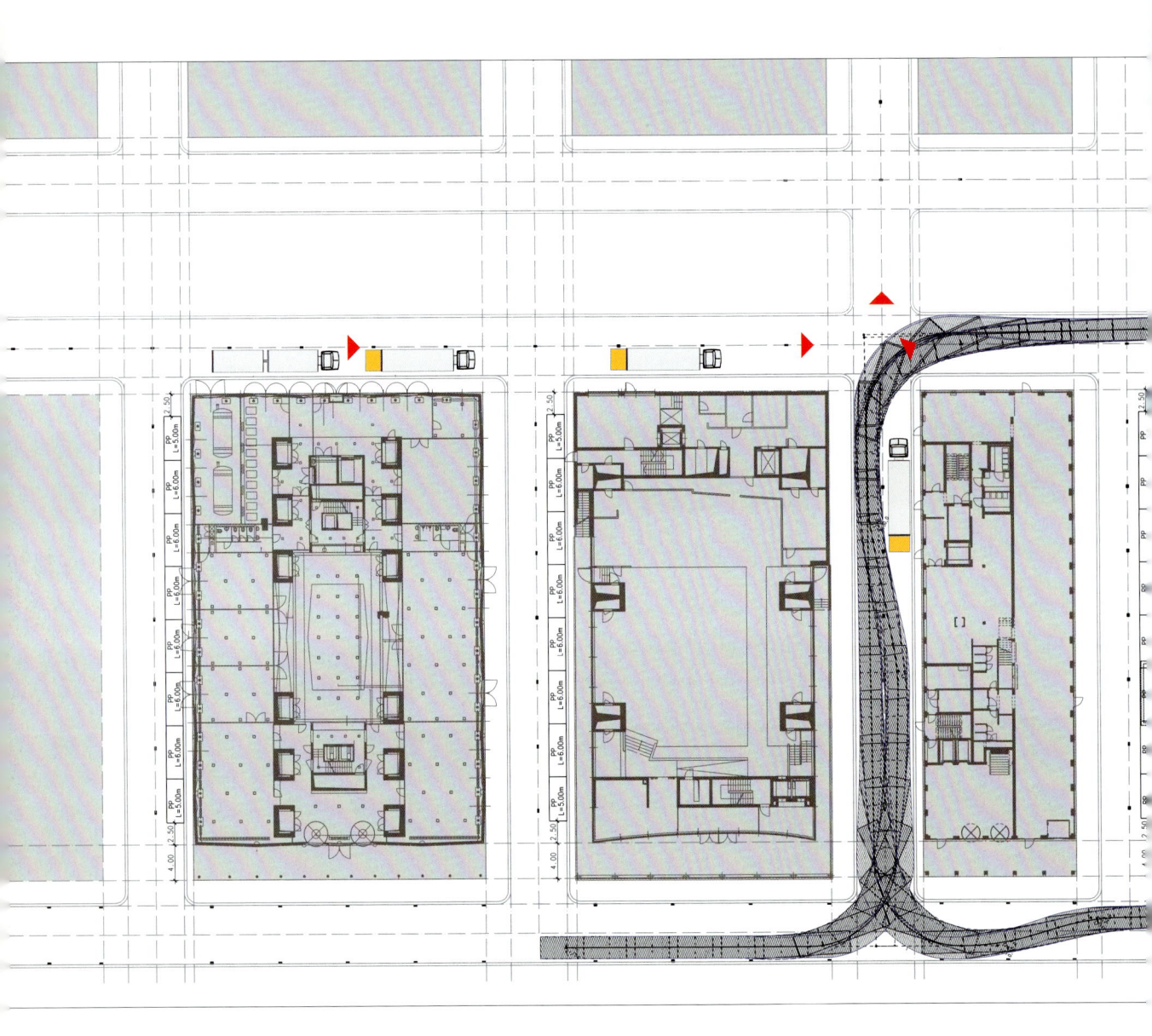

Studies for the curbstone radius on Campus, 2004: The minimum turning curves are drawn in dark grey and violet for the delivery trucks that will supply the buildings. The direction of travel is in red and the delivery points are in yellow.

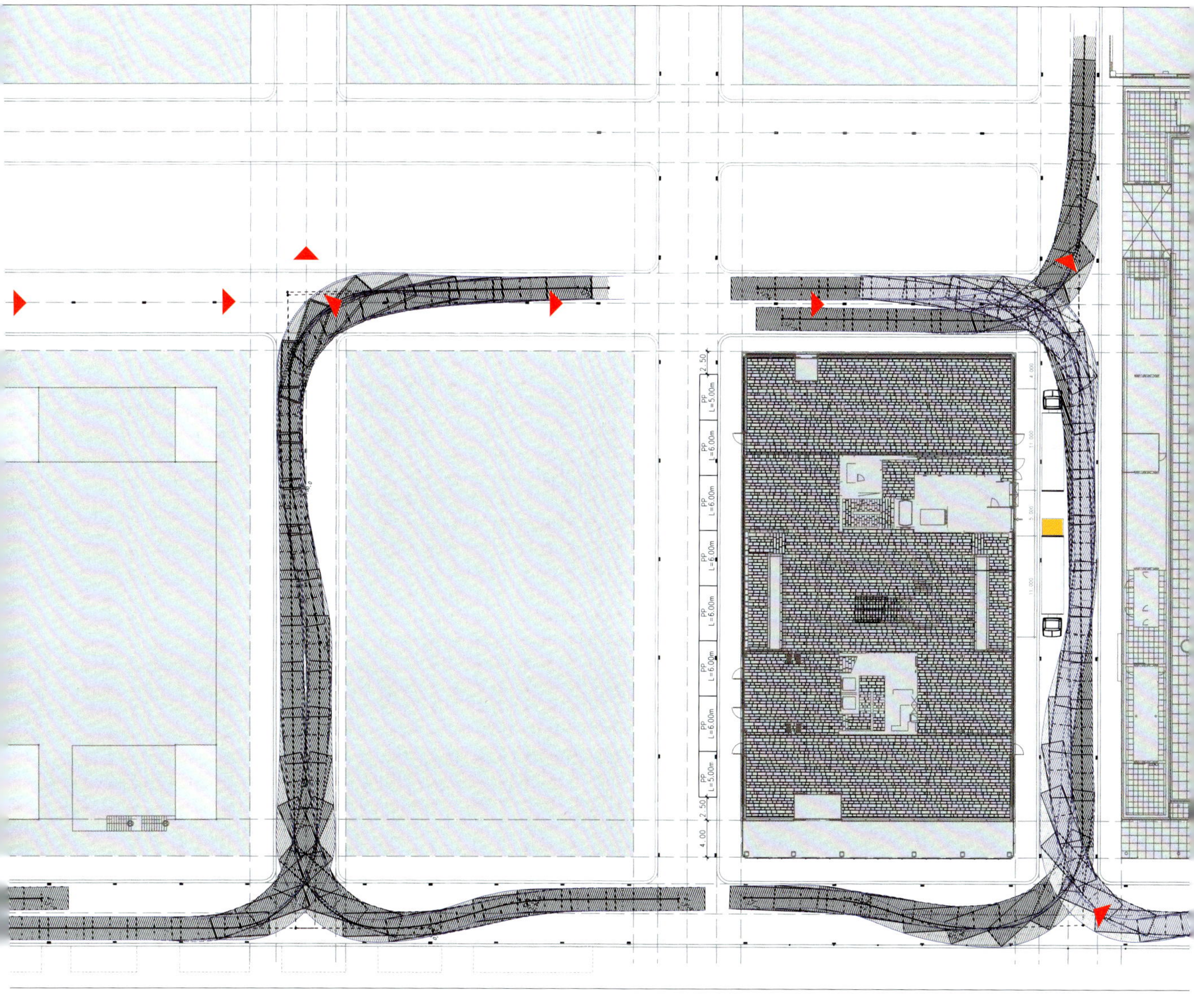

The Building Process

During construction, Facility Management is an integrated component of all Campus projects, because at the beginning of every construction project the various interest groups involved all have differing ideas, which could lead to conflicting goals. While people from the areas of architecture, planning, and design are focused on design and aesthetics, the strategy-oriented Facility Management gives the highest priority to issues of functionality, efficiency, safety, and maintaining value. The point here is not simply to make compromises, but also to bring the experiences of the past into the new projects and to learn from the mistakes that have been made. To cite an example, Facility Management must intervene when the accessibility of certain structures is not guaranteed by the proposed design, whereas a compromise can be found in locations where functionality and safety are not urgently required. Although the Facility Management will often have the necessary foresight to evaluate situations, if it is not in a position to convince everyone of its point of view using lines of argument based on issues of strategy and maintenance, then leniency prevails.

Of course, Facility Management is not permanently caught between persevering and giving in. In order to guarantee the best management of all facilities and buildings with regard to everything from their façades to their basements, additional central processes are need. Facility Management as a strategic organization is not just responsible for compliance with the required standards, maintenance strategies and budgets. It must also keep an eye on quality management, administration, contracts, direction for service providers, and the whole realm of billings and management. It must also find the day-to-day solutions that reflect the architectural intentions with regard to aesthetics and design without impairing the sense of well-being and concentration of the buildings' eventual users. Together with the building operators, Facility Management strives for a smooth operation. A large-scale project like the Novartis Campus encompasses incredibly diverse facilities and services—from building equipment, to telecommunications and information technology, elevators, guidance systems, furnishings, safety, and security, to mail, gardening, dry-cleaning, domestic services, and maintenance. Prevention is important to Campus operations. The satisfaction of stringent demands regarding energy requirements and user expectations are guaranteed by the application of an intense scrutiny of both what is desired and the actual results. The operations side of Facility Management takes care of the operation of all buildings and their maintenance, repair, testing, functional controls, adaptations, and rebuilding. These activities are conditioned by new user requirements, as well as efficiency, regulation, and possible energy savings.

To put it simply, Facility Management's activity is a little like mountain climbing: it is a daily balancing act of what could be and what is out of the question. In pursuing this, Facility Management is usually successful, if nothing unusual occurs. It is when even the the smallest detail is in perfect harmony with the larger picture, and when each and every user feels integrated into their surroundings, then productive, efficient work in a comfortable, creative atmosphere free from disturbance is made possible.

Through close cooperation with all those involved in the construction process, Facility Management ensures the smooth operation of all Campus building sites, 2008.

User Support

The changes to the Novartis Campus's work spaces have as their goal the creation of a work environment which satisfies the requirements of the employees as well as those of the pharmaceutical industry and which at the same time allows for a flexible mode of work in appealing surroundings. For the implementation of the plans, however, more is needed than a management dedicated to the gamut of infrastructural and architectural issues. The interests of the people working on Campus must be also addressed.

In the first phase of the implementation of the Master Plan, it was already determined that the projects realized on Campus would be followed by a team that addressed the psychological aspects incurred by the changes being made to the workplace. The reason for this was the clearly perceived resistance to the changes planned on Campus in the initial phase of the project's development. For instance, there was a basic rejection on the part of some employees of open space or multi-space offices. Two reservations played a major role in the employees' attitude: first, the concern for the apparent lack of confidentiality and privacy in the open-plan offices, and secondly, fears of a probable increase in the control exerted over them by their superiors.

The first meetings in large groups—which, however, did not run smoothly—were followed by meetings in which smaller groups of employees and their representatives, such as the floor managers, were given the opportunity to express their concerns. In this way, the Campus's users were consciously included in the development process. The fact that management issued the invitations to these meetings was an important factor in motivating the employees.

After hearing the employees' reservations, their concerns were taken seriously. They were offered tours and workshops, and their frequent questions were answered. In short, the concerns of the users were attended to with care, thereby assuaging their fears. Even if one were able to refer back to experiences from the first phase of development and utilize those instruments and methods, it gradually became apparent that the approach to user support had to be adapted to each specific situation. Among other things, this concept provides for management training, whereby the requirements of the new offices and their method of working are discussed and analyzed. After this, workshops with all team members are organized.

The examination of mock-ups and visits to the construction sites were deemed especially motivating, and led to a dramatic increase in a project's acceptance. These activities accompanied the intensive preparation phase, which included the preparation of the Welcome Kit, a package consisting of a gift and documentation regarding the relevant project given to users on their first day in the new office. Informal feedback meetings and electronic surveys circulated at regular intervals as well as over longer periods of time allow for a comparison of the various projects and create a broad basis of experience, which in turn can inform future projects.

Although the accompaniment of the projects on Campus by a change management team is costly and intensive, it is both necessary and well worth the effort. However, there are still questions at the end of the day: How can one pass on experiences to someone? And what happens after the projects have been definitively handed over to the users? How is the knowledge gained from earlier projects communicated to those working on new projects and what is the right point in time to do this? The project phases must be defined and structured beforehand. These questions, which are central to the transfer of learning and experiences in their most varied forms, must be more intensively discussed in the future. Those involved with change management continuously gather experiences and document them in word and image, and from this body of information checklists are generated to be used for new projects.

The general resistance to the multi-space offices previously mentioned only partially persists today; employee criticism of the projects has become more differentiated. Even if cherished habits have to be relinquished and the overall learning process is very time-consuming, the result is that communication has already been substantially improved and the speed at which decisions are reached has been markedly increased. Teamwork takes center stage. In addition, employees get to know one another better and a faster, more informal kind of communication is thus promoted. This will exert a long-term influence on work and thinking. Intensive exchange is the basis for good work, which, in turn, can be achieved if employees feel at home in their work environment. To a great extent, the functionality and aesthetics of a workplace contribute to creating this kind of atmosphere, as does well-run, exemplary management. The most important result of all this is the recognition that the work environment must be flexible, that is, adaptable, in response to its future use. The changeover must occur as quickly and simply as possible.

Laboratory Building Requirements

But how are special requirements for the laboratory buildings addressed and which issues demand particular attention?

For the first time in years, the new laboratory buildings on the Novartis Campus offer the chance to fulfill the specific requirements imposed on such structures. In close consultation with both management and users, it was possible to establish what was needed in terms of work spaces and equipment, and how the changes in the various branches of sciences over the last decades affect the building structure. In this context, questions concerning the validity of current standards and the quantity of employees needed in order to be able to do the best work most productively and efficiently were raised. As a very general beginning, the concept of an open structure that provides an inviting, transparent work environment which encourages contact among the employees was formulated. In such an environment, insights and knowledge should be able to be exchanged as quickly and simply as possible, and equipment and work materials should be used in common. The information gleaned from the future laboratory users served as the basis for the first discussion with the research management. The users were then approached with the modified plans. From the very beginning of the laboratory projects, therefore, there was close collaboration with them.

The central question concerning the current needs of those using the laboratory is variously answered depending on the changing perspectives of the different professions involved, as well as the temporal standpoint. At the heart of the matter is an improvement in both the use of equipment and the spatial conditions in which communication primarily takes place. But experience shows that design solutions for complex laboratory buildings are never arrived at immediately; rather, they develop continuously, and considerable time must be allowed for their planning. The logistics of the procedure are extremely important. In the final analysis, the success of the building is the result of several factors.

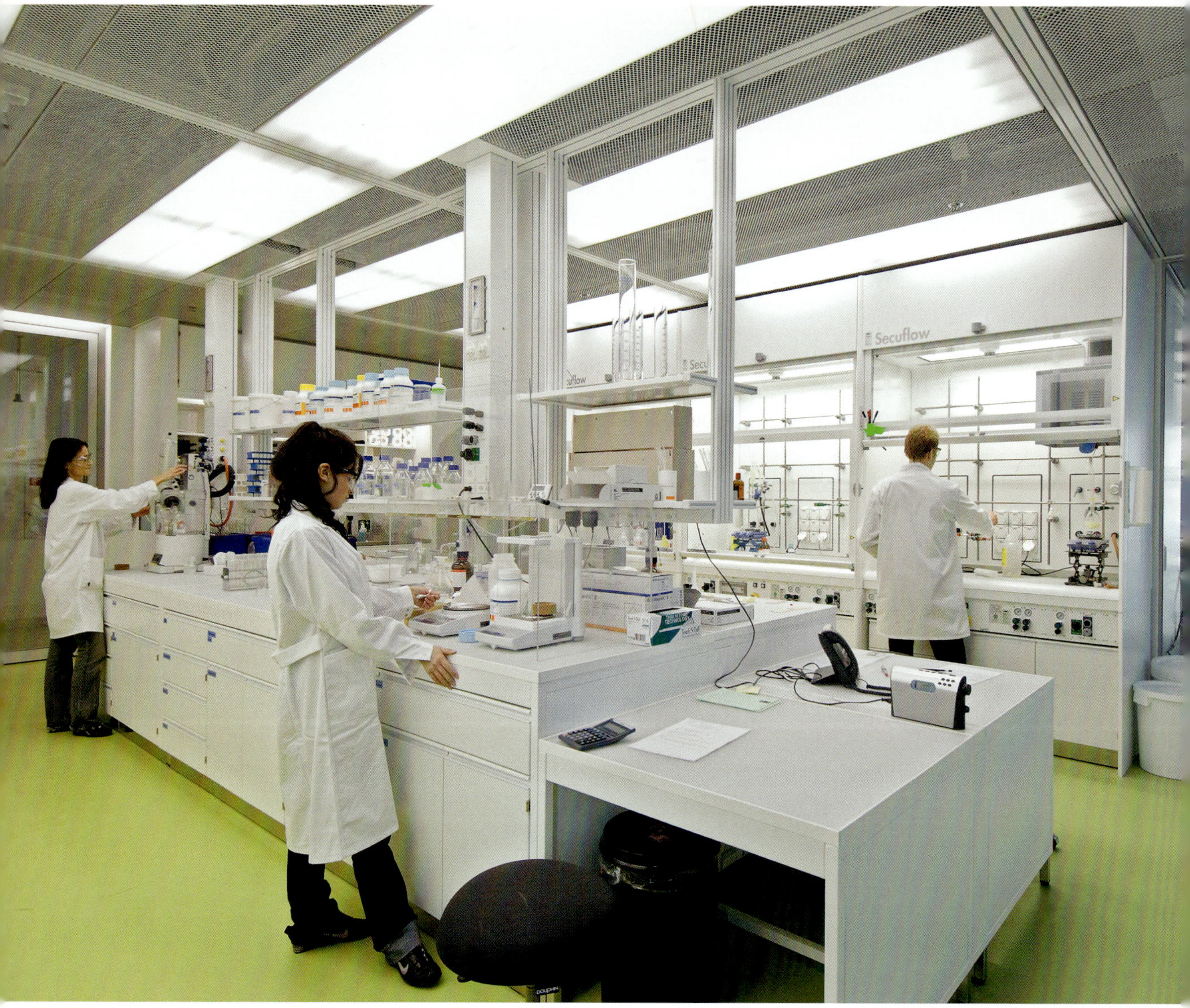
Secuflow

The newly created laboratory
buildings correspond to the
specific needs of the users, 2008.

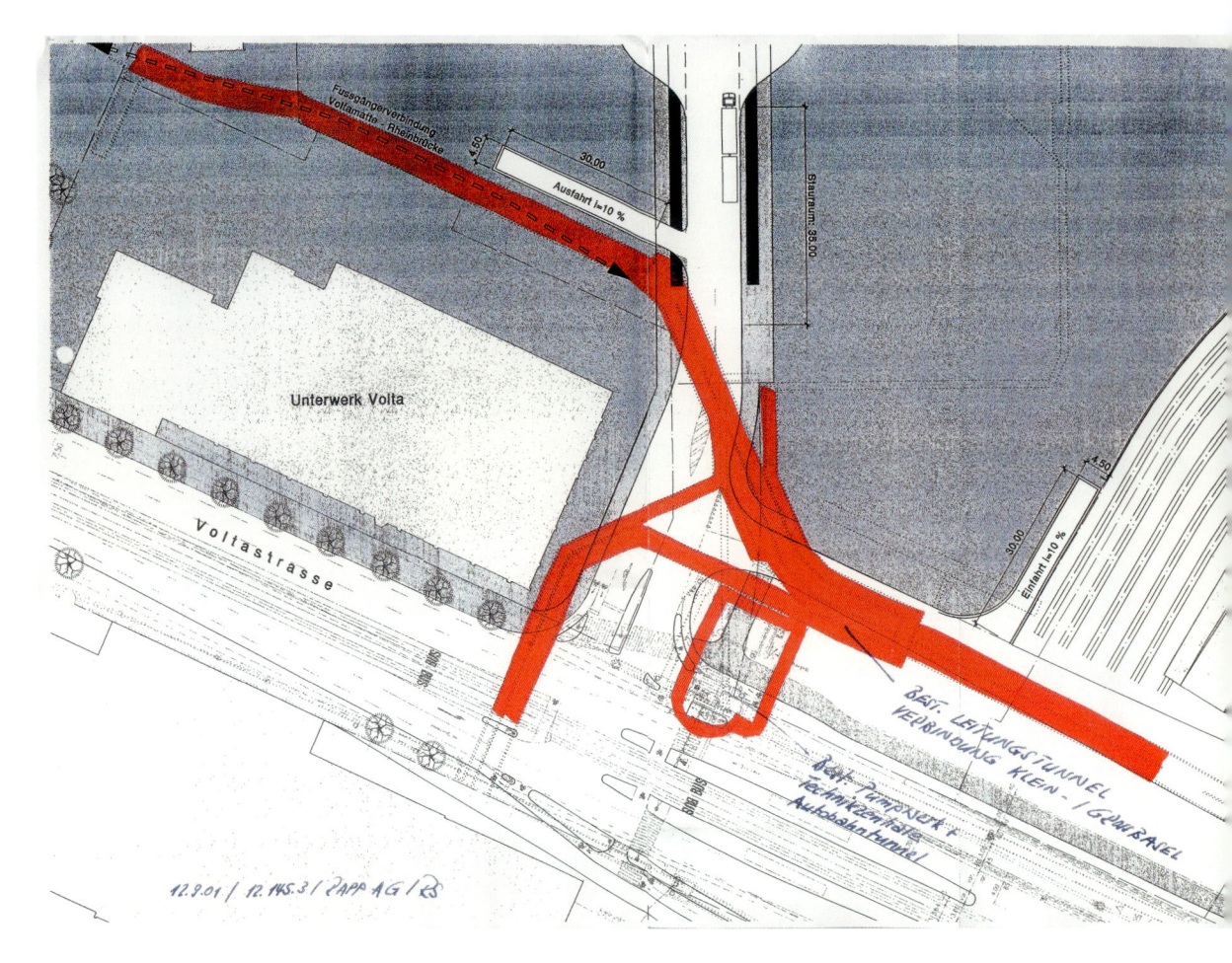

Underground pathways between Voltastrasse and Fabrikstrasse, sketch, 2001: The leeway for design at the entrance of the Campus was and is greatly limited by existing technical infrastructure.

Sustainability

The redesign and transformation of the St. Johann industrial complex into a "Campus of Knowledge and Innovation" offers Novartis a unique opportunity to express its corporate philosophy on social, economic, and ecological levels. Reference will be made here to the ecological aspects.

To begin, the energy goal values for the buildings on Campus is in accordance with the goals of the "2000-watt society," the result of a study conducted by Swiss Federal Laboratories for Materials Testing and Research (EMPA) at the behest of Novartis. As the EMPA study indicates, the Novartis Campus can contribute to reaching the goals of the 2000-watt society by taking three measures: First, by deploying renewable energies to the greatest extent possible. Second, by employing certain construction measures, for instance, using insulating materials or modern heating and air-conditioning equipment. And third, through the use of the most energy-efficient equipment available.

Novartis set itself the goal of supplying all new buildings with exclusively renewable energies and eliminating CO_2 emission on Campus in the mid-term. The new office buildings being built are set up so that they use only a third of the energy of the office buildings constructed earlier. A part of the savings that result from this is being used to purchase one-hundred-percent renewable energies (electricity and heating). The electricity derived from the renewable energies is not generated by burning fossil fuels or using nuclear energy and bears the "naturemade" label of quality. A distinction is made between "naturemade basic" electricity, which is generated from renewable energies, and "naturemade star" electricity, which is of the highest ecological quality and whose ecological added value is scientifically proven and certified. Of the entire electricity needs of the new Campus buildings, ninety-five percent is covered by "naturemade basic" electricity and five percent by "naturemade star." The heating is derived from the refuse incineration plant in Basel, which generates CO2-neutral steam that is sourced as long-distance heating.

In the construction of the new buildings, Novartis adheres to what is known as the Minergie Standard. This means that the energy expended for heating and hot water for these new structures may not exceed a third of their average energy consumption. To meet such a standard, the buildings must have the best possible structural envelope. At the same time, they are designed to provide an ideal indoor climate attuned to the needs of the employees.

Building materials selected according to basic ecological principles are to be used in all new buildings. Novartis set its guidelines according to the standards of the "Koordinationsgruppe Ökologisch Bauen" (KÖB). Highly recyclable building materials—such as recyclable concrete and aluminum profile—are to be used.

The insulation standard set by Novartis goes substantially beyond the guidelines of Swiss energy law. In collaboration with the insulation industry, the insulation thicknesses for the temperatures of various media was calculated, thus allowing the establishment of a standard that achieves the optimal relationship between investment and energy savings over a period of use of twenty years. In the new buildings on Campus, all the heating and cooling mains of the building services and the heating sector component of the energy supply are insulated according to this standard.

In December 2003, Novartis voluntary entered into an energy goal agreement with the Amt für Umwelt und Energie (AUE). In it, an obligatory energy goal value is established for every new Campus building. In the first meetings with the architects, these guidelines are defined and communicated, and adherence to them is subsequently monitored by construction management.

The target value is calculated from the allocation of the energy reference surfaces to eight possible use categories. For office buildings, an average energy coefficient of 300 megajoules per square meter per year were defined for electricity and heating together. All the energy brought into the building is contained in the energy coefficient. In addition to the energy goal value, the thermal insulation values (U-values) of individual building components must correspond to the target values according to standard SIA 380/1. The success of these measures is checked at the end of the first year of operation, and then once a year after that, and the results are communicated to the appropriate officials. Within the framework of the goal agreements, close cooperation with the canton of Basel occurs.

When procuring new electrical equipment in coordination with the technical purchasing department, Novartis follows the recommendations of EnergieSchweiz and favors the use of energy-efficient appliances. These include office equipment—such as computers, printers, copiers, and office lamps—as well as laboratory equipment or household appliances.

The safe and environmentally compatible disposal of waste has a long tradition at Novartis. The handling and disposal of different categories of waste is clearly regulated and operates without a hitch. Within the framework of the Novartis Campus, urban waste became a more significant issue and an investigation of it revealed which categories of waste are generated in the office and laboratory buildings. Guidelines for new and preexisting buildings alike were derived from this information and formulated as a recycling goal, which aims to achieve a recycling quota of eighty percent for the material utilization of urban waste.

The demolition of old buildings, aptly named "deconstruction," is a process that is carefully planned, even on the level of the most minor details. Currently, up to ninety percent of the renatured buildings are recycled in various ways. Building specialists investigate the furnishings and building materials for pollutants. Problematic or contaminated building materials can be separated at an early stage, and handled and disposed of correspondingly. The remaining building materials are recycled in one form or another. The structural shell is also recycled, being directly reclaimed in the concrete recycling and then made available for the construction of new buildings.

The Novartis Campus property is located on a subsurface that, as a consequence of the industrial practices of earlier generations, is contaminated with pollutants on the one hand, but archaeologically significant on the other because it was once the site of a Celtic settlement. In accordance with its building concept of ecological sustainability, Novartis has set the goal of eliminating the existing pollutants where possible and at the same time preserving the archaeological material for future generations. Depending on the type of pollutants found, contaminated earth is divided into batches according to levels of contamination and then disposed of appropriately. By reclaiming broad expanses of contaminated ground, Novartis wants to reach the point at which rainwater can seep in over the entire Campus area and then return in the form of groundwater to the natural hydrological cycle. In order to fulfill these guidelines, the surfaces that are sealed are to be designed in such a way that the rainwater can either be drawn off after being filtered through a leaching facility or directed through a humus- and gravel-filled trough. Surfaces that have been sanitized, and on which neither buildings nor sealed surfaces are to be built, are planted, so that the rainfall can directly seep away. Novartis is setting a new tone with its goal of realizing closed, natural hydrological cycles with soil reclamation on the Campus grounds. All told, about forty percent of the surface has already been reclaimed, and this process is playing a pioneering role in the region.

The supply and disposal concept must be correspondingly adapted to the Campus's concentration on research, development, and administration. The Novartis guidelines pursue different goals. In the case of water, the important issue is its economical use. The Campus plan for the management of wastewater aims for the elimination of industrial run-off, the separation of clean and dirty water, and the use of rainwater. In St. Johann, there are three qualities of water available for use: drinking water, consumptive water, and manufacturing water.

An important supplier of water for Novartis and its future Campus grounds is and will continue to be the Rhine river. The Rhine water—called internally "manufacturing water"—is processed in a Novartis facility and brought into the buildings via a distribution network. Manufacturing water is used in situations in which the quality of drinking water is not needed. The manufacturing water, which is primarily used on Campus for cooling, is fed back into the Rhine after being used. When the temperature of the river water is not cold enough, other cooling systems are used. Together with the Industrielle Werke Basel (IWB) Novartis has created a new product, which from an ecological and economical point of view represents the best alternative: what is called consumptive water on Campus is Rhine water that has been refined with groundwater enhancement and has a temperature of about twelve degrees Celsius. Direct cooling of the buildings with this water works even in the middle of summer. Consumptive water use requires an optimized energy concept and an independent flow measurement. The wastewater from the Campus grounds is divided into two types, which are gathered separately and led off. Investigations have shown that the activities in the new Campus buildings will no longer require an industrial sewage plant.

The Novartis Campus offers the great opportunity to develop standards in the framework of sustainability, which will also become models for other facilities.

Under construction: The heart of the
Novartis Campus—Fabrikstrasse, 2008

From Rehearsal to Real Time: The Pilot Project for a New Workplace Landscape

Sevil Peach

In 2002, Sevil Peach Gence Associates (SPGA) were invited to participate in an international design competition for a Pilot Project to explore and physically embody Novartis's goal of creating a "Campus of Knowledge," an environment that would foster greater communication, interaction, and teamwork.

The project entailed the complete refurbishment of the third floor of one of the existing buildings, which was occupied by part of the Novartis Finance Group and which was organized in a cellular arrangement with continuous individual and shared offices on either side of a central corridor, a space allotment then prevalent throughout the Campus.

The project challenges required us to deal with a building of precast concrete construction originally built in the early 1970s that required the complete refurbishment of both materials and services. In addition, we had to operate within tight budget restrictions, the capacity limitations of the existing centralized plant, rigidly enforced energy consumption requirements, and the lack of both a raised floor and a meaningful depth of floor screed, which meant that planning needed to respect the requirements of the perimeter cableway, so that the supply of power and data could be integrated into specially built elements.

We created an open, dynamic workplace for seventy people that allowed individuals and teams to work within a series of varied environments that supported the various activities at hand, ranging from independent, concentrated work to a working meeting between colleagues or a larger team formed for specific project needs.

Care was taken to divide the space into definable, intimate work areas. The work area is broken down for small groups of eight to sixteen people. A range of workstation types are provided, including one-, two-, and four-person platforms. All allow interaction with colleagues and can be reconfigured to allow the teams to expand or contract. We sought to "bring down the walls" that separated people and to eliminate the outward manifestations of hierarchy by integrating the managers with their teams instead of isolating them in individual rooms.

To emphasize the communal and team aspect of work, a dynamic space is created by locating mailboxes, a coffee point, soft seating, a television, and a large table for events and presentations at the center of the floor.

In either wing, or side, of the office, a central spine acts as a linear and variable shared work bench that can be used for non-territorial or break-away purposes, as well as allowing for the creation of a variety of informal meeting areas. Easily accessible technical support and grouped printing facilities are also located along the length of this spine to further enhance immediate interaction.

At either end of this central spine, enclosed private rooms/cabins allow for concentrated work, confidential discussions, and conference calls as needed. Formal, enclosed meeting and video-conferencing rooms are provided at either end of the floor.

The Workplace Users

At a User level, a strong communications strategy had to be developed in order to manage and overcome the shift from a cellular office environment to an open one. To assist us with this task we invited the collaboration of the late Andrea Finter, a management consultant whose skills complemented our design philosophy.

Our first User Meeting emphasized the enormity of the task we were about to undertake: one staff member's response to the question "How do you identify with the company?" was "I joined this *corridor* three months ago."

From this point onwards it was clear to us that this project was a vehicle for work culture change rather than just an environmental update.

The real challenge we faced was to create a work environment that addressed not only the aspirations of the company, but also the basic needs of the company's employees. The latter concern seem especially important, because letting go of the private, cubicle-style offices was associated with a loss of status. Understandably, most of the employees were concerned about, and some were even openly against, introducing an open plan for fear of risking a loss of concentration and, perhaps, of privacy.

Key to the employees' successful adoption of the project was the User Communication Strategy we established. Its objective was to explain the nature of the new environment and to demonstrate how it could be used to benefit the employees and, by extension, the rest of the company. We had to be prepared to listen, to understand, to respond to any apprehensions, to challenge preconceptions, and, where necessary, to demonstrate our ability to adapt the flexible design in response to major concerns. In short, we had to enter into an honest dialogue whereby trust could be engendered.

The User Communication Strategy involved creating a User Group that was part of the Design Team and in constant communication with us along the way. They were the key people who acted as the link between the designers, management, and the other employees, and they were selected from all levels of the company to represent their colleagues, rather than simply from management. With the User Group we organized visits to other successful open-plan environments, established focus groups and workshops, and presented physical models and drawings of the design to which employees were invited to respond. We established a Web site where we posted articles about new ways of working and, in return, the employees posted their concerns. These measures gave us a deep insight into how the company viewed itself and how its employees viewed themselves within it while maintaining our own perspective as an objective outside party.

Further on in the project, mock-ups of furniture were presented, allowing employees to test and select from a variety of options. Such activities allowed us to encourage them to set up protocols on how to use and behave within the new office culture we were trying to foster, thereby empowering them to make decisions and to resolve issues themselves—in short, familiarizing them with the environment into which they were going to move.

On the architectural level, we proposed solutions that aimed to erase the fears of employees whose vision of open-plan work environments conjured an image of the rubber stamp approach of a sea of desks lacking privacy and personalization. We sought to create definable, defensible group spaces that allowed the individual to work within an understandable landscape and on a familiar scale, a human workplace that offered a variety of possibilities (while recognizing that we work in different ways at different times of day) which would allow employees the freedom to choose the workspace and tools that best suited their tasks in a given moment. We also challenged the employees' belief that work could only occur at their own desks.

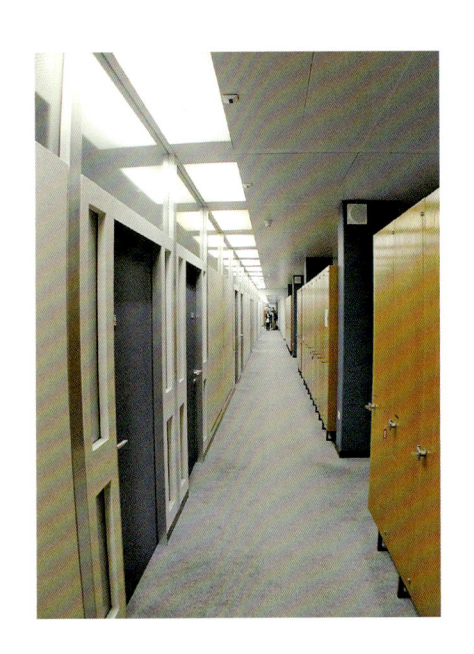

The Forum 2 building (formerly WSJ 202) before the conversion

Above: A corridor and closed work area documents the former office structure, 2003

The Forum 2 building (formerly WSJ 202) after the conversion to the pilot project by SPGA, 2003

Left: Small open meeting room

Below: Shared office space as an instrument and symbol of a new, more communicative work culture

The Occupation of the New Workplace

The User Group, with the help of the Facility Group, organized a seamless move into the new work space. Some of them were with us over the weekend, assisting us in shaping and fine-tuning the work environment, and organizing their communal facilities—essentially, in readying the space and making it homely. The copy area drawers were beautifully set up with stationery already in its proper compartments. Each desk was provisioned with a Welcome Pack. Some of the members of the User Group were inspired enough to stay with us through to the early hours of the morning; there was a fantastic team spirit and buzz, which led to more than one late-night take-away dinner, thus allowing us to christen the Family Table.

Finally, it was heartwarming to welcome the employees on the morning of the project's completion. The management had a breakfast laid out at the Family Table where everyone in the department gathered, perhaps for the first time, as we handed over their new home to them. They all grabbed their coffee and immediately settled in at their desks. There were no problems with finding their shared printers, someone was already collating on the copy bench, and others were already sitting on the sofas having meetings; after just an hour, it felt as if they had always worked in this way and in this environment!

Were There Any Issues?

Of course, there were some minor problems: they wanted more plants, the concentration rooms were not soundproof enough, and it took a little while to learn to keep the coffee point clean. However, some people moved the goalpost even further by wanting the removal of the cupboards between their desks because they found them to be an obstacle to interaction and communication. . . . What a success!

Three months later, we took photos of employee activity within the space for the duration of a working day. They were "changed people" doing things differently than they had before. It was impossible to think that some months ago they had been in their individual rooms along a corridor, denouncing teamwork as useless.

Almost all the employees were in some form of discussion with one another. Most of the informal meeting areas were occupied; the Family Table was used for internal presentations, team breakfast meetings, celebrations, and other events. The coffee point proved to be the heart of interaction, employees were connecting with one another around the platform desks, and the television allowed the group to watch Roger Federer win Wimbledon for the first time. In short, the Finance Group got to know each other, and the photos speak for themselves.

Could We Have Done It Another Way?

Of course. We started the Pilot Project with the goal of launching a learning and development process. For the purpose of the Campus building program, the Pilot Project proved invaluable. It successfully demonstrated that the mission and the aspirations of working in a different way could be both achieved and successfully embraced if appropriate time, communication, and care were given to the people and to the design process. From now on, it will be important that the management, along with the new designers and architects involved, embraces the sensitive issues involved in order to create a successful work environment.

How Are Things Working Four Years On?

On one side of the floor, the users continue to care for and use the environment as we had envisioned, because many of the them have been there since we inaugurated the new workplace on Day One. The spirit of the other side of the floor, however, has unfortunately deteriorated; many of the managers and employees have changed, and with them so has the workplace. The communication necessary for the continuation of employee education with regard to the workplace vision and the motivation behind it has been neglected. We found that the new employees have moved in with their old work habits and transformed the environment to suit these habits and insecurities, rather than embracing the possibilities of the new environment. This has provided an interesting opportunity to take stock of the project and proved that spatial and cultural change in the workplace requires ongoing support and close monitoring as well as sustained passion, commitment, and belief.

A Workplace Conceptualized for Human Beings

We believe that the workplace needs to respond on organizational, physical, and emotional levels in order to create a supportive environment that is inviting and familiar and inspires and motivates its participants by creating a feeling of comfort and confidence while at the same time monitoring the appropriateness for its Users.

It is a given that people's behavior varies in connection with their environment. Therefore, it follows that shaping that environment through design can potentially change how people think and behave.

It is important to think beyond shapes and forms and stylistic interventions when designing workplaces. We need to concentrate on human aspects, activities, and social matrices, which require a different kind of sensibility.

If current business demands require workers who are adaptable and can communicate, share, and interact, then these are the criteria to which we as designers need to respond. We need to look at the familiar, ordinary, normal activities within the workplace and try to bring a new meaning to them in a manner that appears effortless to the workplace's employees, so that the environment, to a certain degree, conforms to their behavior.

It is important to create a strong architectural armature or structure that is non-threatening and enables its users' activity to flow unconsciously in harmony with the environment. The architectural space should be able to respect the individual's need to be able to retreat and be private, to yield to a user's need for personalization and flexibility, and to adapt to change. The design provisions for these activities may not be immediately visible, but they quickly become apparent when people perform these activities without thinking.

We need to challenge the workplace's tools, behavior, routines, bureaucracies, and hierarchies, and, when necessary, redefine and augment them, so that the lives and creativity of the people always take center stage.

Will You Always Succeed?

No. Despite your best efforts, there will always be some who do not want to join you on the journey. Some will want to bring their old chair, or hide themselves behind a wall of plants, or have some piece of equipment right next to them as opposed to having to get up and walk a few meters to where it could have been placed for easier use by everyone. You have to rely on patience and persuasion unless the organization and use of space is a foregone conclusion.

216

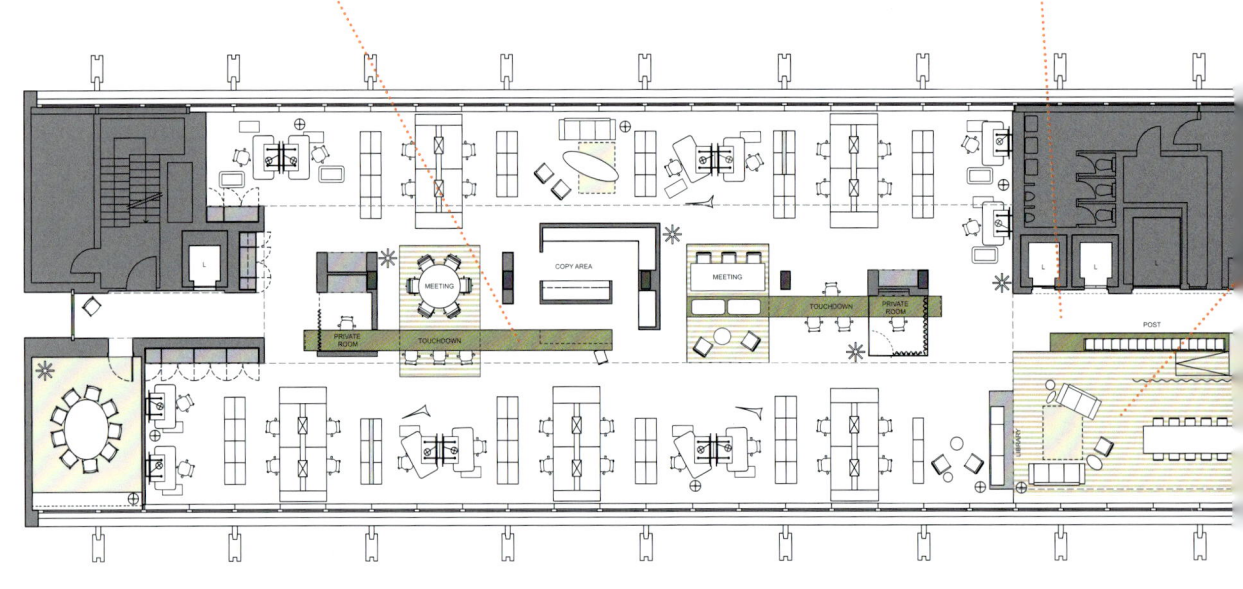

Forum 2 building (formerly WSJ 202), fourth floor, Pilot Project by SPGA, 2003: The floor plan shows the open work areas with desks in groups of four; in between, set off by color, are the common areas with meeting rooms, seating groups, and coffee points. The building cores (in grey) were not altered in the conversion. The photographs transmit the impression of a new brightness, spaciousness, and transparency.

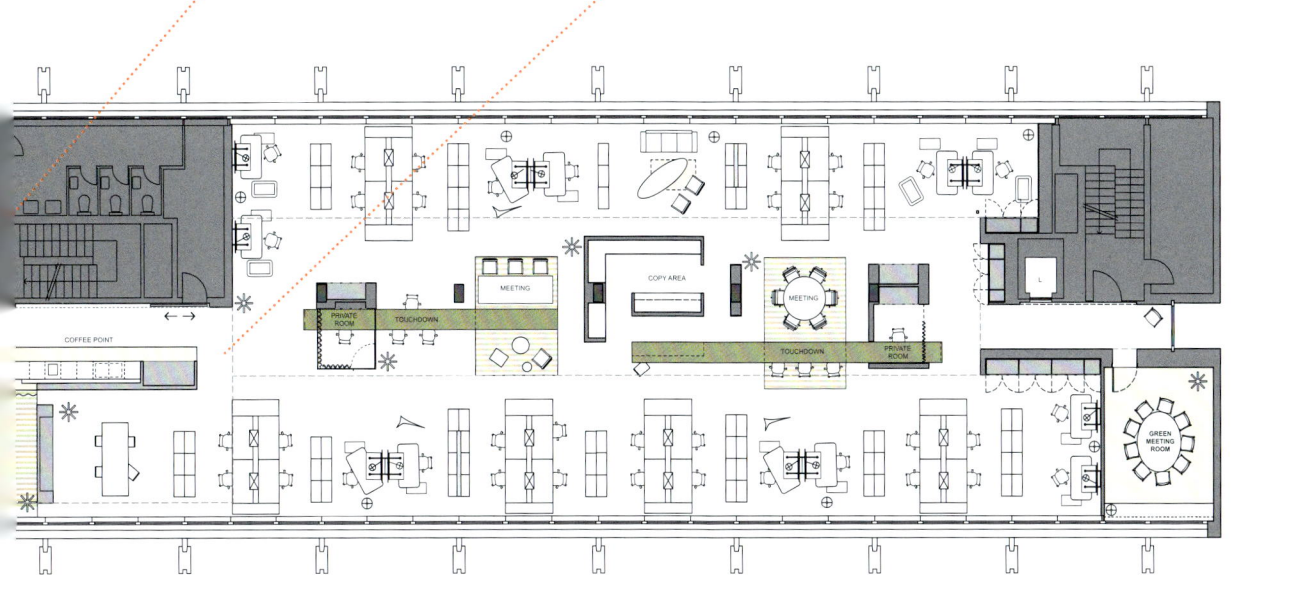

Forum 3: The First New Building

Following our involvement in the Pilot Project, we were invited to join the competition-winning architectural team of Diener & Diener Architekten to bring our space planning, interior design, and workplace expertise to the design team of the Forum 3 building. Consequently, we received two commissions: one as the interior design consultant within Diener & Diener's team, and the other as a direct commission from Novartis to run a User Communication and Training Program.

The task for the new building was bigger, as the number of occupants was much greater and more senior, and we had to balance the two commissions carefully in order to develop a consensus with other members of the design team with regard to the strategy to be applied to the workplace so that employees' concerns were both heard and adapted to.

At the Users' level, a strong communications strategy had to be developed, as we had done for the Pilot Project, in order to manage in particular the issue of confidentiality and the commercially sensitive material with which the workplace's participants deal. We again brought Andrea Finter onto our team, following our successful collaboration on the Pilot Project.

One of the most challenging aspects of this new project was convincing the Division Heads to let go of their private offices and work out in the open with their teams.

Project Description

One of the key features of the Forum 3 building is a double façade with a multicolored glass structure, which naturally introduces color into the more neutral interior. The façade design presents a continuous external balcony on every floor, thus creating a welcoming outdoor space. Tables and chairs have been provided on the external loggias for coffee breaks and to allow employees to work in the fresh air.

At the west end of the building, a four-story room housing a collection of tropical trees also provides an alternative environment for work and relaxation, bringing nature indoors. Such user-friendly architectural features contribute positively to the workplace.

The building's deeply recessed ground floor is designed as a fluid space that in good weather can be opened up to the new Forum/Plaza outside. It also houses the restaurant and lounge, which is open to use by the rest of the Novartis community, as well as a variety of presentation rooms. Now that the square has been fully built, this has turned into a most pleasant communal arena.

Developing on the principles we had created in the Pilot Project, the office floors are designed to be broken down into distinct and definable areas and to provide an open workplace for approximately fifty-five people per floor.

The coffee point and a high table are found near the centrally located spiral staircase, which connects all office floors, thus recognizing the importance of unplanned, informal interactions and meetings within the office environment. The workplace is supported by shared communal and technical support facilities, including a number of informal meeting areas, soft seating, enclosed meeting rooms, and quiet concentration rooms. Given the wireless network in the building, the employees have been encouraged to think of their workplace as being the whole building, not just their individual workstations.

We also reached a compromise with the Senior Managers. While they are now working in the open, they also have physical proximity to an enclosed meeting room, which they can use as required.

Diener & Diener with SPGA, Forum 3, 2007

Left: Space for privacy is offered.

Above: A central stairway interlinks all departments.

Forum 3's Users

In essence, our experience with the Pilot Project set the guidelines for our engagement with the Users of the Forum 3 workplace. However, the new project's timeline and physical manifestation were different from those of the Pilot Project, as they had to complement and work seamlessly with the architecture of the Forum 3 building. The new project also had to recognize the need to mesh together the aspirations and requirements of the many different teams of Global Technical Operations and Pharma Development.

The Forum 3 project's acceptance by its Users was, in the end, a success, and as with the Pilot Project, Day One came off without a hitch, beginning with a guided tour for everyone. The whole experience was greatly assisted by having the Pilot Project as a point of reference, something that was further reinforced by the fact that some of the Users had already worked in the other workplace.

The Meaning-Engendering Surroundings of the Workplace

Fritz Steele

Today's new, innovative work environments are a complex mix of elements and effects, some planned and many unplanned. When you put the various factors together and things are working as intended, what is our sense of a really good workplace? It is the result of both the design of the place and what we bring to it in terms of roles, motives, style, interests, and mood. It includes what we can do there, what we notice, how we feel about the place, and how we feel about ourselves. The following is my sense of what it all feels like when it is working well.

The Workplace a Communal Location

We should begin with a perhaps not irrelevant question: in today's high-tech, high-connectivity world, since people have many more options about how, where, and when to do their work, why bother to bring them together in a common place such as a corporate campus? One reason is gains in efficiency in research and development, for which you would not want the expense of replicating 3,000 small, one-person laboratories, let alone the redundancy of major pieces of expensive equipment. There is also the hope of encouraging contact and information-sharing among scientists and technicians to promote a faster generation and testing of new ideas than tends to happen with solitary work.

For office-type work, the prime rationale is to promote a common identity, engender trust, and enable both quicker and clearer exchanges of information in changing times. In the past, having a single workplace was also a means of checking on who was present or absent. Managers could watch subordinates to ensure that they spent their time working (or, rather, at least *looking* as though they were working). Today most enlightened companies have lost at least some of that suspicious management style and trust their members to be committed to their goals and manage their own time and activities. I assume that today's managers try to measure people's performance by what they accomplish rather than how they look as they are accomplishing it. This requires a shift towards greater tolerance and less judging of one another (by peers as well as managers), or else the evaluation processes and group norms that tend to emphasize being at one's desk and "looking busy" will linger on, even when one's task might call for doing something less obvious, such as changing location to get a fresh perspective on a problem.

My image of the new, dynamic, highly collaborative workplace includes a number of day-to-day experiences and effects: providing us with a sense of common identity and commitment to one another; offering us richer choices of places, tools, materials, information, and the like; promoting effective collaboration and a sense of connection to our colleagues; promoting our health and well-being; and facilitating an environment of development and change rather than just a setting for repetitive activities and tasks.

A Sense of Identity and Community

When people regularly come together in a lively, high-visibility setting they tend to build a shared sense of community identity and a recognition of shared goals, skills, interests, and values. Even though they may not work directly with one another, or even know each other's names, repeated sightings tend, over time, to build a sense of "we" among the people who belong on a particular site or to a given enterprise. That identity can be clearly defined as a particular, small group work site: a single floor of a single building, if people do not leave that area during the day, a single building if they tend to stay there, or the Campus as a whole if the workday involves moving about.

For me, this sense of community is seen best in well-designed university campuses. Faculty, students, researchers, and staff often move around for different activities or events during the day. They do not make the most of these options unless they make the mental shift towards thinking of the whole place as theirs (shared in common with their colleagues), not just their personal assigned workplaces. In the same way, they soon stop using other spaces if they get the feeling that people nearby have not made this shift and resent their presence there.

When I am visiting a client's workplace, I am sometimes given a temporary spot in which to do my individual work. However, I actually move around quite a bit and use the common spaces both inside and outdoors (when the weather permits). I do it partly to see how the new places are working, but I also feel more alert when I am seeing different people and activities rather than when I am tucked away in some hidden cubbyhole.

A Sense of Choice

To me, a great workplace is all about a rich array of available choices: work islands, meeting spaces of varying sizes, very private enclaves, indoor and outdoor informal areas, cafés and other food and beverage places, and pathways that can be special places in and of themselves. I know from both research findings and personal experience that I do not run at the same pace all day as an engine does. I have periods of higher and lower energy, times when I feel creative and times when I feel stuck on a problem, and so on. It feels natural to me to use changes of place as a means of getting re-energized, especially if it includes walking or other forms of physical exercise.

Again, for different locations to be real options, my own attitude is crucial. I want to consciously think of myself as the "designer" of my workdays in both space and time. I need to be free to choose based on tools, technology, people, ambience, my energy level, needs for changes of pace, time of day, weather, what excites me, what calms me down, and all the other factors that influence me. My manager and I have to believe that all of these are legitimate reasons for changes of tempo or scene, and that there is no single "right" way of working.

A Sense of Collaboration and Connection

I believe that the new type of workplace is especially helpful in promoting—and, even more importantly, *not discouraging*—quick and easy communication and collaboration. This does not mean that I have to be collaborating or interacting all the time, but rather that when I need to, I can connect with others easily and quickly. I sense this best when people are visible and accessible spontaneously, as opposed to when they are hidden and one has to make appoinments in order to have even short conversations. Awareness and accessibility are particularly promoted by transparency and visibility through use of glass dividers, open sight lines, atria allowing glimpses of people and activities on different floors, and so on.

In order for this accessibility to have a positive effect, I need to make a mental shift and reverse the usual assumptions about confidentiality. I have to move from keeping most information on a need-to-know basis towards greater trust, which means sharing more information with others unless there is a compelling reason to keep it secret. When relatively open layouts are working well, people also talk at a normal conversational voice level rather than whisper, ideas are often shared more openly, new concepts or issues are visibly posted for people to see and/or react to, and so on. It looks and feels as if people are thinking of themselves as a "we" instead of a collection of "I's."

A Sense of Health and Well-Being

Although historically workplaces have varied considerably in their promotion of workers' health, it seems obvious that one of the primary criteria to be considered in creating every work environment should be the promotion rather than the degradation of our health and sense of well-being. At the most basic level, it should be physically comfortable (temperature, air flow, light/glare control, etc.), ergonomically designed (to avoid back problems or repetitive stress injuries), and free of noxious or toxic substances (gases, smells, chemicals, etc.). Most places where I work today tend to meet these criteria, but I feel still better if they are also *responsive* environments, ones in which I can make small adjustments and in which the system helps resolve bigger problems or make necessary changes.

My personal expectations for a healthy environment include natural light, beverage islands, some varied food choices, and well-designed alternative places to work, such as balconies, interesting sitting areas, and inviting outdoor spaces. Once again, these work best for me when I consciously seek places to match both what I am working on and my energy level and mood at the time. There also needs to be a general understanding that people can use these places for "real work," not just when taking a break. And when they are used for breaks, it is best if people can take breaks when they are most needed, not just when mandated by the company. Formal break times have never made much sense to me, except possibly in labor situations in which workers did not trust management to allow them any rest time at all.

Another important promoter of health on the job is an on-site fitness/exercise facility that is large enough to satisfy the potential user demand, is conveniently located, and is pleasantly designed so that I enjoy being there. Since I am a runner, changing and shower facilities are also a big asset in my eyes. All of these facilities are more useful to me if they are available throughout the day, not just in the early morning and at lunchtime, so that I can do my exercising when it provides the greatest benefit to my energy and mental processes.

❙❙ **One of the most important growth-related design criteria for new workplaces is transparency and the greater visibility of activities and people that result from it.** ❙❙

A Sense of Growth and Development

I also feel more alive in workplaces that help me feel I am learning and growing in skills or understanding. I do not like getting into ruts or seeing the same place and things all day long. One of my favorite stimuli to development is a place with varied displays of information about what other groups are doing, what is happening in the outside world (news, business trends, etc.), and creative developments in various fields (not just my own area of expertise). Workplaces that have physical centers with good current information have helped expand my awareness of issues and possibilities, as well as my notions about what I could do to help make things happen.

To put it more generally, I learn more when I can visually register patterns of events and activities. One of the most important growth-related design criteria for new workplaces is transparency and the greater visibility of activities and people that result from it. As a human being I am a visually-oriented creature, so sights make me more aware of issues, other people, and myself. While it is true that more accessible, transparent workplaces tend to have more potential distractions, they also have a palpable "buzz" which helps keep me informed about what is going on, who is excited about what, and when new opportunities suddenly pop up. As one occupant of a new building put it, "I sometimes get a little less total work done in a day, but I have learned a lot more, and that helps me focus my work and shape it more efficiently."

Finally, since I have been doing consulting for companies making major physical changes, I have become aware of an unexpected source of growth and awareness: functioning day to day in the environment of ongoing renovation and construction projects. This may sound a little strange, since it is often noisy, irritating, and sometimes even looks quite chaotic. But it also provides a continuous learning environment where history is revealed: how old structures were built, how new ones are put together, and the dynamic nature of organizations that are no longer static for long periods of time. This especially happens when new temporary walking paths are set up (and old ones closed off), so that new bottlenecks/meeting points occur almost by accident and the number of useful chance meetings increases significantly.

I know I am a different person due to having naturally absorbed these experiences. Of course, it can be noisy and distracting at times, but I am convinced that it is a force that expands awareness for all of us who live with it, even when we do not consciously recognize it. It is hard to hold on to old notions and static expectations about place, groupings, and work style in the midst of such dynamic change. I just naturally appreciate workplaces more because I know how they got that way. This effect is even stronger when user groups are involved in detailed design choices for their own areas: they identify with and "own" them more strongly because they know how and why they were created.

To sum up briefly, when I am using a new workplace that has the right mix and feel, less is hidden and I have a greater visual awareness of the people and activities around me. This helps create a general sense of identification and trust among all of us, with less concern about confidentiality and fewer secrets. There are more choices about where and how to work, and I feel free to pick spaces that suit my task, mood, or inclination, rather than having to stay put just to prove that I am busy. I choose places because they are both useful and fun at the same time. There is less of a turf mentality, and there are fewer places considered off-limits and more people using common facilities. Since there are usually more quick interchanges and fewer long, scheduled meetings, I can check my ideas with others more efficiently, get reactions, and move on to the next step. Groupings, organizational structures, and physical settings are all more fluid and less fixed. I feel healthy when I am working, and I move around or exercise when it helps re-energize me, not just when it is scheduled. Finally, it is a more demanding environment, because I have to make my own choices about how and where to do different things, and if I am not doing that, the fault is mine.

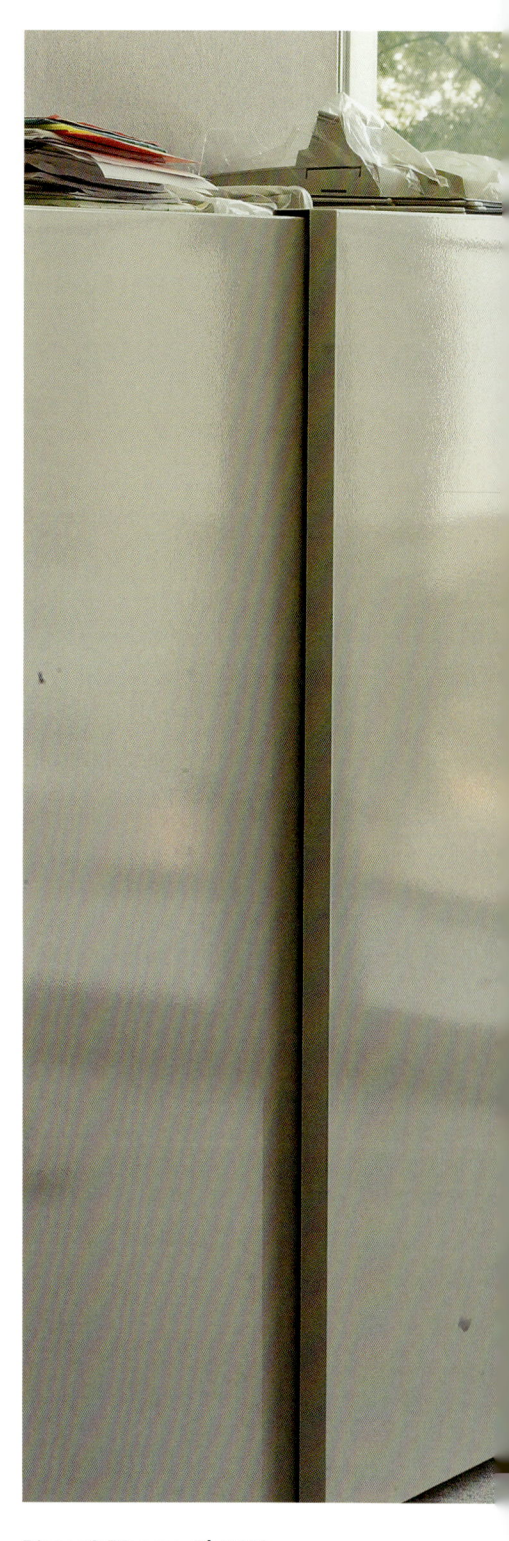

Diener & Diener with SPGA, Forum 3, 2007: In spite of their spatial openness, the newly installed work stations allow for the development of an individualized work style.

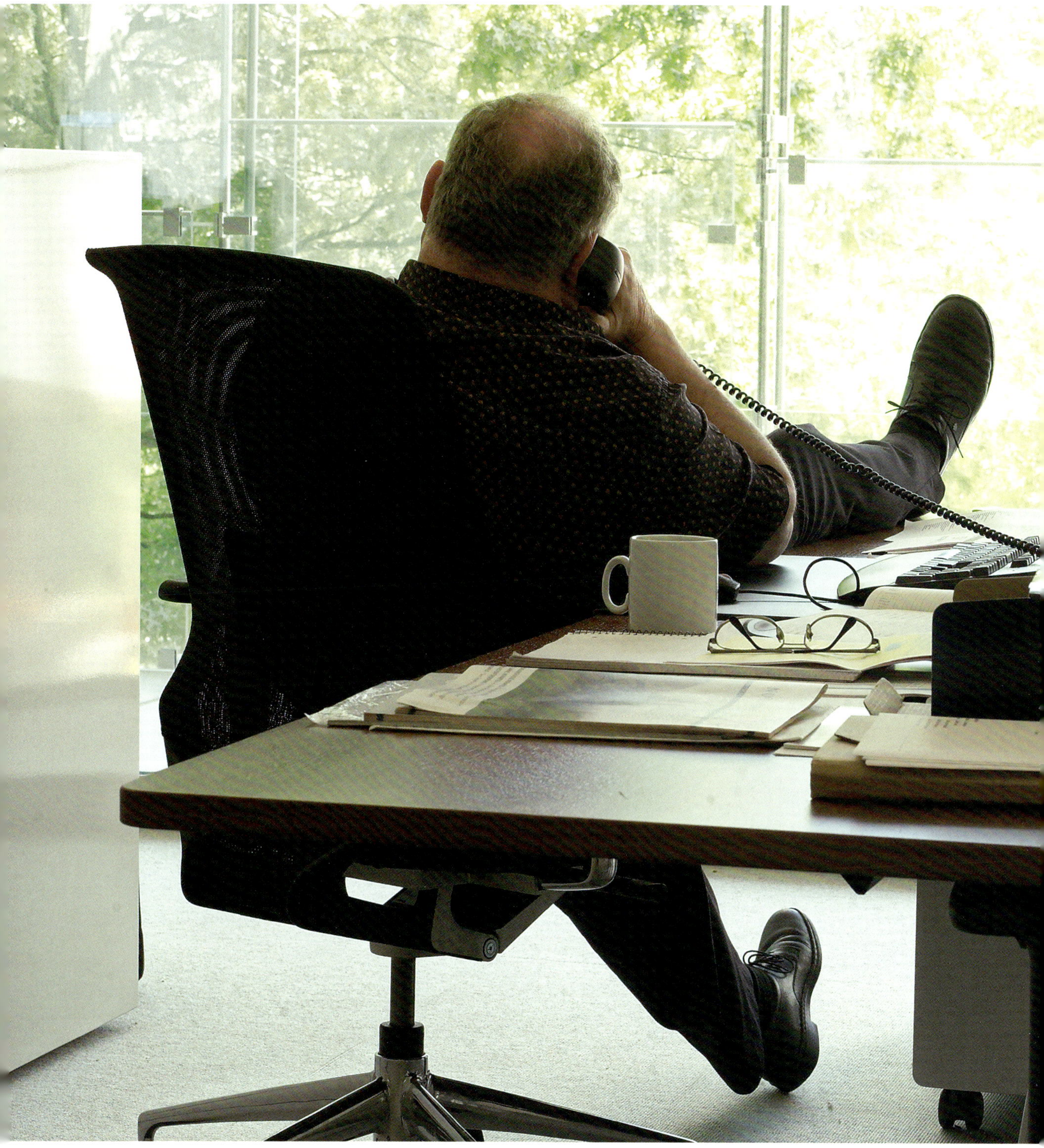

Office Space and Creativity

Roman Boutellier

Modern Homo sapiens spends his time primarily in meetings. More than eighty percent of all economic transactions are directed from above within organizations and are not negotiated on the open market. Some conclusions may be drawn from the many complaints of those employed in research and development about the negative effects these hierarchies and coordinations have on their work: Where should creativity originate? What time is left to think about customer needs, to estimate the effects of new technological developments, to exchange ideas, and to introduce new medications to the market if the large organization in which one is bound intervenes to direct these creative processes?

How did these structures arise? Let us look back for a moment: the first signs of human creativity in Switzerland occurred in the Wildkirchli, in three caves near to Ebenalp in Appenzellerland, where, during the Ice Age, hunters and gatherers withdrew from the glaciers and constantly improved their lives with mural painting, simple tools, and primitive "green biotechnology." Were these human beings creative? Most ethnologists agree that they were at least as creative as we are now, 50,000 years later. But from today's perspective they had two great disadvantages. They died young—the average life span was only twenty-five—and they had very little contact with others outside their own clans. Specialization was therefore not possible, and very few people lived long enough to gather long-term experience and pass it on to the next generation. Today it is known that technologies developed in small, isolated communities are very quickly lost, and short life expectancies offer very little motivation to execute radical changes. Isolated groups of less than 1,000 members dissipate knowledge, while groups of more than 250 have problems exchanging knowledge rapidly and intensively among themselves. Science and technology, therefore, developed slowly and were heavily dependent for thousands of years on individual extraordinary minds: Aristotle, Plato, Galileo Galilei, Isaac Newton, Gottfried Wilhelm Leibniz, and the last universal genius, Leonardo da Vinci—all of them knew more or less all of the academics of their times and all of them lived to an advanced age. But they were mavericks, and in their eras no critical mass of scientists was ever reached.

Even the exceptionally talented had to work for longer periods of time before they became experts. Modern creativity research shows that even Wolfgang Amadeus Mozart and The Beatles needed between 5,000 and 10,000 hours in order to realize their creative ideas. Until 1963, The Beatles played the usual rock 'n' roll, and only after that—after more than 1,200 concerts—did they establish their own style. In the case of Mozart, many are of the opinion that his breakthrough occurred with the Köchel Catalogue No. 271 at the age of twenty. What he had composed until that time was still very strongly influenced by his father. According to Herbert Simon, a Nobel Prize winner for economics, 5,000 to 10,000 hours mean five to ten years of intensive work in a world-class "scientific community"! Creativity does not just mean producing original ideas; it also means the ability to judge whether these ideas can be realized, for growth comes only from their realization!

Today it is known that the gross national product (GNP) per capita remained constant for thousands of years, while the life expectancy in the emerging cities, for reasons of hygiene, even went down. Our fledgling technology could barely keep up with the population growth until about 1850. Since then the GNP has doubled every twenty years! According to Paul Samuelson, another Nobel Prize winner for economics, this is the most important economic fact of the entire history of mankind. Before 1850 technology was based on the principal of "trial and error," whereas since 1850 it has been based on scientific insight. Gu Binglin, the president of the most important Chinese university, the Tsinghua University in Peking, expressed his understanding of this when he said at the ETH Zurich in 2005 that "China needs two things to become rich: capital and engineers."

> **In spite of a raised life expectancy and increased technological growth, motivated, exceptional minds and intensive teamwork are still the most important corporate capital.**

One might add that, on the other hand, scientists and engineers need an appropriate environment and organizational background in order to be productive. In spite of a raised life expectancy and increased technological growth, motivated, exceptional minds and intensive teamwork are still the most important corporate capital. Some psychological-scientific experiments demonstrate this: In an experiment that was repeated several times, fifty married couples were briefly given a certain amount of information and later checked to see how much of this information they had retained. Later, the couples were mixed so that none of the married couples were together. The result was a surprise for many people: the married couples remembered much more. The currently accepted explanation of this is that people who know each other very well build up an organizational memory—each knows what the other knows; there is an informal division of labor that has an especially positive effect on the overall efficiency of research groups. It appears that these effects are lost as soon as the size of the group exceeds 250 people. Some researchers see this as the reason that the smallest military fighting unit, the company, has for centuries consisted of 200 soldiers, irrespective of technological developments and modern means of communication.

Tom Allen of the Massachusetts Institute of Technology (MIT) has shown that the intensity of communication at distances greater than fifty meters drops to zero. Whether offices are fifty or five hundred meters apart does not have a significant effect on the intensity or quality of the communication between the offices. In both cases, one must resort to technical or formal means in order to guarantee communication. But formal means are already critical for the emergence of creativity in a group: they destroy the uncertainty of informal contacts that is indispensable in the early stages of the creative process, as German Nobel Prize winner for physics Werner Heisenberg has remarked. This is because creativity thrives on casual relationships, on chance encounters with people one knows from work or whose reputation one esteems and who live in a scientific world different from one's own. It is precisely such people who provide the impulse for new ideas. In this sense, the stairways, corridors, and company cafeterias play a role that cannot be overestimated as stimuli to innovation.

Steven Pinker, a professor of psychology at Harvard University, has shown that human beings have a sophisticated "lie detector" at our disposal, but it only works when we have our interlocutor directly in front of us. Our body language is many times more efficient at transmitting information than e-mails or telephone conversations. Direct contact facilitates the rapid establishment of reputation and, along with it, trust. Without trust, very few people are ready to expose their new creative ideas to the possibility of "public ridicule," as Sir Karl Popper once said.

Now, certain things have changed since the eras of Leonardo and Leibniz. Knowledge has grown exponentially and almost exploded since World War II. Humanity produces more than one million new commercial articles per year. The amount of knowledge that must converge so that a new medication can successfully be brought to market does not just cost

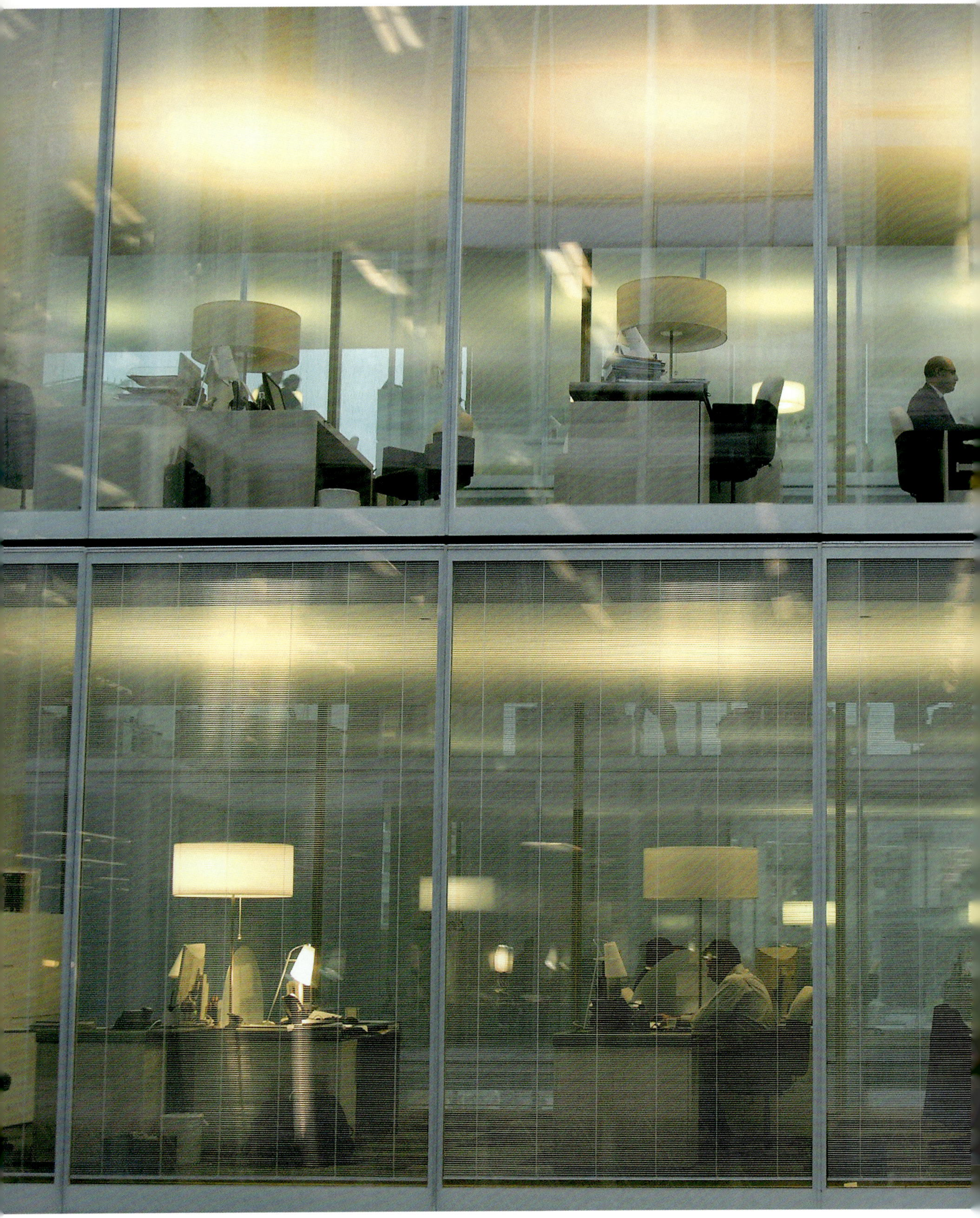

Sejima & Nishizawa (SANAA) with Andrée Putman, side view of the office building at 2 Fabrikstrasse, 2007: Working behind a completely transparent façade

hundreds of millions of Swiss francs, but it also means the deployment of hundreds of specialists. For every large organization this poses the dilemma of facilitating the creative efforts of individuals while at the same time coordinating them and encouraging collaboration. In universities, the initiative, or specialization, is given priority—professors cooperate only reluctantly. Large projects, such as the hunt for elementary particles at the Conseil Européen pour la Recherche Nucléaire (CERN) in Geneva, are the exception. In industry, which wants to develop applications from fundamental research and does not have unlimited time, coordination and cooperation are imperative. In order that this coordination does not limit the scope for freedom too early in the development stages, and thereby impair creativity, it should occur informally and be experienced by the researchers and developers as a natural sort of arrangement.

The monasteries fulfilled this task in the Middle Ages by architectural means: the monks could withdraw to their individual cells, where they could concentrate and pursue their own ideas undisturbed. The coordination of the group occurred on an informal basis in the cloister, where one met with fellow brothers every day and, while conversing, one could "test" one's ideas. Modern scientific research no longer views the era of the medieval monasteries as the Dark Ages, but rather as an innovative period that, with powered mills, open-field agriculture, and the new horse's harness, brought about a significant increase in food production and thereby laid the foundation for later specialization. Recently, the architectural ideas of the monastery have been applied successfully again at the elite Technical University in Munich, in the BMW Development Center, also in Munich, and on the new Novartis Campus in Basel.

A comparison of the old cubicle-style offices with the new open-plan ones shows that communication changes dramatically if people move out of the former into the latter. A study lasting approximately sixty hours of each work setting generated surprising results. In the old cubicle-based environment, discussions took an average of three to five times longer, while in the more open office space, which facilitated four times more social contact, there was nonetheless more time to pursue one's own train of thought.

The individual buildings in the new Campus provide space for about 250 employees, and on every floor the office layout allows for a choice between spaces for large team meetings, short, informal exchanges, or concentrated, individual work. On the ground floor the security measures are reduced to a minimum, thus easing contact with outsiders. The Novartis Campus thereby offers the ideal preconditions for creativity, namely, options. The employees have a choice between communicating or not communicating with others, but at the same time they are operating in an architectural environment that naturally supports communication and coordination, thus ensuring, by the many unplanned moments of social contact, the formation of the new friendships that are so crucial to the generation of new ideas. The Campus itself provides many opportunities for exchange. The challenge has now become the modularization of knowledge, so that less information must flow between the individual buildings of the Campus, but so that within the buildings a very intensive exchange may take place.

Sejima & Nishizawa (SANAA) with
Andrée Putman, 4 Fabrikstrasse, 2007:
A shared, open-plan workplace

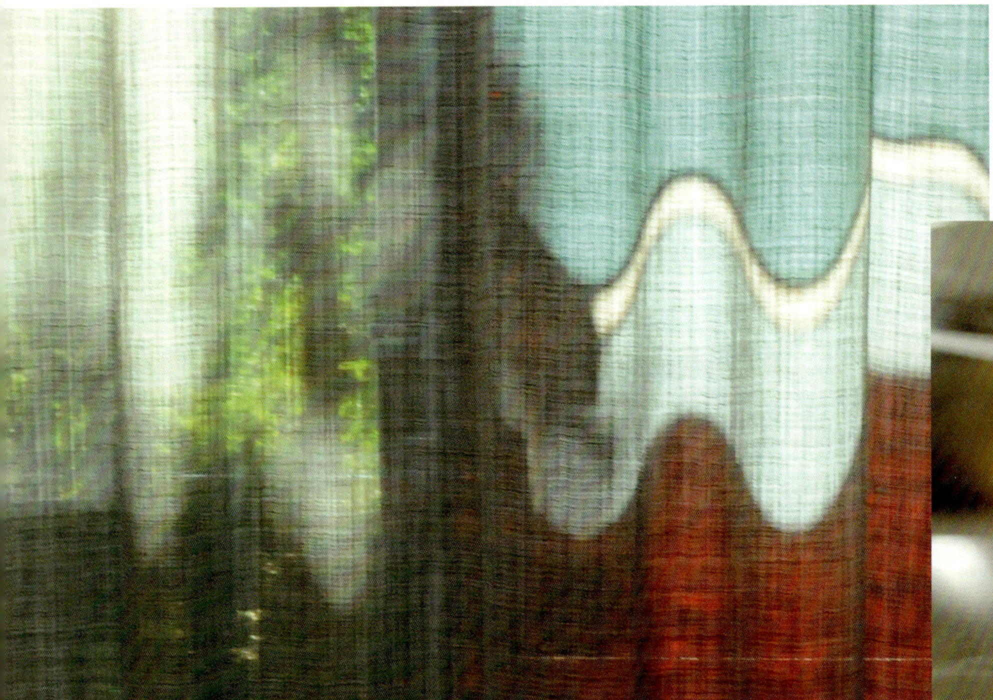

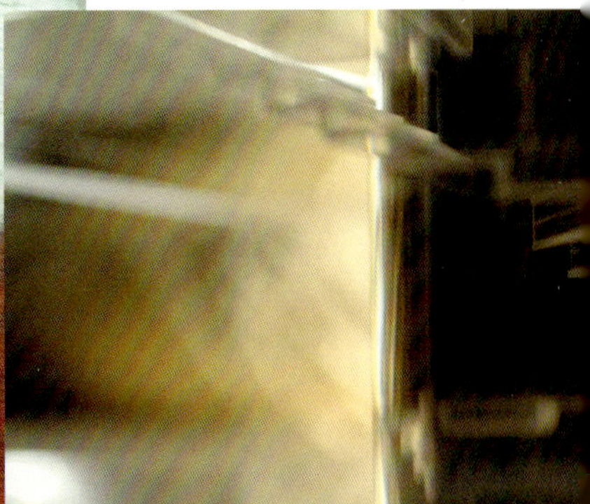

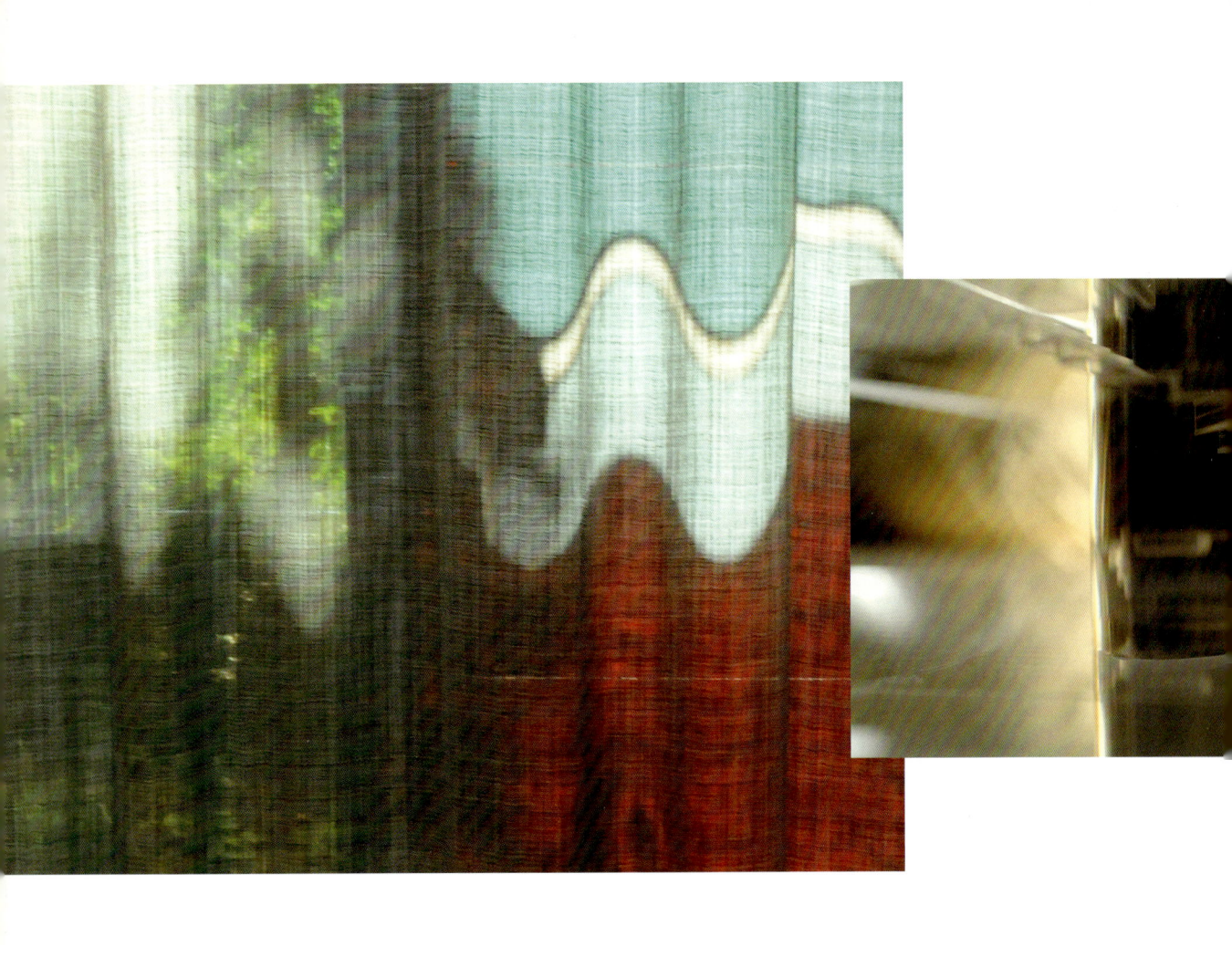

PERSPECTIVES

The Relocation of the Harbor and the Consolidation of the Campus

Markus Christen

In April 2005 the cantonal city government of Basel reached a groundbreaking agreement with the management of Novartis. Under the heading of "The New Use of St. Johann Harbor–Campus Plus," the visions of the Novartis "Campus of Knowledge" that had been launched in 2001 were united with the urban development goals of the canton.

For both partners, the project offers unusual opportunities to realize regional economic and urban development goals in a manner that is both financially sustainable and expedient. At the same time this joint endeavor, given the scale upon which it has been planned, represents a unique collaboration between the public and private sectors.

The canton of the city of Basel is responsible for the renaturation and decontamination of the St. Johann harbor, the establishment of public pedestrian and bicycle paths along the Rhine to Hüningen, and the creation of high-quality living spaces in Schoren.

For its part, Novartis is responsible for the consolidation of the St. Johann Campus, the extension of the park to the Rhine, the impropriation of Hüningerstrasse, and the building of a high-rise area in the north part of the Campus.

The settlement devoted to college activity in the Life Sciences area at the Dreirosen bridgehead will be pursued jointly.

Aerial photograph of the Novartis Campus and its surroundings, 2008

The most important sub-projects of the "Campus Plus" operation are:

1 Relocation, renaturation, and redesigning of the St. Johann harbor
2 Construction site for college use
3 Impropriation of Hüningerstrasse
4 new Hüningen-Basel connection
5 Impropriation of the corner lot at Elsässerstrasse and Hüningerstrasse
6 High-rise "Campus Plus" zone

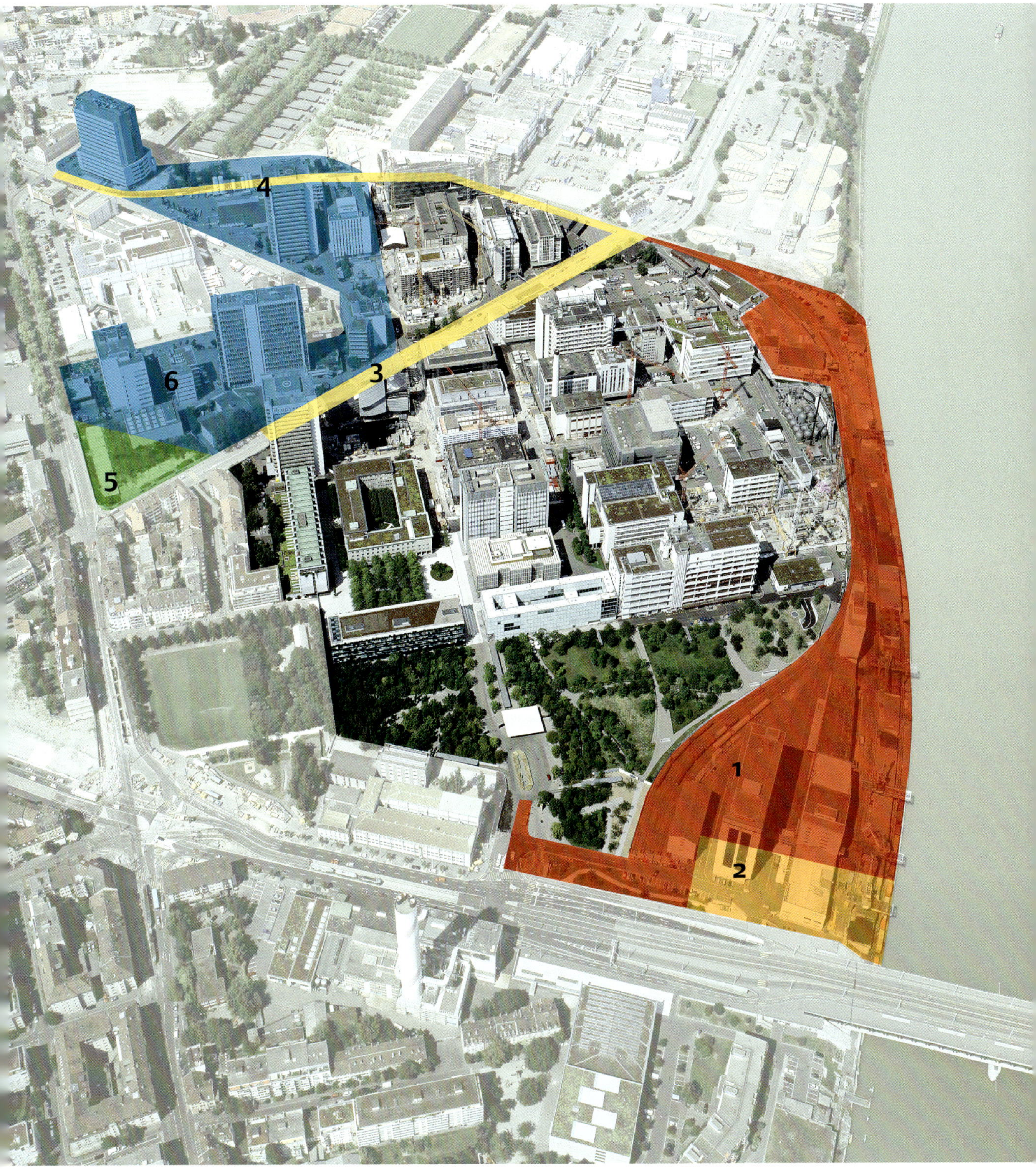
4
3
6
5
1
2

wyhlen

4000 kg
10000 kg

Relicts of the previous use of the St. Johann harbor, 2008: The harbor is relocated in the direction of the city, and an attractive public promenade takes its place along the Rhine.

St. Johann Harbor

In the framework of urban development, the task of transforming the St. Johann Harbor is one of the mid-range goals of the governing council. The project's realization failed at first due to a lack of financing. The agreement reached with Novartis, however, now makes this unique project possible. The negotiations with the firms involved have led to the decision to transfer Dock 2 (Silo) in St. Johann Harbor to Muttenz. At the same time, a public competition for the design of the bank of the Rhine was announced, which Hager International AG won in September 2007.

After the harbor is cleared by the end of 2009, the realization of this project will begin. Once finished, for the first time it will be possible to travel directly to Hüningen from the downtown area on the Basel side of the Rhine.

View from the Rhine of the Novartis Campus with its group of high-rises, rendering by Wettstein Architekten, 2008

Hüningerstrasse

Hüningerstrasse divides the current Novartis grounds in St. Johann into two areas and therefore poses a logistical hurdle. The impropriation will noticeably increase the security of both employees and visitors—thousands of people every day—because the transfer will no longer occur via a public thoroughfare. In this way, Novartis achieves a decided improvement of the functionality of, communication within, and movement on the Campus. Novartis has provided an area in the adjacent community of Hüningen–St. Louis as an adequate replacement for Hüningerstrasse.

The politically responsible entities from the Elsass—the Département du Haut-Rhin, the Sous-Préfecture de Mulhouse, and the communities of St. Louis and Hüningen, as well as the Communauté de Communes des Trois Frontières—together with the superintendents of the Departments of Construction, Economics, and Social Welfare of the canton of the city of Basel and representatives of Novartis analyzed several versions of the street routing and arrived at the best solution, which involves the use of French territory and which was ratified in a framework agreement in May 2007.

With the closing of Hüningerstrassse, the new Avenue de Bale, which was completed in 2008, opened new dimensions for the development of the Novartis Campus.

The High-Rise Zone

The high-rise zone is another strategically significant element of the basic agreement. It is closely related to the purchase and demolition of the residential housing on the corner of Elsässerstrasse and Hüningerstrasse. The high-rise zone gains the needed additional space for expansion from this area.

The interaction of the new, relatively low buildings occupying a large part of the area with preexisting and new high-rises reflects the design concern of the Master Plan and is at the same time important for the efficiency of the use of the northwestern part of the Campus. Therefore, in the interest of optimum land utilization, the previously separated functional groups are being consolidated in high-rises and reorganized. The new building plan was developed by a group of experts comprised of Novartis, canton representatives, and independent experts in close cooperation with the EuroAirport, and other business neighbors. As a first phase, the plan allows for the construction of two high-rises with a maximum height of 120 meters on the property border of the Bell company.

Campus Plus

"The New Use of St. Johann Harbor–Campus Plus" project is an ambitious and very demanding project, which is being realized together with the public sector. It represents a great opportunity for the development of northern Basel (Volta/St. Johann) and makes the optimum development of the Campus possible for Novartis. Since the signing of the basic agreement on April 20, 2005, the project has been implemented and realized step by step. This requires an ongoing dialogue between Novartis and the public sector and offers significant benefits for both.

Above: Urban option of the Rhine bank promenade with paved roadway, Studio di Architettura, rendering, 2006

Right: Landscape option of the Rhine bank promenade with roadway surface framed by water, Studio di Architettura, rendering, 2006: This option was selected and was the basis of the winning competition entry by Hager Landschaftsarchitekten.

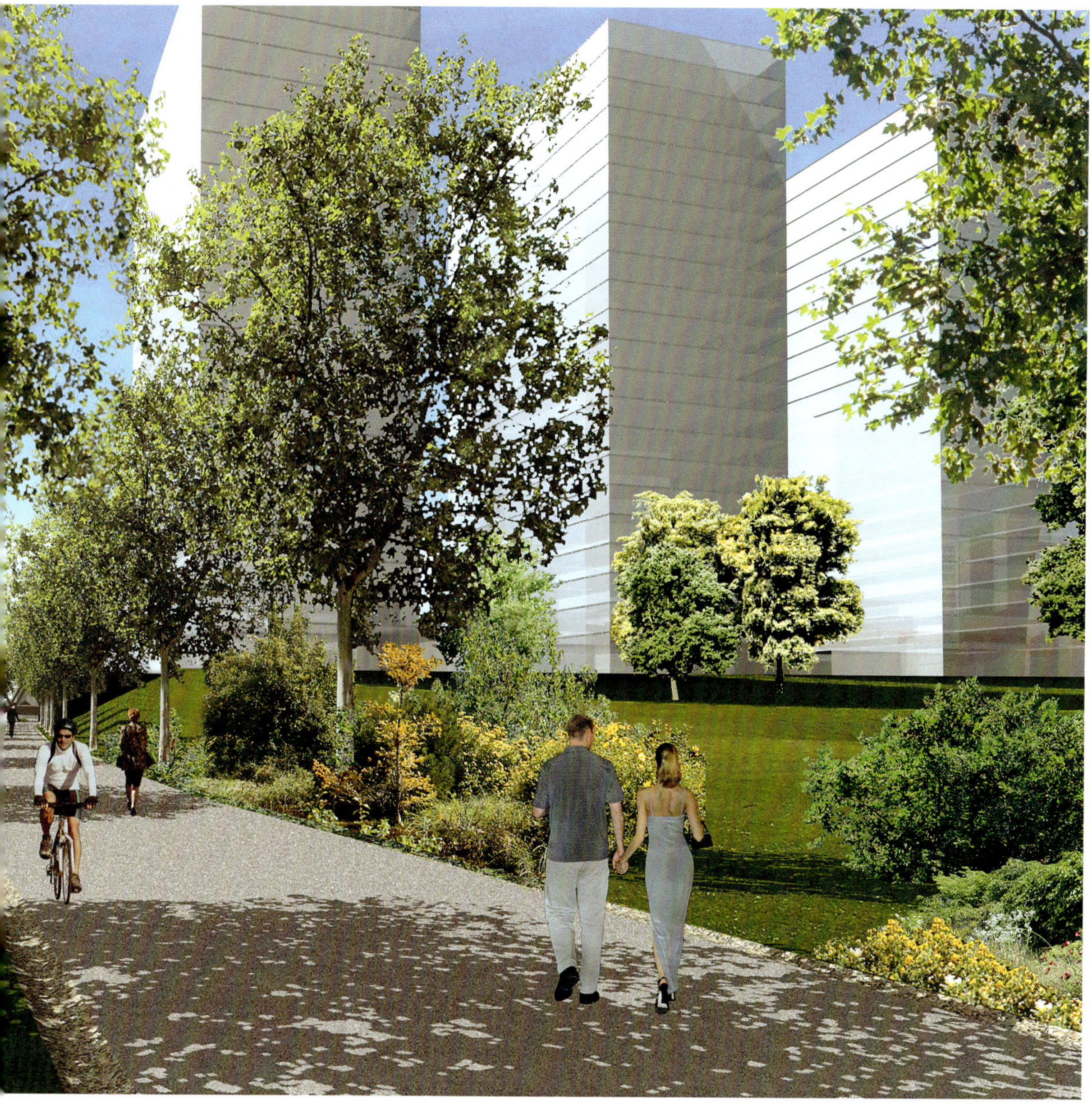

The Design of the Promenade along the Rhine
Guido Hager

Every stretch of waterside in Basel between the Rhine bridges features a different formal character. For the section of the former St. Johann harbor, which is to be transformed into a public promenade, another completely new waterside design was conceived. It is derived from the science of hydraulics. Turbulences occur where impediments like bridgeheads or buildings protrude from the river bank and disturb the quiet flow of the river. In the design, the stream sets the walls optically in oscillation as if they were part of the river, an image of the force of the water. The sweeping lines and the terraced topography are simultaneously developed from the Novartis Campus Park. In spite of the physical boundary between the private Park and the public promenade the whole area is being designed as a whole and not as two independent subunits. The two spheres, that of the Park and that of the Rhine waterside promenade, are woven together. The terracing and the integration of ramps and stairs lead to a situation in which walls arranged in different horizontal layers merge into each other, and separate again. They seem by chance to seek their own ways. Other parameters and constituent magnitudes of the shaping process are minimal path widths and maximum ramp grades as well as various safety aspects.

The Details: Dry Walls, Ramps, and Terraces

Mastering the considerable height difference (ten meters on average) through walls, terraces, ramps, and stairs provides the grounds with a striking profile. The different elements generate a sculptural character and an emphasized volume. The walls are formed from natural stone slabs of varying thicknesses that stand on each other and tilt slightly backwards. This gives them a light, filigree effect that suggests fabric. The result is a widening path profile, which in turn opens the view and connects the walls with the partial meadow embankments. Although the Novartis Campus stands on a stony pedestal overlooking the Rhine, it is not at all forbidding or monumental, but rather playfully scales the differences in height.

The Promenade along the Rhine

The flood-proof Rhine waterside promenade in the area of interest is defined by the supporting walls. The minimal width of the pedestrian and bicycle paths is 4.5 meters and can extend to 11 meters, in order to provide space to linger thanks to the provision of benches and drinking fountains. Wide and narrow zones alternate. Stairs and ramps provide access to the pier at the level of the former Rhine harbor. Changing cubicles, showers, and washrooms are built into the supporting walls.

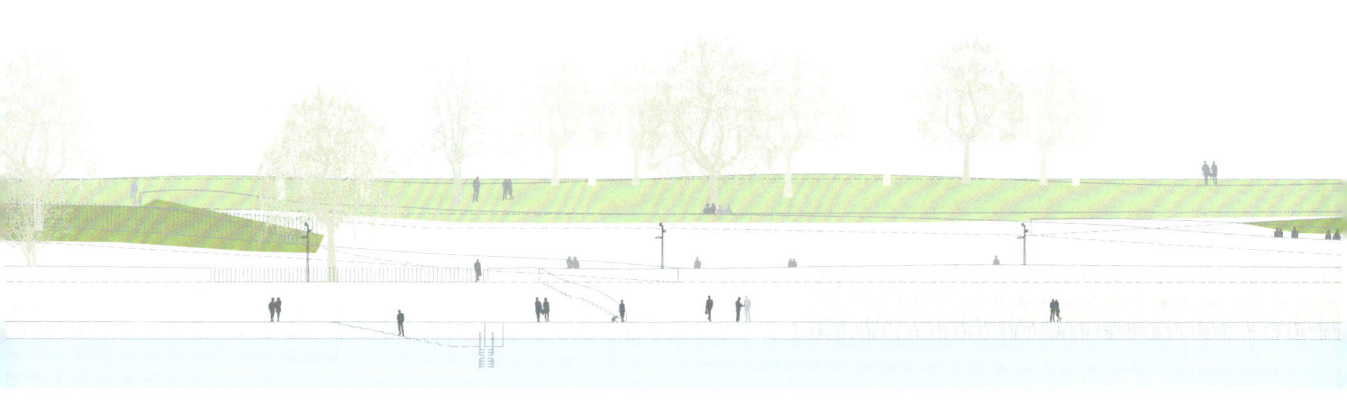

Vegetation and Ecology

On the one hand, the porosity of the dry walls, the paving with dirt-filled joints, and the macadamized surfaces make possible an ecological treatment of the rainwater and on the other hand they provide a dry habitat for warmth-loving plants and animals. The spontaneous growth of grasses, ferns, and moss will accumulate to create a sort of green patina, and as the area becomes successively settled, the walls will slowly be transformed into a hanging garden. The value and significance of the waterside will increase with time, if the ecological niches are successfully established and living communities accommodate one another.

In addition, solitary silver and weeping willows line the waterside promenade. They provide places to relax and hang a vegetative curtain in front of the support walls. They break up the geometry and give the scenery a casual quality. Trees on the ramps and on the terraces provide a thematic as well as spatial connection to the adjacent Novartis Campus Park.

Hager Landschaftsarchitekten, 2008: Embankments and walls extend from the Novartis Park to the two public levels of the Rhine bank paths. A few trees provide a visual connection between the Park and the water. In spite of their height of up to ten meters, the walls look light because of the variability of the terrace height and the integration of ramps and stairs.

Hager Landschaftsarchitekten, 2008: The design of the riverbank introduces a new element in the Basel cityscape. It connects the downtown with Hüningen. The execution of curving lines is inspired by the flow of the river and refers to the design of the Novartis Park.

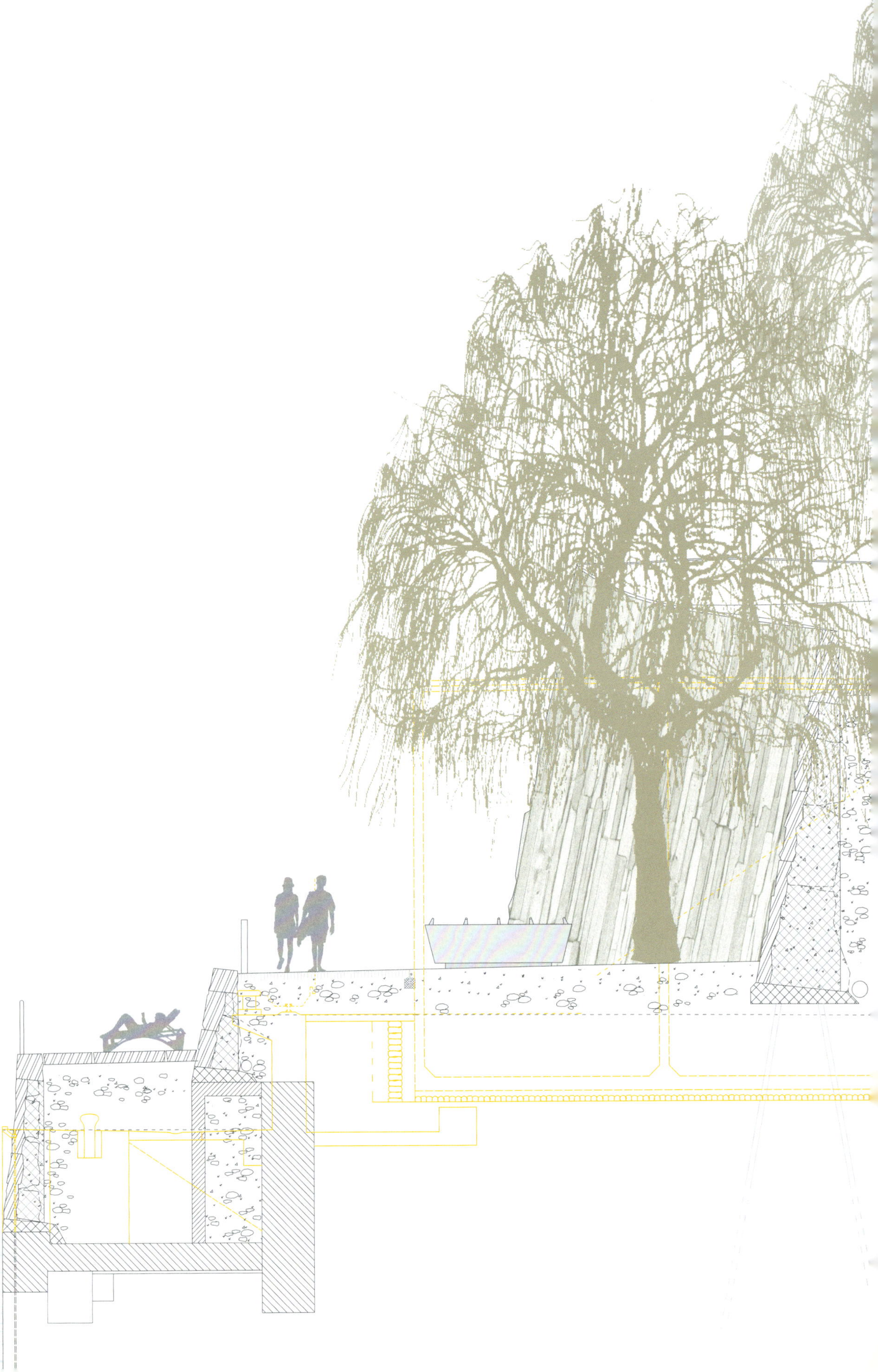

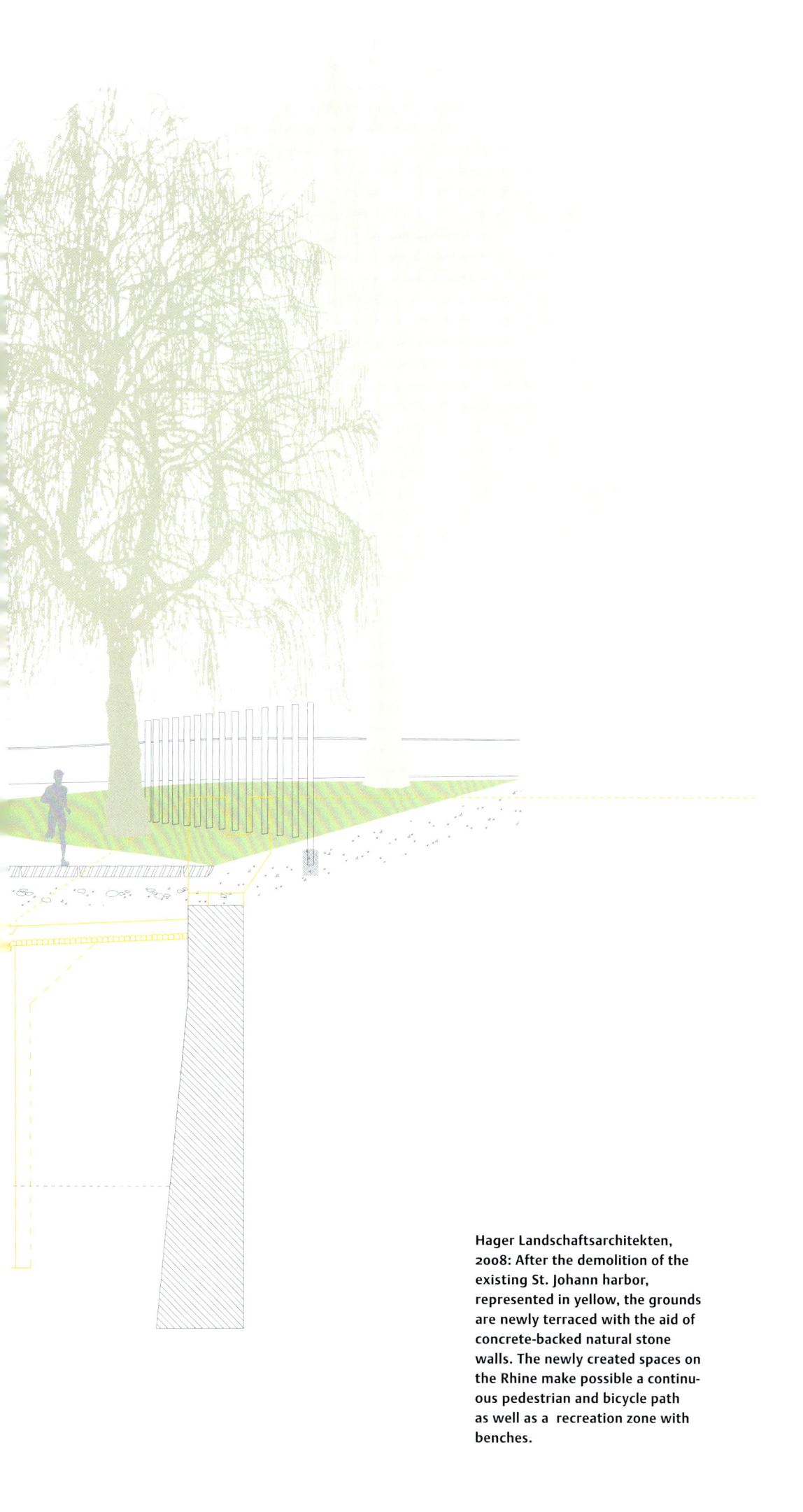

Hager Landschaftsarchitekten, 2008: After the demolition of the existing St. Johann harbor, represented in yellow, the grounds are newly terraced with the aid of concrete-backed natural stone walls. The newly created spaces on the Rhine make possible a continuous pedestrian and bicycle path as well as a recreation zone with benches.

The Extension of the Campus: A Possible Strategy
Vittorio Magnago Lampugnani

In order to investigate the possibility of acommodating more employees on the St. Johann Campus, and to give up provisional locations that have been rented in the city and prepare for the future growth of the company, building expansion of the Campus area was a logical consideration. The adjoining properties in the north would be appropriate for such construction, particularly since the other boundaries of the Campus are defined by Voltastrasse, Elsässerstrasse, and the Rhine. Since such an expansion cannot yet be quantified nor its deadline specified, and since the necessary information is not yet available, only an architectural proposal has been developed.

Both the functional needs and the urban planning conditions in the existing cluster of high-rise buildings encourage further high-rise development. This has been systematized and designed to exploit the maximum approved height of 120 meters, in deliberate contrast to the comparatively low buildings on the rest of the Campus.

Six more high-rises are now to be added to the two high-rise buildings that had already been included in the original Master Plan, forming a large and striking urban form enclosing an equally large park that runs almost east to west. Arranged in two rows and at slightly varying distances from each other, the high-rise buildings are generously spaced, but, at the same time, they lose their isolated quality and gain an urban dimension. The high-rise buildings immediately adjoin Fabrikstrasse, the park by means of a twenty-three-meter-high building that provides an open passage at ground level. Towards Elsässerstrasse, the slightly angled high-rises come right up to the street space, and the park is completely open, offering a generous visual expansion of

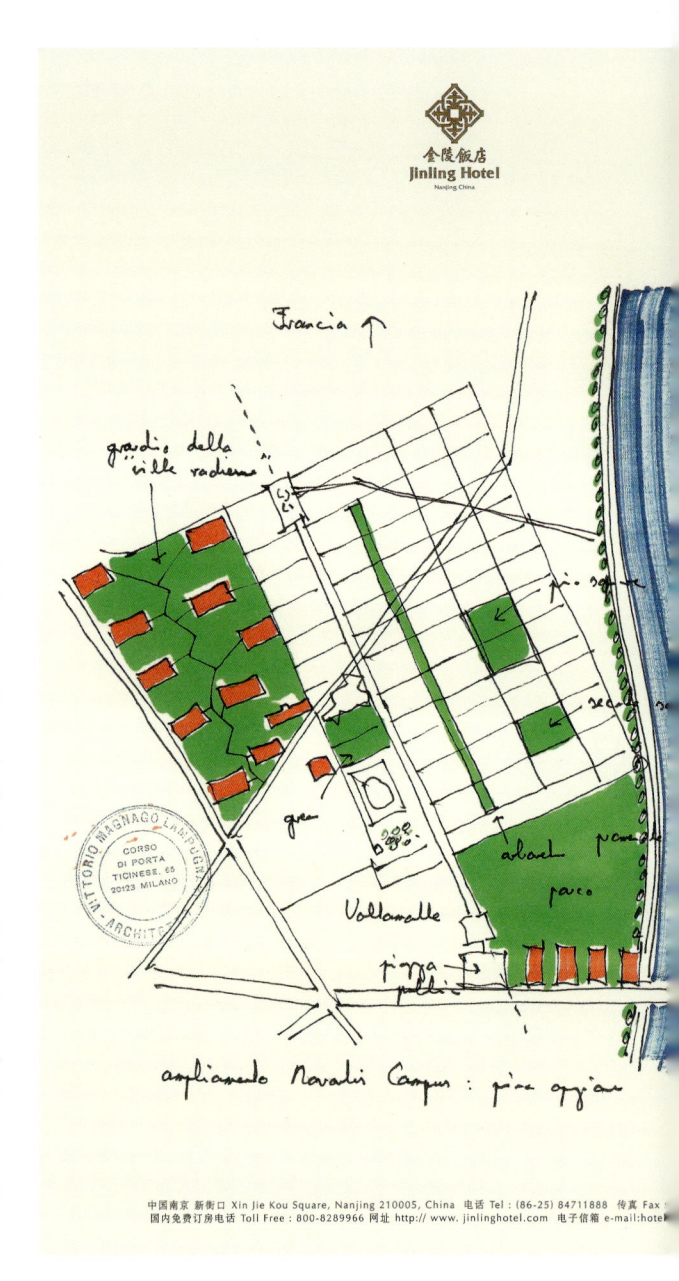

Studies for the high-rise zone,
Vittorio Magnago Lampugnani,
2005

Above: Expansion option with freely arranged high-rises in green

Right: Expansion option with a high-rise group that forms a new open space within the Campus's geometry: This variation will be pursued.

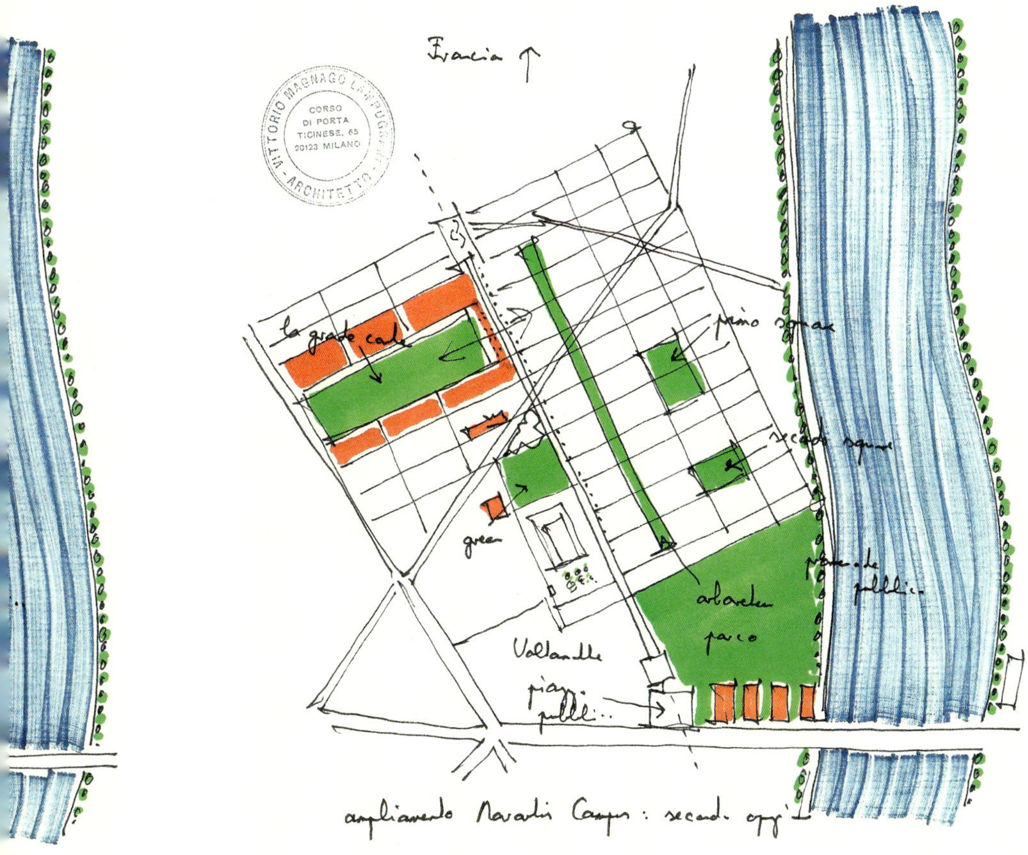

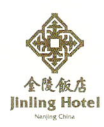

the street itself and a wide opening through which the afternoon sun will be able to shine. Towards the park, the high-rise buildings present a smooth façade that defines the space clearly and sharply; towards the streets, the buildings become smaller step by step in order to let more light in and allow economic ground plans. Overall, the park—which is enclosed by high-rise buildings and corresponds to the Piazzetta on the other side of Fabrikstrasse—creates the appearance of a powerful (and unusual) transverse axis to the street. It not only shapes a location, but also forms a new center of development within the Campus complex.

Around the monumental heart of this complex, the structure of streets and squares continues regularly and quietly to the north without any surprises, and to the south with another high-rise that mediates between "The Quadrangle" ensemble and the existing hundred-meter-tall building on Hüningerstrasse.

The decision not only to incorporate Hüningerstrasse into the Campus, but also to build over it, relieved the Master Plan of a geometric problem that had historical roots, although it contributed to its spatial richness. A comparable enrichment was therefore needed in order to replace it, but it was not possible to force this upon the Cartesian arrangement pattern arbitrarily. For this reason, the transverse axis—half of which was already marked out by the high-rise structure with the central park—was continued towards the northeast, once again as a wide green strip, but enclosed this time not by high-rises, but instead asymmetrically by twenty-three-meter-high laboratory buildings on one side and narrow service buildings on the other. This produced an easy link to the Piazzetta, which thus becomes part of the axis, as well as a generous opening towards the river area of the Rhine and the hills on the other shore.

The Novartis Campus, working model, 2007: Eight high-rises frame a large park (The Quadrangle), which together with the Piazzetta forms an impressive lateral axis with Fabrikstrasse.

This opening not only represents a spatialization of the principle of an openness towards the Rhine, on which the whole Master Plan is based, but also provides a new potential developmental line for future expansion, since the closure of the waste treatment plant on the other side of the French border will free up areas there that will be suitable for leisure and sports facilities, as well as for further building.

The City and the Campus
Fritz Schumacher

A discussion between Fritz Schumacher, a canton architect, and Ulrike Zophoniasson, an architecture journalist

Ulrike Zophoniasson: In its structure the Novartis Campus has a very urban effect, and with the expanded services it offers it also displays the characteristics of a city. But city districts are permeable as a rule. In contrast, this area is a closed piece of private property. From an overall urban standpoint, is the Campus thereby a part of the city or is it a city within the city?

Fritz Schumacher: As long as something is being produced on the grounds, then fencing them off will always be necessary for security reasons. The Master Plan, however, in no way sees this as compulsory. Maybe the opening (of the Campus grounds) is only a question of time. Basically, the metamorphosis from "work area" to "Campus" should be understood as a definite sign of a change in self-conception. In that regard, what the Campus offers is actually moving quite far in the direction of autonomous self-sufficiency and thereby represents increased competition for the city. What is involved here is without a doubt a certain resemblance to the classic Anglo-Saxon campus. But unlike that model, just because it incorporates certain elements of a basic urban provision of services, it is not an "ersatz city"; it is by no means an autarkical system. In that sense, in spite of its close proximity to the existing city, it in no way represents a threat or competition. The city would exist without the Campus. On the other hand, the Campus needs the city, because with its manifold residential, cultural, recreational, and, last but not least, transportation services it provides the needed infrastructure. This is something the Campus does not provide itself, but urgently requires—especially because it wishes to attract scientists from the around the world with its appealing surroundings. The word "campus" may be a misnomer here. In central Europe today, the term calls to mind a large, interdisciplinary research complex that is a by and large autonomous, citylike organism. It would thereby not be living space but merely one work location among many and clearly therefore part of the city.

UZ: It is a part of the city, but one which as a private entity of an internationally active firm is organized differently and lays claim to a high degree of freedom in its development and decisions. How does one approach the Campus in a responsible way from the standpoint of the city as a whole?

FS: The firm has a great economic significance for the city canton. It is therefore in the interest of the city as a whole that the framework conditions necessary to Novartis's development and growth be achieved politically. In addition, the government is naturally responsible for the physical city. On company property itself—as long as the development occurs within the prescribed zones—the freedom for design is great. The first point of interest for the city as a whole are the interfaces, that is to say, those areas where city and Campus meet one another. And since the area is not located in a "green pasture" like an American campus, the question of what these places of contact must provide and how they are designed is of great significance for both sides. If the city and Novartis both put the larger urban planning connections in the foreground, and thereby pull together and act in concert, the development of these interfaces will be a gain in synergy for the city as a whole. And the Campus in turn will profit as a part of that whole.

UZ: Where are these areas of interface exactly?

FS: They have already been envisioned in the Master Plan of the Campus and concretely defined in "The New Use of St. Johann Harbor–Campus Plus." "Campus Plus" was developed jointly by representatives of the city of Basel and Novartis and connects the urban planning concerns with the intended extension of the Campus. The project itself consists of several sub-projects. For the city as a whole, an important component of the cooperation agreement is the sale of the St. Johann harbor area. In return,

Visualization of the ProVolta buildings seen from Kannenfeldplatz (view from the high-rises at Kannenfeldplatz in the direction of the Novartis Campus), Kunz und Mösch Architekten, 2008

a new pedestrian and bicycle promenade will be built along the Rhine. The area on the Dreirosen bridgehead will become a location for university training and research facilities with a focus on life sciences. In addition, the canton will turn over Hüningerstrasse to the Campus, and Novartis will withdraw from the Schoren area, in order to make room for the construction of new housing.

UZ: But what does that mean in terms of a gain in synergy? And can this agreement become something more than a give and take, a mutual transaction?

FS: For instance, the desire to beautify the Rhine's riverbank and the indispensable elimination of certain "urban blockades" were matters that had already been addressed by the urban planners. But without an acute need to act, the city simply did not have the energy to initiate the necessary political decisions. The reconstruction plans for the adjoining Novartis grounds actually created a window of opportunity, and the "Campus Plus" plan set in motion the dynamic that was necessary to expedite and proceed in a financially affordable way.

The reorganization of the harbor facility represented a similar opportunity. In this case, also the decision to dismantle the St. Johann harbor was in no way a threat for the water management. Quite to the contrary, it was the trigger to reorganize the entire harbor area and to modernize its facilities. It was once again the activity in St. Johann that generated the boost needed to propel the development of the harbor and the logistical hub of Basel.

In my eyes, from an overall urban development perspective the most important element of the basic agreement is in fact the bridgehead building area. In the ranking of international colleges, the size and the quality of the institutions play an important role. The university will seize the opportunity and establish a new area for teaching and research in cooperation with the ETH Zürich and the Friedrich-Miescher-Institut. Meanwhile, the test planning to define the location of the university has begun, and the invitation to bid for the commission will be issued over the course of next year.

This bridgehead will be the "city partner" of the Campus, because we will uphold the European tradition that believes that the private and public spheres should not mix, but rather approach one another in a relationship of mutual excitement. This statement should also become visible in the realms of architecture and urban planning.

UZ: Is there not a danger that through collaboration with other institutes of the university and the ETH Zürich that a part of the college will take on a life of its own and mutate into an independent campus?

FS: No. The college is and will remain a part of the city. It is already true that individual points of focus are locally concentrated, which in no way contradicts this policy. The scientific institutes have long since taken the leap outside the city ring and are lining up in a row in the direction of St. Johann. Rather, I see that with this additional step the city is advancing beyond Voltastrasse and thereby reaching a city district that is currently involved in an exciting process of renovation and fresh design.

UZ: A process, however, that was not initiated by the Campus, but rather by the construction of the city autobahn, which now crosses all of Basel-North underground?

FS: Yes. Here it was also clear from the beginning that the construction of the northern highway tangent would not only relieve through traffic in the affected city district, but an added value would accrue to the benefit of the city district. The urban planning annexation program "Pro-Volta" was in that sense never thought of as a palliative measure, but was intended instead to provide the needed impulse for long-term upgrading. This program has been conspicuously successful. It was particularly gratifying that large scale projects initiated by the government along Voltastrasse have in the meantime been joined by many private initiatives, a development which guarantees the sustainability of the upgrade. The transformation of an until now rather egregiously unattractive industrial area into an architecturally ambitious urban planning-designed "Campus of Knowledge" is a happy coincidence that will now give an added boost to development in the district. The establishment of 10,000 highly qualified jobs will without a doubt have a positive effect on the area's user structure. And those in charge will see to it that, with yet other new living, working, and recreational aspirations, the unavoidable displacement in such circumstances does not get out of hand and that "development" also means a chance for advancement for the local population.

UZ: What will this city district look like in the future?

FS: It will be a denser, livelier, and more attractive residential and work area whose transformation will become inscribed in the cityscape, which will be even further enhanced by the new Campus high-rises. With its new waterside design along the Rhine, it will expand more self-consciously in the direction of Alsace and in its urbanity it will be prized by its users, because it will have successfully graduated from a migration stopover to a city district with international flair.

Visualization of the ProVolta buildings as seen from the Novartis Campus (view from Novartis high-rise Building 210 to the southwest), Kunz und Mösch Architekten, 2008

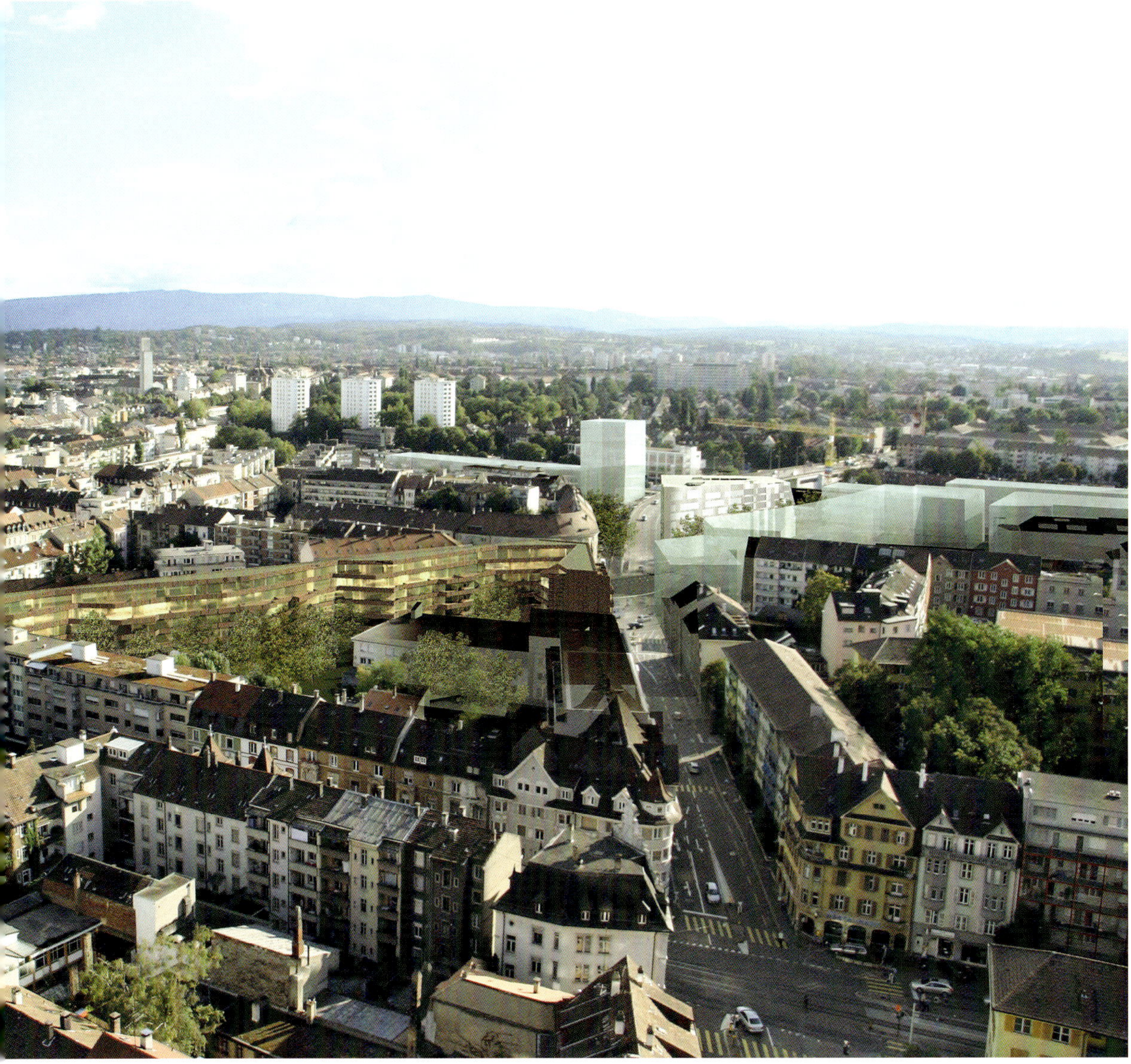

From the Confinement of Heterotopia to the Urbanity of Novartis Ville

Richard Ingersoll

Although mankind has always toiled, the concept of "work," whereby one's time to perform a service is assigned a monetary value, is a relatively recent one. During the early nineteenth century, as the system of wage labor took hold in industrialized cities, new building types and urban arrangements were created exclusively for work, both for manufacture and for management. The mills and warehouses of Manchester, along with the counting halls and bureaus of London's banks and insurance companies, established the prototypes that would dramatically alter the scale and social mix of modern cities. Buildings became little cities unto themselves while entire streets and districts were taken over by a single type of activity. No one lived in the superb, vaulted chambers of John Soane's Bank of England, nor did anyone work, except for the domestic servants, in John Nash's palatial terrace houses overlooking Regent's Park. As the distinction between work and life grew, cities began to grow according to a logic of segregation that was eventually consecrated by zoning legislation in the twentieth century. The contemporary city in the developed world has been increasingly broken into discreet enclaves by the demands of industrial compounds, commercial centers, and business parks.

Looking back to the outset of the industrial revolution, the most significant precedents resulted in grand landscapes of complete architectural unity, such as Claude-Nicholas Ledoux's Saltworks at Chaux and Thomas Jefferson's University of Virginia in Charlottesville. Although the Salines de Chaux, built in the 1770s near Besançon with the royal sponsorship of Louis XV, were only partly completed as a half oval, the project beautifully represents the desire to exercise complete architectural control over the work environment and, by extension, to exercise physical and psychological authority over the workers. The colossal, rusticated temple front of the director's building in the center is locked in a radial relationship with the surrounding workers' lodges, as a theater's stage is to its auditorium. At a time when workers were treated only slightly better than slaves and prisoners, the fortified and surveilled environment met the real need to prevent workers from running away.[1]

By contrast, Thomas Jefferson's campus project in Charlottesville, built during the first quarter of the nineteenth century, was without repressive intentions, even if it initially included housing for the African slaves who accompanied their young masters to college. As

[1] Vidler, Anthony. *Claude-Nicolas Ledoux: Architecture and Social Reform at the End of the Ancien Régime* (Cambridge, Mass., 1990).

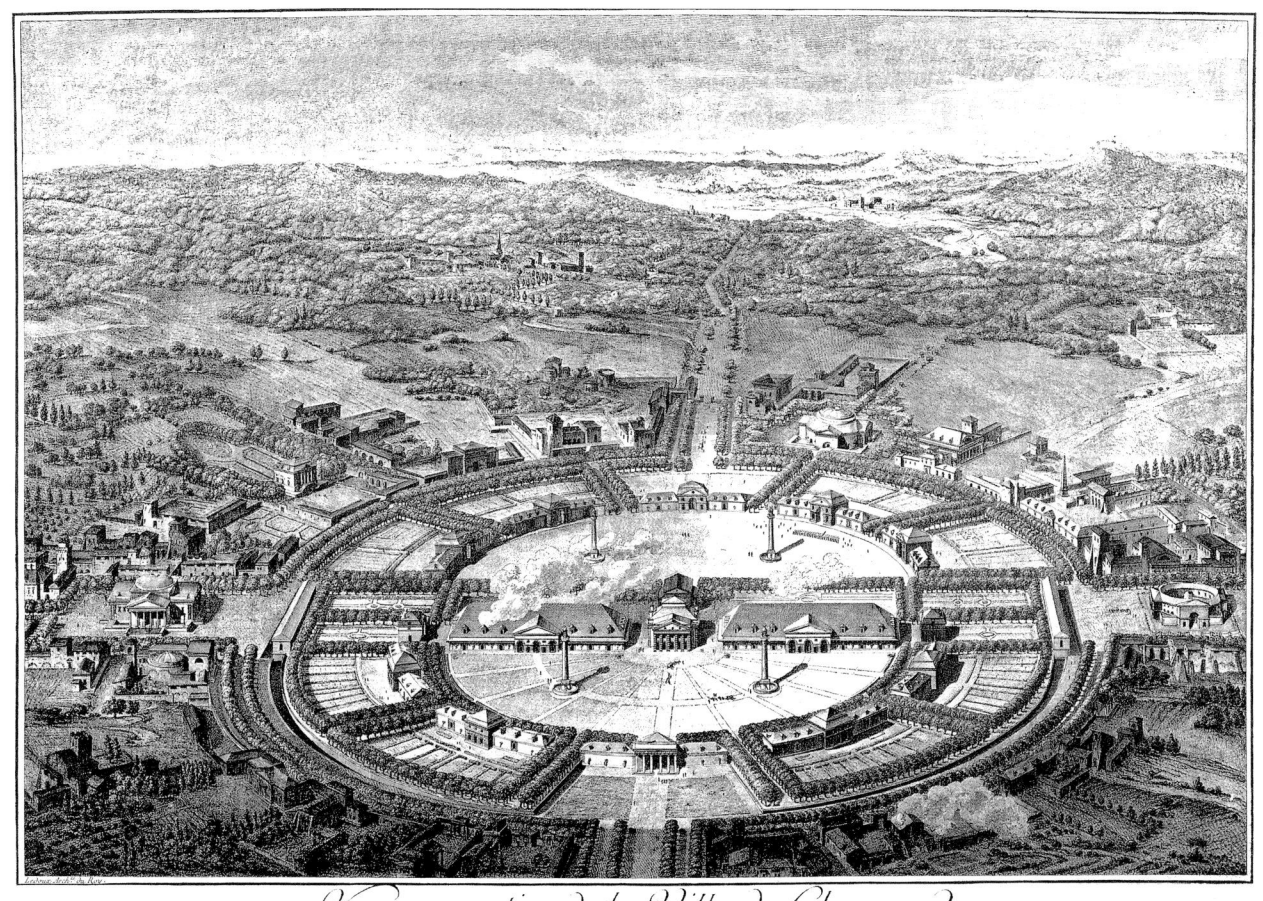

Bird's-Eye View of Salines de Chaux
by Claude-Nicolas Ledoux, 1804,
copper engraving

the world's first completely secular university, it was intended to serve as a place for the exchange of ideas in complete freedom. Nonetheless, Jefferson set the campus in isolation from the distractions of the town and hoped to shape and control the tastes and lifestyle of the students through his architectural code of white columns and grand vistas. A half-scale simulacrum of the Pantheon stands at the head of a series of ten individually decorated Neoclassical houses linked by classical colonnades on either side of the vast, grassy mall. The effect is like perusing an encyclopedia of classical architecture against the backdrop of the greater world of nature at the end of the mall. The University of Virginia, like Chaux, pursued a totalizing architectural vision in which all of the pieces were congruous elements of a grand geometric scheme.

Such early enclaves, autarchic in nature, led the contemporary philosopher Michel Foucault to speculate in 1967 on their social implications as landscapes of control, a category he called "heterotopia."[2] Foucault's heterotopia can be defined as an isolated environment, usually boasting a distinct architectural identity, that is set apart from the city to follow its own rules and reproduce society on its own terms. According to Foucault, places such as company towns and university campuses that are autonomous in terms of time and place tend to "create a space that is other, another real space, as perfect, as meticulous, as well arranged as ours is messy, ill constructed, and jumbled."[3] The order of the medieval monastery set off against the disorder of the city established a type that has been repeated for a wide variety of different spaces, such as cemeteries, prisons, schools, hospitals, and, during the twentieth century, universities and office parks.

Many of the efforts to reform the working environment during the past two centuries have involved investments in the culture and welfare of the workers. Among the most successful was Saltaire, a complete Victorian company town designed in 1851 for Titus Salt's alpaca wool factory. The patron, who was a key political figure in the Bradford region, provided solidly built, well-ventilated workers' housing, a church, a cultural center, a mess hall, public baths, allotment orchards, and a large public park with sports fields, while eliminating the tavern from the urban context. The settlement's most original feature was an almshouse for retired workers. While a strictly paternalistic proposition, Saltaire furnished the earliest demonstration that industry did not have to be a completely degrading experience and set the liberal agenda for housing reform for the next few decades.

[2] Jack Quinan, *Frank Lloyd Wright's Larkin Building: Myth and Fact* (Cambridge, Mass., 1987).
[3] Michel Foucault, "Of Other Spaces," in *Diacritics* 16 (Spring 1986), 22–27.

The limits in the internal cohesion of modern heterotopias become clear when the enclave is forced to confront the conflict of urban reality. The static and intolerant order of the enclave proves incompatible with the changing and dynamic situation of the city. In the Pullman strike of 1894, for example, the workers who lived in a well-planned company town with many of the features of Saltaire rebelled against the uncompromising dictates of their heterotopia. They could no longer endure the situation of wage-slavery, in which they were forced to pay almost everything they earned as rent to the factory owner. One way to avoid such conflict was to include the workers in the business. This was the strategy of Jean-Baptiste André Godin, an ardent follower of the socialist theories of Charles Fourier. During the 1860s he established the Familstère at Guise, a small city in the industrial triangle of northern France. In a single complex he provided apartments of a variety of sizes, collective dining halls, educational facilities and nurseries, and a theater as an adjunct to his factory for cast-iron goods. In 1880, Godin converted the operation into a cooperative, owned and managed by the workers. As the physical realization of socialism, the Familstère, an enclave composed of three linked courtyard structures roofed over by glass ceilings, took on heroic proportions. For a few generations, utopia inhabited heterotopia, but as Émile Zola remarked after his visit, the dull regimentation of the Familstère lacked the vitality of the city.

Among the most innovative efforts to improve the comfort and social life of the enclave type without collectivization came with the Larkin Administration Building (demolished in 1950) in Buffalo, New York, designed in 1904 by Frank Lloyd Wright. The architect and his patron, Darwin T. Martin, attempted to create a palace of labor for this mail-order soap company, fitted with sculptures, fountains, an organ for noontime concerts, a hothouse for a botanical garden, a dignified dining hall, and democratic inscriptions: "Honest labor needs no master, simple justice needs no slaves." Wright radically altered the office genre, placing the major typing pool in a central four-story atrium. The smaller offices were stacked around this inner court with open balconies overlooking it. Many of the features that are taken for granted in contemporary buildings can be traced back to Wright's innovations: the open plan office, built-in filing cabinets, radiant floor heating, air-conditioning, steel furniture, and wall-hung toilets. The Larkin Building's windowless elevations enforced its role as a sort of fish tank for labor, yielding a classic heterotopia sealed off from the rest of the city.

Frank Lloyd Wright, Larkin
Company Administration Building,
Buffalo, New York, 1902–06

[4] Antonio Román, *Eero Saarinen: An Architecture of Multiplicity* (New York, 2003).

The business enclave reached a new level of development in the 1950s and '60s during the postwar automobile industry boom in the U.S. The earliest corporate headquarters to relocate from the center cities to the suburbs willfully imitated the aesthetic of the university campuses. They elaborated on the Jeffersonian ideal of juxtaposing culture and nature. Eero Saarinen, with his compounds for General Motors in Warren, Michigan (1949–56), and the Deere & Company headquarters (manufacturers of tractors) in Moline, Illinois (1957–63), introduced the prototype for idyllic, parklike settings supplemented with convivial clublike dining halls.[4] Many imitations have ensued, such as IBM's corporate suburb of Solana, built in the mid 1980s twenty kilometers west of Dallas by Mitchell/Giurgola and Ricardo Legorreta, or the B. Braun pharmaceutical headquarters by Stirling and Wilford in rural Melsungen, Germany (twenty kilometers south of Kassel), completed in 1992. These projects, located in faraway suburbs, are efficient in simplifying working relations and providing more space, but consume precious rural lands and force the workers to commute long distances.

Aside from wasting land and diverting resources away from the crossing paths of the city, suburban corporate enclaves are frequently alienating. A heterotopia makes people aware of their status within the enclave but insecure in their relations with the rest of the world. Working in the controlled enclave environment is almost like being trapped in a reality show. Despite the pleasant landscapes and sense of protection of corporate campuses, their isolation eliminates the possibility of acquiring "street smarts," that special type of intelligent adaptation that occurs in the urban setting where there is a lot of unpredictable social interaction. Even a large headquarters that has remained in the downtown core of a city will often produce the same sort of anomie found in the isolated rural heterotopia. One of America's leading corporations, Proctor & Gamble, threatened to move elsewhere if it were not granted permission to expand into a four-block area of downtown Cincinnati. Between 1982 and 1985, their architects Kohn Pedersen Fox forged an emphatic vision of power centered on twin octagonal towers linked to long wings of offices with glistening marble facades. The large private gardens, ringed with trellises and patrolled by private police, have been carefully studied to create a *"cordon sanitaire"* to buffer the shiny, white headquarters buildings from the rest of the city. Despite its central urban position, Proctor & Gamble remains as divorced from the rest of Cincinnati as the Vatican is from Rome; the badge-wearing employees move about like collar-clad priests, remote from the secular affairs of urban life.

Architects have been to some degree to blame for the proliferation of heterotopias when they propose perfected models of containment to their clients. In 1959, Louis I. Kahn was approached by Nobel laureate Jonas Salk to design a research center in La Jolla, California to which the scientist "might also invite Picasso." Kahn produced an ingenious interlocking system of loftlike laboratories, with their services tucked into the deep trusses. The work space is connected by a few steps to secluded, wood-paneled studies that obliquely overlook a central court. This space, more of a void than a court, was designed with the advice of the Mexican architect Luis Barragàn as a stark travertine plane interrupted by a ribbon of water borrowed from the Alhambra. The space frames a magnificent panorama of the Pacific coast, a hard materials variation on Jefferson's grassy mall. Like a primeval *temenos,* the enclosure has become a space of dread that few people dare to enter. While astonishingly beautiful, the atmosphere of the Salk Institute is so abstract that even the proverbial absent-minded professor, swept up in his research, feels a greater degree of solitude here than he would desire, or than is healthy.

Nearly forty years later, Gerald Edelstein of the nearby Neuroscience Institute proposed to his architects, Todd Williams and Billy Tsien, that they subvert Kahn's antisocial prototype and fill the center with pathways and activities, so that "one's point of view would change with each step." They built a concert hall as the central focus of a public plaza and exposed the laboratories to a partial view from this same space. Various pedestrian paths meander through the plaza and over the rooftops of the labs, allowing visual contact among the parts at various points. People pass through the space for a variety of reasons, including just loitering.

One of the more successful corporate headquarters of the last two decades, the ING bank built by Alberts and Van Huut in the Bijlmer suburb of Amsterdam in 1982 (and first known as the NMB bank), demonstrates that a large office complex can meaningfully mingle with the urban environment. The expressionistic design of the towers was partly generated by numerous ecological considerations, which made the buildings the most energy-efficient offices in Europe. The ING bank project's most interesting feature, however, was to conceive of the campus as a series of ten linked towers casually clustered around an urban plaza that connects to the metro station. As in all banks, the entries are carefully controlled, but around the plaza the corporate structure shares space with shops and housing and participates in the daily life of the city. Both the pleasant interior conditions of the offices and the feeling of permeability with the urban setting engage the bank with the city. The new headquarters measurably increased worker productivity, and the office environment became a sensual experience that inspired a sense of community. The enclave remained but gracefully dissimulated its role as a heterotopia.

The capacity to assimilate urban qualities is what will allow the new Novartis Campus to move beyond the conventions of the typical corporate enclave. Perhaps one day it will be known as Novartis Ville, a place that will seem as vital as Basel's historic center. What once was an uninviting cul-de-sac crowded predominantly with industrial structures is being transformed into a stunning, post-industrial office park with buildings and artworks by celebrated designers. Considering the site, however, there is no way that it could *not* be perceived as an enclave: the area is hemmed in by the French border on the north, the River Rhine on the east, a multi-lane highway to the south, and a fragmented residential neighborhood on the west. Once infamous for its pollution and a disastrous chemical fire, the renewed district will in time be admired as a paragon of urban hygiene and environmentally friendly architecture.

While the promoters currently refer to the Novartis plan as a "campus," like an American university campus, the underlying goal is in fact to produce the feeling of a small city. The layout thus follows a rational grid of well-proportioned pedestrian streets in which each of the fifty or more buildings takes the form of an urban block. Both the company's mercurial CEO, Dr. Daniel Vasella, and his level-headed planner, architect Vittorio Magnago Lampugnani of Milan, insist that the urban analogy will stimulate the most creative working environment. They hope in time to approximate the historic city's wealth of social and cultural networks and the serendipity of its dense urban situations. The Novartis plan, while kept separate from the rest of Basel by a broad glacis of landscaping, attempts to echo the urban weave of the historic city. Rather than emphasizing its isolation, the architects have consciously made the Campus appear as if the buildings belong to the fabric, scale, and variety of the greater urban whole. Lampugnani has enforced the analogue of the little city in an effort to break out of the alienating effects of heterotopia.

Perhaps the most interesting part of the Novartis process has been the clash between Lampugnani's idea of architecture and that of his patron. The architect, squarely in the rationalist tradition, aspires to the no-nonsense *kleinstadt* approach of the early-twentieth-century German architect Heinrich Tessenow. His perspective drawing of Fabrikstrasse, published in the Master Plan of 2002, shows a series of sensible buildings that defer to the scale and materiality of the original headquarters building. The uniform, stone-clad façades are intended to convey a solid sense of utilitarian purpose. Vasella's idea, however, is closer to that of the art collector. He acquired a conspicuous Richard Serra sculpture, *Dirk's Pod,* to use as a filter for the entry from the parking lot across the French border, and then commissioned the Frank O. Gehry building as a centerpiece for the Campus. In this he seems to be keeping up with another "collector of architecture," Rolf Fehlbaum, CEO of Vitra, a prominent Basel-based corporation that commissioned the first Gehry building in Europe, as well as projects by Tadao Ando and Zaha Hadid. Vasella's ambition in hiring famous architects is that each new building will be a potential masterpiece that adds symbolic capital to his company's profile.

Aside from works by coveted architects, Vasella also wanted each building to have some special attractions, including a noteworthy work of art and a good restaurant. SANAA's building is so transparent it nearly disappears and, like the sets in Jacques Tati's film *Playtime,* it keeps people guessing as to where the doorway is. On the ground floor it hosts a delicately appointed Japanese restaurant. Diener & Diener's headquarters building, aside from its scintillating chromatic façade, contains a magnificent rosewood spiral staircase connecting the second and third levels and a tropical arboretum on the upper four floors of its west end. Märkli's building displays a prominent Jenny Holzer LED screen on the attic of its portico. The flickering moralisms of the artist's sayings tease those who work for the multinational: "you are a victim of the rules you live by," "everyone's work is equally important," "the abuse of power comes as no surprise." The words pass so quickly that one can hardly grasp the messages, and one can almost imagine reading a line inspired by the recent

Film still from Jacques Tati's
Playtime, 1965

ethical skirmish with India: "drugs should not be the privilege of wealth." The possibility that this sort of ideological contradiction could occur is what makes the Novartis Campus already feel urban. The attitude of the buildings and the artworks challenges the stuffy conformism of the typical corporate enclave. The openness, transparency, and variety found in the nascent little city of Novartis Ville give it a critical advantage as a place of creativity. By fostering a contrast between the utilitarian repetition of the urban block type with the hedonist variety of their contents and cladding, the planners have generated a dynamic scenario that promises to supplant the heterotopian beginnings of a corporate campus with an increasingly urban way of life.

Author Biographies

Roman Boutellier (born in 1950) has been a professor of technology and innovation management at the Swiss Federal Institute of Technology Zurich since 2004 and an honorary professor at the university in St. Gallen since 1999. In the past, he has also occupied leading positions at various firms.

Albert Buchmüller (born in 1957) has been responsible for the coordination of the exterior design aspect of the Novartis Campus's Master Plan and Novartis plant requirements since 2001. After studying process engineering, he went to work for Ciba-Geigy AG in 1980, and then for Novartis in engineering services.

Jacqueline Burckhardt (born in 1947) is an art historian and critic who serves as art advisor for the Novartis Campus. She is co-publisher and editor of the art magazine *Parkett,* a reader at the Accademia di architettura of the Università della Svizzera italiana in Mendrisio, and director of the Summer Academy of the Zentrum Paul Klee in Bern.

Markus Christen (born in 1959) is currently directing the "New Use of St. Johann Harbor–Campus Plus" project for Novartis and is responsible for the collaboration with the city canton of Basel that this project requires. In 1988 he completed his studies, and in 1992 he joined Sandoz AG—which later became Novartis—as a medical chemist, acting in different leadership capacities.

Walter Dettwiler (born in 1960) is director of the Novartis company archive. He studied history and philosophy, and has worked at the Schweizerische Landesmuseum in Zurich as well as the Historisches Museum in Basel. In addition, he has been active as a freelance historian. He has realized several exhibitions and published on a variety of historical subjects.

Robert A. Ettlin (born in 1946) directed Development Site Operations from 1998 to 2008. He studied medicine at the universities in Zurich and Vienna and completed postgraduate training in experimental medicine. After working for several institutes, hospitals, and a chemical firm, he joined Sandoz AG in Basel in 1987 and went to Japan as a preclinical director.

Mark C. Fishman (born in 1951) was named president of the Novartis Institute for BioMedical Research in 2002 and since then he has been part of Novartis Executive Committee. Previously, he had been the head of cardiology and the director of the Cardiovascular Research Center at Massachusetts General Hospital in Boston, as well as a professor of medicine at Harvard Medical School.

Alan Fletcher (born in 1931, died in 2006) was responsible for graphic design on the Novartis Campus and was involved in the Campus's planning from the beginning. Over his career, he worked for *Fortune,* the Container Corporation, and IBM. In London he co-founded Fletcher/Forbes/Gill in 1962 and in 1972 he helped found Pentagram, which he left after twenty years to open his own studio.

Alice Foxley (born in 1978) has worked since 2003 for Vogt Landschaftsarchitekten in Zurich. Her main responsibilities at Vogt are research and design, and she has played a significant role in the design of the Novartis Campus Park. Foxley studied in Newcastle and Bath. From 1999 to 2002, she worked in several architectural firms, including Herzog & de Meuron.

Andreas U. Fürst (born in 1966) has been working for Novartis Site Operations in Basel as a licensed hotelier and restauranteur since 2003. From 1992 to 2003, he was responsible for the implementation of new restaurant concepts and was the food and beverage expert of various firms and associations.

Guido Hager (born in 1958) is the managing director of Hager Landschaftsarchitektur AG and Hager International AG in Zurich, which he runs in partnership with Patrick Altermatt and Pascal Posset. The broad spectrum of his activities includes involvement with questions of landmark preservation and contributions to contemporary landscape architecture.

Richard Ingersoll (born in 1949) is an architectural critic and urban historian who for the past three decades has lived mostly in Italy. His recent books include *Sprawltown, Looking for the City on Its Edges* (2006) and *Ticino Modernism. The University of Lugano* (with Kenneth Frampton; 2004).

Gaby Keuerleber-Burk (born in 1957) has been responsible since the fall of 2004 for the establishment of change management on the Novartis Campus. After being trained as a physiotherapist, Keuerleber-Burk took a teaching position at the Colegio Suizo de México, the Swiss School in Mexico. She has also studied economics at the university in Basel.

Martin Kieser (born in 1965) has been responsible for the implementation of the Novartis Campus project since 2002. He studied architecture at the Swiss Federal Institute of Technology Zurich. From 1994 to 2001, Kieser worked in the architectural firm of Wirth + Wirth AG in Basel and opened his own firm, Kieser Architektur und Projekt Management, in 2000.

Vittorio Magnago Lampugnani (born in 1951) was contracted to do the overall urban planning of the Novartis Campus in 2001. He studied architecture in Rome and Stuttgart and graduated in 1977. From 1990 to 1995, he was the publisher of the magazine *Domus* and director of the Deutsche Architekturmuseum in Frankfurt am Main. He has been a tenured professor of the history of city building at the Swiss Federal Institute of Technology Zurich since 1994 and has his own architectural firm (Studio di Architettura) in Milan.

Lize Mifflin (born in 1956) is a consultant on brand identity and design for a variety of Swiss and international companies. She studied Fine Art at Columbia University Teacher's College (MFA) and Carnegie Mellon University (BFA). In 1986, after moving from New York, she joined Kaspar Schmid to found the Zurich design partnership Mifflin-Schmid Design. She has lectured at Lucerne's University of Applied Sciences and Arts, The Museum of Design Zurich's Poster Collection, and Zurich University of the Arts.

Roger Müller (born in 1975) has been responsible for sustainability aspects of Novartis's plant in Basel since 2006. He studied process engineering and graduated from the Swiss Federal Institute of Technology Zurich. In 2004 Müller completed a postdoctoral year at Novartis before becoming a project manager for Linde-KCA-Dresden GmbH.

Reto Naef (born in 1954) has led Novartis's Swiss Research Operations division since 2001. He studied chemistry at the Swiss Federal Institute of Technology Zurich and then did two postdoctoral placements in the U.S. He has worked in different branches of research, first at Sandoz AG and then at Novartis.

Markus Oser (born in 1958) has been a member of different committees of the Novartis Campus project since 2001, with a focus on area development and external relations. He completed training in architecture and facility management and has worked in different areas of facility management and plant planning strategy since 1987, first at Sandoz AG and then at Novartis.

Sevil Peach (born in 1949) and her partner Gary Turnbull, who together formed their own design and architecture studio in 1994, were involved with a Pilot Project designed to shape the new workplace environment on the Novartis Campus.

René Rebmann (born in 1951) has been in charge of the management of Novartis's real estate in the Basel area as head of facility management since 1997. After studying structural engineering, in 1976 he started working for Ciba-Geigy AG—and subsequently for Novartis—as a project manager of industrial development projects in the Basel area.

Jörg Reinhardt (born in 1956) was appointed Chief Operating Officer of Novartis in 2008. He received his doctorate in pharmaceutics in 1981 and has held numerous leading positions in the areas of Research and Development for both Sandoz Pharma AG and Novartis since 1982. He was named Chief Executive Officer of the new Novartis division "Vaccines and Diagnostics" in 2006 and has been a member of the board of directors of Novartis since 2007.

Gottfried Schatz (born in 1936) presided over the Schweizerische Wissenschafts- und Technologierat (Swiss Council on Science and Technology) from 2000 to 2003. He studied chemistry in Graz and did biochemical research at the university of Vienna, Cornell University, and the Biozentrum in Basel. In his youth, he played violin in several opera houses.

Silke Schmeing (born in 1971) has been working in public relations at Vogt Landschaftsarchitekten in Zurich since 2007. Seven years before, she had worked in advertising and communication as a copy writer and concept creator. Schmeing studied landscape architecture at the Technikum Rapperswil.

Kaspar Schmid (born in 1954) was invited by Alan Fletcher to join him in developing the new Novartis Campus corporate design. After graduating from the Kunstgewerbeschule Zürich and working as a graphic designer for various Zurich agencies, he worked at Pentagram Design, London, and at Pentagram, New York. In 1986, he founded the Zurich design agency Mifflin-Schmid Design with partner Lize Mifflin. Today, he is a design and identity consultant for a variety of Swiss and international companies.

Andreas Schulz (born in 1959) is responsible for lighting design on the Novartis Campus. After completing his studies in electrical engineering in Cologne and lighting design in Ilmenau, he founded the lighting design office Licht Kunst Licht in Bonn and Berlin. He is a guest reader at the university in Düsseldorf and the first professor of lighting design at the University for Science and Art in Hildesheim.

Fritz Schumacher (born in 1950) has been the master builder and director of the Structural Engineering and Planning Office in the building department of the canton of Basel since 1994. In 1980 he started working in St. Gallen as an urban planner. He has diplomas in urban planning and architecture.

Wolfdietrich Schutz (born in 1940) has been entrusted with the coordination of the Novartis Campus project since 2001. He studied mathematics at the university in Munich. Beginning in 1967, Schutz worked at Sandoz AG, and then for Novartis, in various responsibilities within the areas of pharmaceutical marketing and planning.

Marco Serra (born in 1970) has been the planning coordinator for the Novartis Campus project since 2003. He graduated in architecture at the Swiss Federal Institute of Technology Zurich in 1996, after which he worked in several firms. In 2004 he realized the reception pavilion and underground parking garage on the Novartis Campus. He has also been responsible for the reconstruction of the Abadia Santa Maria de Retuerta in Valladolid since 2007.

Fritz Steele (born in 1938) consults about, writes about, and occasionally teaches organizational change and workplace design/use. He resides in Brookline, Massachusetts. His books include *The Sense of Place, Physical Settings and Organizational Development*, and *Workplace by Design: Mapping the High-Performance Workscape* (with Franklin Becker).

Harald Szeemann (born in 1933, died in 2005) was involved in the layout of the Novartis Campus in the capacities of art critic and curator from 2001. From 1961 to 1969, he was the director of the Kunsthalle Bern and from 1981 to 1991 he was the independent curator for the Kunsthaus Zürich. In 1969 he founded the Agentur für geistige Gastarbeit, and in 1974, the Museum der Obsessionen, going on to found other museums later. In 1972 he was appointed director of documenta 5 in Kassel.

Daniel Vasella (born in 1953) has been a member of the Board of Directors, as well as the Chief Executive Officer of Novartis AG since the founding of the company in 1996 and was appointed to the position of Chairman of the Board of Directors in 1999.

Günther Vogt (born in 1957) is a landscape architect, as well as a lover of plants and literature. With the assistance of his thirty coworkers at the company he founded in 2000, he has realized nationally and internationally acclaimed projects in Zurich and Munich, including several projects for the landscape architecture design of the Novartis Campus. He is also an adjunct professor of landscape architecture at the Swiss Federal Institute of Technology Zurich, where he directs the Netzwerk Stadt und Landschaft.

Peter von Matt (born in 1937) was a professor of German literature at the university in Zurich and writes books and essays about literature and art history. Among his most important publications are *Liebesverrat. Die Treulosen in der Literatur* (1989), *Verkommene Söhne, mißratene Töchter. Familiendesaster in der Literatur* (1995), and *Die Intrige. Theorie und Praxis der Hinterlist* (2006).

Peter Walker (born in 1932) was involved in the landscaping design of the Novartis Campus from the very beginning. He was educated at the University of California at Berkeley and the Harvard University Graduate School of Design. Walker has taught, lectured, and written for, as well as served as an advisor to, numerous public agencies. His projects around the world range from small gardens to new city centers.

Image Credits

Comet Photoshopping GmbH / Dieter Enz: 60/61, 86/87, 235

Deutsche Kinemathek: 265

Fachhochschule Nordwestschweiz, Hochschule für Gestaltung und Kunst, Institut Visuelle Kommunikation, Basel:
Pouya Ahmadi: 178 (Poster 23)
Jinsu Ahn: 10/11, 90/91, 100, 101 below
Zeynep Basay: 178 (Poster 20)
Katharina Blanke: 178 (Poster 8)
Patrick Bürdel: 178 (Posters 12, 15)
Theodore Davis: Cover Photos, 2/3, 178 (Poster 19)
Cornelia Descloux: 178 (Posters 10, 11)
Jonas Jäggy: 126 above, 126/127, 194 (18.2.2005–30.5.2006)
Philippe Karrer: 178 (Poster 18)
Susanne Käser: 6/7, 18/19, 56/57, 85, 88/89, 92/93, 94/95, 96/97, 101 above, 141, 148, 158/159, 159, 169 above, 178 (Poster 3, 9, 13, 22), 181, 183, 184 below, 185 above, 194 (10.7.2006–20.3.2007), 195 (26.4.2007–29.7.2008), 201, 209, 236/237, 250/251
Nicole Lachenmeier: 102, 103 above / below, 104, 105 above / below, 166, 168, 190 above
Angelo Lüdin: 84
Gokhan Numanoglu: 178 (Poster 17)
Roland Schär: 142 (1–4), 143
Theo Scherrer: 99, 224/225
Christian Schmid: 178 (Poster 1)
David Schwarz: 93 below, 131 above/below, 178 (Posters 2, 5, 6, 21, 25)
Christian Stindl: 178 (Poster 18)
Simon Stotz: 90 above / below, 167, 178 (Posters 7, 14)
Ivan Verovic: 178 (Poster 4)
Oliver Walthard: 178 (Poster 24)

Hager Landschaftsarchitektur AG: 243, 244/245, 246/247

Véronique Hoegger: 232/233 middle

Canton of Basel, Kunz und Mösch Architekten: 253, 254/255

Christian Kurz: 212 right, 228/229

Claude-Nicolas Ledoux, *L'architecture considérée sous le rapport de l'art, des moeurs et de la législation* (Paris 1804), pl. 15: 257

Mathias Leemann: 97 above / below, 98, 204/205, 205 above / below

Licht Kunst Licht: 185 middle / below

Yann Mingard: 130

Novartis International AG, Firmenarchiv: 13, 45, 46/47, 48/49, 50 (1–6), 51, 52/53, 54/55, 89 below, 118, 140, 158 above, 162, 188/189, 198/199

Jörg Pfäffinger: 94 above

Goran Potkonjak: 231

©2009, ProLitteris, Zurich, David Larkin (ed.), *Frank Lloyd Wright. Die Meisterwerke* (Stuttgart/Berlin/Cologne, 1993), p. 68: 260

PWP Landscape Architecture: 121, 124 left

Christian Richters: 89 above, 119

Corinne Rose, Berlin: 32/33, 42/43, 93 above, 112/113, 146, 147, 150, 151, 152/153, 153, 191 above, 193

Lukas Roth: 94 below, 124/125, 154/155, 156/157, 190 below, 191 below

Kaspar Schmid: 161, 170/171, 172, 173, 179, 180, 232 left, 233 right

Sevil Peach Gence Associates (SPGA): 216/217 below

Gary Turnbull (SPGA): 212 left, 213, 216 above, 217 above, 219

Studio Azzuro, Milano: 78/79

Studio di Architettura, Milano: 59, 62/63, 65, 66/67, 68 (1–4), 70, 72/73 (1–8), 74/75, 75, 76, 78/79, 107, 108, 110, 111, 116/117, 184 above, 187, 206, 240, 240/241, 241, 248/249, 249

Christian Vogt: 132/133, 136/137, 169 below

Vogt Landschaftsarchitekten AG, Zurich: 128/129, 134

Jean Goujon, *Illustrations de architecture ou art de bien bastir, mis de latin en fraçoys par Ian Martin* (Paris, 1547), p. 124: 22

Wettstein Architekten: 238/239

Patrizia Zanola, graphics: 39, 40, 86/87, 234/235

269

Editing:
Novartis International AG

Concept:
Vittorio Magnago Lampugnani

Editorial team:
Jacqueline Burckhardt
Martine Francotte
Vittorio Magnago Lampugnani
Michael Renner
Wolfdietrich Schutz

Coordination:
Martine Francotte

Editorial:
Sibylle Hoiman

Copyediting:
Krystina Stermole

Translations:
Michael Robertson,
Geoffrey Steinherz,
CLS Communucation AG

Graphic design:
Patrizia Zanola

Cover illustration and
frontispiece:
Design: Mifflin-Schmid Design
Photos: Fachhochschule
Nordwestschweiz, Hochschule für
Gestaltung und Kunst, Institut Visuelle
Kommunikation, Basel,
Theodore Davis, 2007/08

Production:
Stefanie Langner

Typeface:
Akkurat, Campus, DTL Argo

Reproductions:
LVD Gesellschaft für Datenverarbeitung mbH

Paper:
Galaxi Supermat, 170 g/m²

Binding:
Verlagsbuchbinderei Dieringer,
Gerlingen

Printed by:
Dr. Cantz'sche Druckerei, Ostfildern

© 2009 Hatje Cantz Verlag,
Ostfildern; Novartis International AG,
Basel; and authors

© 2009 for the reproduced
works by Jenny Holzer, Eva Schlegel,
and Frank Lloyd Wright:
ProLitteris, Zurich, as well as the
artists and their legal successors

Published by
Hatje Cantz Verlag
Zeppelinstrasse 32
73760 Ostfildern
Tel. +49 711 4405-200
Fax +49 711 4405-220
www.hatjecantz.com

ISBN 978-3-7757-2053-3 (English)
ISBN 978-3-7757-2054-0 (German)

Printed in Germany

Special thanks go to:
Simon Heusser
Susanne Käser
Cäcilia Mantegani
Michael Rock
Fiona Scherkamp
Marco Serra
Francine Zimmermann